A PRACTICAL INTRODUCTION TO

RESTORATIVE
PRACTICE
IN SCHOOLS

of related interest

Implementing Restorative Practice in Schools
A Practical Guide to Transforming School Communities
Margaret Thorsborne and Peta Blood
Foreword by Graham Robb
ISBN 978 1 84905 377 8
eISBN 978 0 85700 737 7

Restorative Practice and Special Needs
A Practical Guide to Working Restoratively with Young People
Nick Burnett and Margaret Thorsborne
Foreword by Nancy Riestenberg
ISBN 978 1 84905 543 7
eISBN 978 0 85700 968 5

Restorative Theory in Practice
Insights Into What Works and Why
Edited by Belinda Hopkins
ISBN 978 1 84905 468 3
eISBN 978 0 85700 847 3

The Psychology of Emotion in Restorative Practice
How Affect Script Psychology Explains How and Why Restorative Practice Works
Edited by Vernon C. Kelly, Jr. and Margaret Thorsborne
Foreword by Andrew Becroft
ISBN 978 1 84905 974 9
eISBN 978 0 85700 866 4

The Pocket Guide to Restorative Justice
Pete Wallis and Barbara Tudor
ISBN 978 1 84310 629 6
eISBN 978 1 84642 748 0

Restorative Justice
How It Works
Marian Liebmann
ISBN 978 1 84310 074 4
eISBN 978 1 84642 631 5

Just Schools
A Whole School Approach to Restorative Justice
Belinda Hopkins
Foreword and Introduction by Guy Masters
ISBN 978 1 84310 132 1
eISBN 978 1 84642 432 8

A PRACTICAL INTRODUCTION TO

RESTORATIVE PRACTICE IN SCHOOLS

THEORY, SKILLS AND GUIDANCE

Bill Hansberry
Foreword by Margaret Thorsborne

Jessica Kingsley *Publishers*
London and Philadelphia

The quote on page 85 is reproduced from Kelly and Thorsborne 2014 with kind permission from the editors.
The quote on page 97 is reproduced from Nathanson 2004 with kind permission from The Silvan S Tomkins Institute.
Excerpt from the *Restorative Justice Pocketbook* (page 117) used with the kind permission of Teachers' Pocketbooks.

First published as *A Practical Introduction to Restorative Practice in Schools* in 2016
by Jessica Kingsley Publishers
73 Collier Street
London N1 9BE, UK
and
400 Market Street, Suite 400
Philadelphia, PA 19106, USA

www.jkp.com

Copyright © William Hansberry 2009, 2016
Foreword copyright © Margaret Thorsborne 2016

Originally published in 2009 as *Working Restoratively in Schools* by Inyahead Press.

Available to purchase from Jessica Kingsley Publishers in all territories excluding Australasia.

Front cover image source: iStockphoto®

Library of Congress Cataloging in Publication Data
A CIP catalog record for this book is available from the Library of Congress.

British Library Cataloguing in Publication Data
A CIP catalogue record for this book is available from the British Library.

ISBN 978 1 84905 707 3
eISBN 978 1 78450 232 4

Printed and bound in Great Britain

This book is dedicated to the memory of Geoff Blair.

As well as being a truly wonderful fellow, Geoff was a highly skilled secondary school teacher, restorative conference facilitator and a private consultant to schools. Geoff worked tirelessly with schools to develop more humane and peaceful cultures. Geoff's influence permeates my thinking and the pages of this book. Thanks to Geoff's wife, Stephanie, I have been able to use some of Geoff's unpublished work in this book.

'Never make someone wrong.'

Geoff first said this to me when we were discussing restorative conference facilitation. At the time I didn't understand how it was possible to help a person take responsibility for harm they'd caused others without pushing them to admit that their actions were wrong. Years later, with many more restorative conferences under my belt and a deeper understanding of the psychology of emotion of restorative practice, Geoff's words have proved right.

Contents

List of Figures, Tables and Forms

Figures

Tables

Forms

Foreword

This is a book about relationships – and healing – in schools, the place where we spend a great deal of our time in our formative years and where experiences can profoundly shape our view of the world. It's a book about the healing of harm done when someone, adult or child, in a school, does something to hurt another adult or child. It's a book about all the ways that healing can be accomplished, and how to build relationships that we care enough about in the first place, so that healing matters.

'The healing of one is in the hands of the other.'

I first heard this quote from Bill Hubbard, a Deputy Principal at Rosehill College, a high school known for its 'restorativeness' in a somewhat deprived area of Auckland, New Zealand. I'm not sure where he found it (and neither is he) or whether or not he wrote it or spoke it, but it has stuck with me. It captures the essence of the messages in this book and in the work that restorative practitioners strive for every day. That healing for those harmed by incidents of inappropriate behavior is central to this work, but so is the healing of those responsible – a concept that is foreign to many. It is vital we understand that much of the more serious wrongdoing we have to deal with in schools comes from the impact of the trauma of adverse childhood experiences on our young people.

Restorative approaches to problem-solving, from a slow start some two decades ago, have enjoyed increasing interest and uptake from schools all over the world, as it finally sinks in with educators and policy makers that retributive discipline and zero tolerance policies do not deliver what we had hoped for; that positive relationships lie at the heart of effective teaching and learning; and that punishment is not empowered to heal. I do not need to outline in these few words here the extensive research and evaluations that show that a more relational approach to problem-solving creates a more positive school climate, a greater sense of connectedness and well-being for all members of the school community, and greater engagement in learning. Bill Hubbard (2007) writes in his blog:[1]

1. Schools must create a climate so patently fair that the school cannot be reasonably accused of bullying students (several adults that I have met over the past few years have told me that their secondary schools had been the biggest bullies that they had ever encountered).

2. Schools must compete for the hearts and minds of the 'peer group' (that 80% of students who are essentially bystanders) in the daily battle that unfolds between the school and the heroes/heroines. I have often seen bystanders swap allegiances from the hero to the school during a conference because the school was being more honourable than the hero.

3. Schools can do more to give students something to be grateful for. From what I have seen in my trip so far and from what I have witnessed in conferences at Rosehill College, I believe that students are genuinely grateful to the school for building their character through restorative experiences.

4. [Restorative practice could be improved in schools] by better marketing restorative practices as an element of 'character education' – which I believe it is. Every parent wants their child to become a fully functioning and responsible member of adult society. If these same parents understood that the restorative practices that their son/daughter was involved with on a consistent basis at school was character building, schools would better win their favour and support.

These words, written in 2007, still, in my opinion, hold true. Restorative practice, and the philosophy underpinning it, is a great platform for culture change in a school, particularly so if a school realises that for this approach to work best, there needs to be an understanding about how vitally important relationships are; and energy invested in building and maintaining positive, robust and healthy relationships so that learning is maximised. After all, we need to have something to restore to (Thorsborne and Blood 2013).

Latest research in neuroscience also supports our restorative efforts in helping to mature the parts of a young person's brain that help them process the

---

1   Bill Hubbard's blog, written during a study tour of Australian schools in 2007: http://rcrp.blogspot.co.nz.

world around them, manage their impulses and self-regulate, make decisions, plan, *think*… This knowledge demands us, as the adults in their world, to manage our own thought processes, self-regulate, think things through from a different perspective, perhaps differently to the way we were raised; and to understand that if we wish to help young people change their behavior *we must manage our own first*. This is why, with the increasing uptake of programs like PB4L/PBS/SWPBS[2] around the world, I would much rather we called what we are trying to do PC4L – Positive CLIMATES for Learning (York Region District School Board, in Thorsborne and Blood 2013). The emphasis with the change in one word, 'behavior' to 'climate', hands serious responsibility to the adults to preside over and develop a classroom and school culture where the emotional climate is one of inclusion and belonging, where interest and enjoyment are maximised for children and adults alike, where engagement in learning is a mutual responsibility, where children and their families are not *blamed* for their disengagement, but helped and supported to overcome any obstacles. We would do much better thinking about behavior *development*[3] than behavior *management*; this latter implies a kind of command and control authoritarian approach.

Becoming more fascinated by new knowledge about how the brain works, I have read, with great enthusiasm, Canadian psychiatrist and psychoanalyst Norman Doidge's books[4] and recently attended a seminar with him in Brisbane, Australia. If only I could keep all these new ideas and research in my own head! In one telling passage in his newest book on healing brains, he writes of the parasympathetic half of the autonomic nervous system:

> The second branch is the parasympathetic nervous system, which turns off the sympathetic nervous system and puts a person into a calm state in which he or she can think or reflect. While the sympathetic system is often called the fight-or-flight system, the parasympathetic system is sometimes called the rest-digest-repair system. (Doidge 2015, p.111)

It remains, and I stress again, that if we are the adults in the child's life (caregivers and educators), we must *manage our own emotional states*, to regulate ourselves into a state of parasympathetic calmness when we have to deal with the fallout of their behavior, especially when it directly affects us, and to decrease

---

2   Positive Behaviours for Learning/Positive Behaviour Support/School-wide Positive Behavior Support.
3   Thanks to Terence Bevington for these words. Terence is the Restorative Approaches Coordinator for the Borough of Hackney Learning Trust in London, UK.
4   Doidge's 'The Brain that Changes Itself' (2007) and the 'Brain's Way of Healing' (2015).

the likelihood that our own behaviors will trigger unnecessary sympathetic arousal in our young people. In my own workshops, training educators and managers in restorative practice, I stress the need for us to remain, as much as humanly possible, and despite sometimes quite serious provocation; *calm, curious, polite, respectful,* and *gently relentless.* And we need to continue the hard work of creating a climate in the classroom and wider school that maximises interest and enjoyment.

This book contains an extremely comprehensive and detailed account of the 'what' and 'how' a school might do its restorative practice – a complete 'one-stop shop' for those amongst us genuinely interested in the possibilities of culture change that restorative problem-solving offers. I have enjoyed the helpful way Bill has set his work out into four sections: *Thinking Restoratively* (mindsets), *Feeling Restoratively* (understanding the emotions involved), *Working Restoratively* (practice along the restorative continuum from preventative to responsive), and finally *Following Through Restoratively* (the work that doesn't finish once the meeting or Circle is done).

Bill is a master storyteller. He has woven many stories into his book and done this so well that the characters and situations leap off the page into our heads and hearts – we can all identify with the challenges. I wondered if perhaps the next step for him might be playwright – he understands the characters so well!

Of the many gifts in this book, I'd like to emphasise a few. Bill mounts compelling arguments for restorative approaches to problem-solving. These arguments are presented in a comprehensive way that will be useful for readers wishing to influence others. Bill's conference preparation, told through his case studies, is impeccable – challenging us to lift our practice, I believe, to new levels. His detailed follow-up work described in Part 4 also reminds us that *the game is not over* once a process has happened. His insights into how children and young people feel and think is very helpful, again helping us to think carefully about our own practice, thoughts and feelings. Finally, though, the whole section called *Feeling Restoratively* is a must-read, if we still need convincing that we need to change the way we work with young people. Bill's grasp of Affect and Script Psychology (Human Being Theory) allows the reader to understand in a deep way, our emotional selves as humans – we are after all, social animals, and we are wired to live in good relationship with others. Important issues around accountability, responsibility, mercy, forgiveness and redemption must be tackled if we are to change our schools, and eventually our communities and world. This book is full of useful ideas and I hope it will become a well-thumbed resource for restorative practitioners. It's a great read.

I would like to finish by endorsing Bill's dedication to our colleague Geoff Blair, who went about his passion for restorative problem-solving quietly, imaginatively and effectively. He is missed.

Margaret Thorsborne
Restorative practitioner, author and trainer

References

Doidge, N. (2015) *The Brain's Way of Healing.* Australia and London: Scribe.

Hubbard, W. (2007) *Restorative Practices in Australian Schools.* Available at http://rcrp. blogspot.co.nz, accessed on 24 May 2016.

Thorsborne, M. and Blood, P. (2013) *Implementing Restorative Practices in Schools: A Practical Guide to Transforming School Communities.* London: Jessica Kingsley Publishers.

York Region District School Board (2013) 'Positive climates for learning'. Available at www.yrdsb.edu.on.ca/pdfs/w/council/PositiveClimateforLearningIntroductory. pdf, accessed on 24 May 2016.

Acknowledgements

I thank Jane Langley whose work is recognised as being at the forefront of restorative practice in the early years. Jane and I have been restorative partners in crime for many years and have co-written *The Grab and Go Kit for Teaching Restorative Behaviour* (Inyahead Press) and the 'Early Years Restorative Conference script cards' (also available from Inyahead Press). We have more early years restorative practice resources in the pipeline.

I also thank Margaret Thorsborne who is internationally recognised as a leader in restorative practice in schools, workplaces and justice settings. Margaret co-wrote Chapter 21 of this book to help teachers to get deeper engagement from young people ('from their heads and hearts' as Marg would say) during restorative interventions. Marg has been a continuing support and mentor to me for over a decade and has opened many doors for me that may have otherwise remained closed.

I acknowledge Travis Bartlett, one of the most gifted communicators and leaders with whom I have had the good fortune to work with. Travis co-wrote part of Chapter 5 and poured every bit of his passion for social justice into the task.

Every now and then I come across someone who just 'gets' restorative practice, and Robyn Trabilsie is one of these people. I've had the good fortune to have worked with Robyn and her school since 2014 on implementing a whole-school approach to restorative practice after first teaching staff and students about affect and shame. We have seen the stunning results first hand in terms of reduced behavioural incidents in her school. Robyn tirelessly edited and made helpful suggestions for several sections of this book.

I thank John Hall who generously juggled work and family commitments to find time to edit and make suggestions for several sections of this book. John's steady friendship and mentorship have been a guiding light for many years.

Liz Stewart and I have worked together on and off since 2011, and I was thrilled when she offered to run her discerning eye over sections of this book while it was in draft. Liz is an incredible teacher, behaviour coach and a true believer in a restorative way of working in schools, and I am grateful for her contribution.

I also thank Joshua Morrall, a fine young man who I've had the pleasure to mentor since 2014. Joshua is a gifted writer with an amazing intellect, and he was kind enough to share some of his thoughts for developing Chapter 10.

I acknowledge the late Geoff Blair, to whose memory this book is dedicated and who influenced so much of the thinking in this book. Our conversations were invaluable to my understanding of restorative practice and the psychology of emotion that makes it work.

Many of the concepts and ideas in this guide have been borne from generations of modifications and changes. Restorative justice is by no means a new field; however, its application in schools is relatively recent. It is common to see one idea evolve into another as it is adapted to suit different contexts and situations. Wherever possible, the obvious and traceable sources have been acknowledged. If, by chance, an original source has been omitted, I sincerely apologise. The overriding intention in writing this guide is to help my committed and passionate colleagues apply restorative values and approaches to their work to benefit young people in schools.

Preface

If you are new to restorative justice in schools, this book will introduce you to the incredible possibilities that restorative practice can bring by way of creating gentler, calmer and kinder places of learning. Yes, restorative schools are kinder schools, and research from all over the world is now beginning to confirm what we have known for years now: young people learn better in schools that have committed to a restorative way of life.

I have written this book as a wide-ranging introduction to what it can look like to work restoratively in a school. It will take you on a journey across the wide range of restorative and preventative responses to things that can go wrong between people in schools. If you have started to implement restorative practice, you will find this guide useful in providing some important background and theory about where restorative practice comes from and what makes it work. Years of training schools has helped me to realise that, at its heart, restorative practice is about people learning to understand better their own emotions and the emotions of others. Affect script psychology – a theory of emotion and motivation developed by the late Silvan Tomkins – does this well and is surprisingly easy to teach to young people and adults. If understanding feelings doesn't interest you, put this book down and forget about restorative practice because it's not for you!

Schools that are at the stage of building a restorative conferencing programme and the necessary systems of record-keeping, communication and conference follow-up processes will find this book a valuable resource with straightforward advice on the finer details of supporting their restorative conferencing programme.

For me, a restorative view of the world holds that although sometimes people do bad things, we are all essentially moral and good, and when we are not acting in a way that is moral and good, we can be shown how to do so by a community that sees the best in us. We all share the same basic building blocks of emotion and a primal urge to be connected to one another. Because of this, we care. When we forget this, things go awfully wrong for individuals and communities.

Restorative people are overwhelmingly optimistic about the nature of people and, because of this, operate from a place of love rather than fear. Through their bold work, restorative people see the worst of human behaviour and its awful consequences, yet continue to have a steadfast belief that people are innately good. Restorative people want to help others put things back together when they break.

Whole-school training

It is strongly recommended that schools wishing to implement restorative practice undertake whole-school training as well as drawing on guides like this one to develop practice. Regrettably, my experience in working with many schools and teachers has led me to believe that restorative practice is one of the most misunderstood approaches to school discipline and, as a consequence, can be poorly implemented. Because of this, it is important that schools commit to a long-term, strategic and whole-school approach to learning about restorative practice. This should involve hands-on training, professional reading and structured conversations about what working restoratively means for individual teachers and whole-school practice.

Ideas for formal restorative conferencing and the ongoing management of conference agreements are presented in detail later in the book. Included are examples of pro formas that schools can use as a springboard to develop their own forms and letters to support their restorative processes.

How people are referred to in this book

In this book I refer to the grown-ups in schools (i.e. school staff) as either 'teachers' or 'adults' to acknowledge that a range of people will engage restoratively with young people. I use these terms interchangeably but not exclusively. When referring to students, I interchangeably use the nouns 'young people', 'students' or 'people'.

PART 1

Thinking Restoratively

*Challenging Paradigms about What to
Do when Things Go Wrong*

Chapter 1

An Intractable Conflict

Case study: Tristan and Jason

To give you a strong sense of what restorative practice is, and how it works, I use real stories drawn from school life throughout the book. Below I start with the story of two boys, Tristan and Jason, and their intractable conflict. (Note: Jason and Tristan's story is based on a real situation that I became involved with as an external consultant to the school. I facilitated the process. The names and places have been changed.)

The conflict

Things had become bad between Jason, a 13-year-old boy, and Tristan, a 12-year-old boy in the same class. At the beginning of the school year something had sparked a conflict. Nobody really knew what, but since then, the boys' interactions had been characterised by regular episodes of teasing, and even awful comments about each other's families. This had sometimes escalated into defacing one another's schoolbooks, deliberately hiding belongings from one another and, on occasions, the boys had come to blows, although Jason, a much bigger boy, had a physical advantage.

There were times of ceasefire between the boys, when they managed to go about their day spending time in the same friendship group without confrontation. This was temporary, as both boys had developed a hair trigger when it came to one another's words and actions, so something as small as a sideways glance or a difference of opinion would quickly descend into taunts, insults and challenges to fight at the school gates after school. Some of the other students in the class saw this as great entertainment and sometimes said and did things to set the scene for more conflict between Jason and Tristan.

Due to the escalating nature of the incidents and the rising distress of the boys' parents and staff, the school principal, Mr Barker, felt that he had no choice but to separate the boys at break times. This arrangement saw Jason or

Tristan spending break times in the school's computer suite, on alternate days, while the other was free to move about the play areas. Mr Barker had invested hours of his time and energy trying to minimise the harm the boys could bring to one another. It seemed as though this was the only solution to an ongoing conflict where both boys believed that they were the victim.

The boys' profiles

Jason

Jason was older, taller and physically stronger than Tristan. He presented as a quietly spoken and kind boy and had an air of self-assurance about him, which perhaps came from the fact that he was taller than most of the other boys. On occasion, Jason used his physical supremacy to gain status or to get his way. Like most boys his age, Jason's mask of quiet confidence hid a scared little boy who spent a lot of time worrying about how he fitted in and what he was good at achieving.

Tristan

Tristan was Jason's physical opposite: he was short for his age and all of the other boys stood taller. Tristan had an engaging personality and was more of an open book than Jason when it came to discussing life, friends and school. Tristan's insecurities were easy to see and he was socially immature for his age. He was eager to ask questions about friendship and life and was yet to develop some of the finer skills for making and keeping friends. Tristan, however, had a quick mouth and an expansive vocabulary that made him a formidable opponent for anyone who engaged him in a battle of words. Tristan had learned to manipulate, divide and conquer to keep a hold on friendships. It was all he knew, and mild social anxiety drove many of his social decisions.

More about the conflict

What had been happening? How had people been affected?

Over several months, Mr Barker had investigated issue after issue between Jason and Tristan, ranging from reports of teasing to pushing, giving each other dead arms (a punch in the bicep), as well as a few public verbal exchanges, including taunts and threats at the school gates. Both boys had been suspended for their roles in these incidents. Each time, this only seemed to further galvanise each boy into seeing himself as the victim and further inflamed the boys' parents, especially Tristan's mother, Louise, who believed that these responses were unfair to Tristan while letting Jason get away with bullying.

Louise had made enquiries about legal action against the school for the harm that she believed had come to Tristan. A law student herself, Louise was deeply distressed by the stories that Tristan was telling and believed that the separation order that Mr Barker had put in place was impacting Tristan's ability to maintain his friendships with other boys in his class and, therefore, damaging his mental health.

In a moment of extreme stress, Louise had, a few weeks earlier, entered the boys' classroom unannounced, without signing in to the school, and publically threatened Jason that she was watching him and would involve the police if he didn't leave Tristan alone. This incident embarrassed Tristan, made Jason fearful, distressed Mrs Jansen (the class teacher) and caused a stir within the community. Mr Barker was concerned with Louise's disregard of the school's child safety procedures and wrote her a formal letter, cleared by the school district's legal team, indicating that she had breached child safety policies. The letter stated that, from then on, Louise was only to move within the school grounds accompanied by a member of the school's leadership. Louise steeled herself for a legal challenge to this letter and was preparing her case against the school.

Galina, Jason's mother, took a different view of the situation. The quarrelling between the boys concerned her, but she viewed the issue as something from which both boys could learn valuable lessons. In her opinion, what was happening between Jason and Tristan was part of growing up and could be overcome with sensible guidance from adults. Galina had encouraged Jason to make better choices when Tristan did something that insulted him. Galina did not know Louise well but had been made aware of how Louise had entered Jason's classroom and confronted him. Galina felt angry with Louise for this but felt some empathy towards Louise, understanding that she must have been very distressed to have chosen this course of action.

Tristan and Jason's class teacher, Mrs Jansen, was run off her feet from having to closely monitor the boys' every interaction within the classroom and document her observations. There was a growing likelihood that these notes would become evidence in a courtroom some time in the future. As well as teaching a class of 30 students ranging from 11 to 13 years of age, Mrs Jansen had to constantly think about how any classroom activity might bring Tristan and Jason into contact with one another, and the potential consequences of this contact. Group work, class sports, excursions – even just eating time – all had become an exercise in risk management for Mrs Jansen. This was taking its toll.

Tristan and Jason shared a group of friends. These friends felt like the meat in the sandwich and were finding the constant bickering and one-upmanship between Jason and Tristan exhausting. Having to second-guess the potential consequences of spending time with either of the boys was taking up a lot of head space for the boys' friends, particularly Adam and Aston. Understandably, Tristan and Jason would subtly encourage the boys to side with them, using their rostered play times to desperately re-establish their friendships, anxious that they had lost ground to the other during their previous stay in the computer suite. How else would boys of this age act under these circumstances?

Mr Barker phoned me to see whether I could work with the school to find a solution to the problems. He wondered whether a fresh set of eyes and a restorative approach could be the catalyst for positive change. This was a difficult step for Mr Barker, because involving an outside person in this situation was, perhaps, an admission that what the school had done to date had not been effective. Mr Barker was also adroit enough to know that Louise no longer trusted him to make decisions that she felt were in Tristan's best interests. Communications with Louise were strained and this was, of course, impacting on how Mr Barker could work with Tristan. It had got to the stage that every interaction Mr Barker had with Tristan would result in another strongly worded, legalistic email from Louise, who had become so anguished that there was nothing Mr Barker could do that wasn't immediately misinterpreted by her as a deliberate attempt to make Tristan's existence at school miserable. Of course, Tristan was doing what most children in this position would do, that is, taking every possible opportunity to complain to Louise about Jason's and Mr Barker's unfairness and mistreatment of him. After all, this got his mother's attention.

I'm sure elements of this story will be familiar to many readers. In the next chapter we look at restorative approaches as an effective alternative to addressing situations like this one, and we will return to Tristan and Jason's story later in the book.

Chapter 2

Courage, Connectedness and Restorative Work

Restorative practice is a constructivist, learning-based approach to conflict and wrongdoing that distinguishes between 'managing behaviour' and 'managing relationships'. Those who've worked with restorative practice understand that when we change the way people see one another and feel about one another, people's behaviour can change quickly. Underlying this is a truism that people's behaviour is heavily influenced by the quality of their relationships.

Morrison (2007), in her analysis of research carried out by Baumeister and colleagues on the effects of social exclusion and rejection, sums things up by saying that the inference Baumeister is making is that who we are as individuals is 'intimately caught up with who we are as a member of society' and that our 'social identities, understood as the psychological link between individuals and social groups, mould who we are and how we behave' (p.29).

Based on the principles of restorative justice, restorative practice involves those who've become entangled in an incident of harm or conflict working together to find solutions and ways forward. A restorative mindset holds that the best way to deal with a problem or incident is to bring those involved, and affected, together (if possible) to discuss what has happened and how people have been affected. The next task is to help people to take responsibility for their misdeeds and bad decisions, and decide on a way that the harm might be repaired. This is a far more sophisticated approach than simply punishing those we judge to have wronged others. So restorative practice is essentially a face-to-face response to disruption and wrongdoing in schools. The ability to do this face-to-face restorative work is something that we can teach young people to do, beginning the moment they enter formal education settings. It is useful to think of restorative practice as a pedagogy rather than a bag of tricks that we pull out to use with some students in some situations.

The alternative to face-to-face work is the business of separating young people after a conflict, or after one has hurt the other, and making all of the decisions about how the problem will be dealt with on their behalf. The effort involved with keeping people who have been in conflict apart and trying to impose our solutions, or punishments, to their problems wastes precious time and energy in schools and rarely brings lasting behaviour change. This divide-and-conquer approach almost always further damages relationships, increasing the chance that the same issues will reappear. Schools need to ask themselves whether their approaches to wrongdoing and disruption strengthen relationships between people or whether these approaches erode relationships. In other words, do people feel better or worse about one another after the school has intervened?

Better relationships, better behaviour

Restorative practice improves behaviour by improving relationships between people in schools, particularly in the wake of incidents where relationships have been strained or fractured by the inevitable bumps and scrapes of school life. Yes, upset and conflict in schools is inevitable; things do go awfully wrong from time to time in classrooms, hallways and schoolyards; good people sometimes say and do bad things to one another. But we do young people and their parents a terrible disservice when we send messages like 'what happens at school will always be fair' and that 'if something goes wrong at school, then someone isn't doing their job properly'. A clever principal I worked with once said, 'We can teach kids to cross the road but we can't stop the traffic.' This is how I see restorative practice working: we give young people the skills to cross life's many roads knowing that the traffic will probably not stop for them.

One of the greatest gifts we can give the next generation is emotional intelligence and a set of skills and attitudes to apply this intelligence to address conflict and wrongdoing more effectively than generations before them. Restorative practice is a stunningly effective pedagogy for achieving this outcome. I have had the good fortune to have been part of the cultural transformation that restorative practice brings and have come to see restorative practice as a vehicle for school improvement, not just a way of managing behaviour and improving relationships in schools.

When schools commit to restorative practice, a spirit of dialogue and an ability to understand one another's perspective begins to take precedence over the primal urge for retribution and quick fixes. Peace 'breaks out' because restorative practice allows us all to be human with one another again. Growing research from around the globe is building a compelling picture: going to work on the quality of relationships between people and dealing with conflict in positive, collaborative ways delivers us safer schools. The International Institute for Restorative Practices (IIRP) produced a document titled 'Findings from Schools Implementing Restorative Practices' (Lewis 2009) which shows significant reductions in incidents of violence in schools across the research schools. In light of recent attacks across the globe by radicalised extremist minorities, the call from academics and informed commentators is that we need to value and protect the connections that hold our communities together and challenge practices that push people to the fringes of our communities. Schools seem an obvious place to start.

School connectedness

School connectedness is about the quality of relationships that young people have with others (teachers and peers) at school. Connectedness is often explained as the extent to which students feel accepted, valued, respected and included in the school, and has recently surfaced as one of the most important predictors of adolescent mental health (Shochet, Smyth and Homel 2007, p.2). When young people (particularly adolescents) feel connected to and cared for by people at their school, they are less likely to use substances, engage in violence and become sexually active at an early age. Feeling connected to school has been strongly correlated with higher levels of emotional well-being (McNeely, Nonnemaker and Blum 2002, p.138). Connectedness to school has also been proven by numerous researchers to be a protective factor against delinquency and gang membership. For example, McNeely *et al.* (2002) state:

> When teachers are empathic, consistent, encourage student self-management and allow students to make decisions, the classroom management climate improves. The overall level of school connectedness is lower in schools that temporarily expel students for relatively minor infractions such as possessing alcohol, compared to schools with more lenient discipline policies... Zero tolerance policies...seek to make schools safer. Yet students in schools with harsh discipline policies report feeling less safe at school than do students in schools with more moderate policies. (p.145)

Risk management?

In the current climate many school systems have become over-cautious around issues of student safety and well-being. The crushing burden of trying to foresee, manage and respond to every possible risk to student well-being has resulted in schools spending inordinate amounts of time on reports and bureaucracy about what's being done to stop things from going wrong in schools. We have lost the plot, and the result is ever-increasing numbers of overwhelmed school leaders, disenchanted teachers and less-well young people.

Going back to our earlier metaphor, trying to stop the traffic for young people has taken the focus away from teaching, learning, relationships and connectedness. So, when restorative justice advocates talk about bringing distressed young people and their distressed, possibly angry parents or caregivers together to sit in a Circle to talk about incidents of harm, many school leaders go wobbly at the knees. It can seem too risky, and many schools do whatever possible to avoid conflict.

However, schools that are skilled in doing this type of wobbly-knee work – that acknowledge conflict and meet it head on – do best when it comes to the task of keeping young people connected, behaving well and learning well. Morrison (2007) states:

> Johnson and Johnson (1995) have acknowledged the failure of many schools to deal with conflict head on. They differentiated between 'conflict negative' schools, those that manage conflict destructively, and 'conflict positive' schools, those that manage conflict constructively. They note that most schools today are conflict negative, where conflict is dealt with through denial, suppression or avoidance. They advocate a cultural change to conflict positive schools, where conflict is addressed openly. Through using restorative justice practices, students will have the opportunity to learn productively from their experiences of conflict. (p.101)

Over-paternalistic styles of dealing with conflict and wrongdoing makes schools conflict negative. In these cultures, young people are robbed of opportunities to learn from conflict and develop resilience. All of us need to challenge the belief that young people aren't able to develop the skills to be part of the problem-solving process and that they must be shielded from conflict by grown-ups. We have been underestimating our young people for too long, and their resilience has been the casualty. Has our preoccupation with safety and student well-being created less-well young people?

Restorative discipline

By contrast, as Stutzman Amstutz and Mullet (2005, pp.26–29) point out, restorative discipline is an approach which:

- acknowledges that relationships are central to building community

- builds systems that address misbehaviour and harm in a way that strengthens relationships

- focuses on the harm done rather than only on rule-breaking

- gives voice to people who have been harmed

- engages in collaborative problem-solving

- empowers change and growth

- enhances student responsibility.

As you read this book I hope that you will come to see that restorative practice is not for the faint-hearted. Working restoratively requires courage, because it demands that we come face to face with the negative emotions that are stirred up when things go wrong. Working restoratively is highly emotional work. This is why a large section of this book is dedicated to a theory of emotion that explains restorative practice. (Skip this section at your peril!)

Working restoratively simultaneously demands the best from young people and those who work with them in schools. So my question to you is the same question I've asked thousands of young people faced with the scary prospect of sitting down with others to sort out conflicts, upsets and problems, or to face up to their misdeeds: Are you up for the challenge? (I think you are!)

The next chapter introduces you to the social control window, a powerful way to conceptualise the role of adults (those in charge) and the different ways adults exert control on, and provide support to, young people in the pursuit of learning environments that are safe and productive.

Chapter 3

How to be in Charge – Four Modes of Discipline and Control
More Asking and Less Telling

The social control window (Wachtel 1999) is a mainstay of restorative thinking. This model describes how restorative justice (i.e. restorative practice) differs from other modes of being in charge or having authority over people. Its four quadrants eloquently explain four sets of ways that people in charge generally behave. These four patterns of leadership styles are each based in particular beliefs about the nature of people and ways of interacting with people that gets results. Who am I referring to when I talk about leaders? In schools, this is any situation when one person has some level of authority or responsibility over another person. In schools, these may be:

- principals leading assistant principals, heads of house, grade coordinators or administrative support staff

- assistant principals, heads of house or grade coordinators leading teaching staff

- teaching staff leading students

- teaching staff leading teacher assistants

- student leaders leading students.

Regardless of the hierarchical structure in a school (or any other organisation), somewhere along the line someone will have authority over someone else. Even in so-called flat leadership models, certain individuals eventually rise to the top and inherit particular responsibilities that see them calling the shots in one way or another. In my work helping organisations address conflict and harm in the workplace through restorative practice, a lack of clarity about who is in charge of whom has been a common ingredient contributing to breakdowns in good will and the emergence of destructive behaviour.

Social control window

The social control window (see Figure 3.1) teaches us that when someone has responsibility or authority over other people, their leadership or management style can be experienced in two main ways: somewhere on a continuum of low to high support, or on a continuum of low to high control.

Low support ◄————————————————————————► High support

At the high-support end of this continuum, high levels of understanding, nurturance, encouragement and flexibility are offered to those being led. If asked, the people being led would typically describe the person with authority as friendly, patient, supportive and perhaps even lenient. In this zone, the person with authority is very interested in people feeling looked after, because after all, he or she takes a keen interest in how people feel. That person wants to see those being led achieving and feeling good about themselves, so he or she works hard at explicitly teaching, reminding, encouraging and coaching. The feedback given to people by the person with authority is overwhelmingly positive. In the endeavour to be warm and supportive, such a person is highly flexible in accommodating different personalities and styles, and will often bend expectations so that everyone feels taken care of.

At the opposite end of this support continuum, low support, the person with authority works in a way where he or she offers very little in the way of support, nurturance and understanding. That person is generally indifferent to how people feel. He or she believes that whether or not people thrive under his or her supervision is up to them, so that person doesn't see it as their job to go out of their way to help people. Such a person would be described as the type of leader who leaves people to their own devices and has an air of 'don't bother me – work it out for yourself'. He or she doesn't provide feedback in any form and doesn't change anything about how work is performed to accommodate others.

Low control ◄————————————————————————► High control

At the high-control extreme of this continuum, the person with authority micromanages and takes an almost obsessive interest in things being done their way. He or she is big on rules and routines, and people know what expected behaviour looks like. Such a person would be described as overbearing, controlling and a disciplinarian. Behavioural and performance boundaries are clearly laid out and well communicated. When people fail to live up to such a person's expectations, the person holds them accountable and never shies away from giving negative feedback. Things need to be done the way the person with authority expects, because after all, that way is the best way.

At the other extreme of this continuum, the person with authority adopts an approach that offers others nothing in the way of guidance about expected behaviour. He or she leaves people alone to decide how they will do things – and even if they *will* do things! Structure and routine are not part of what such a person values. Their style would be described by others as 'anything goes'. Because such a person lacks any clarity about what they want from others, they don't provide performance-based feedback in any form.

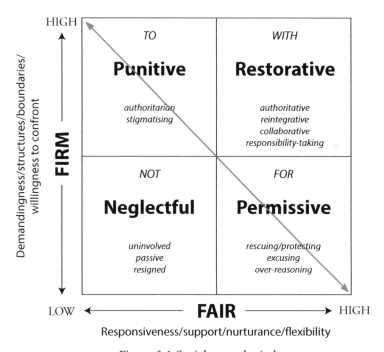

Figure 3.1 Social control window

Combining the support and control continuums

When one brings a continuum of support together with a continuum of control, a powerful way of thinking emerges about how leadership should occur. In explaining the social control window from here on, I will place it in the context of students and adults (teachers and teacher leaders) in school settings.

Being punitive

This section explains the 'TO' quadrant shown in Figure 3.1. Here the person with authority combines a strong need to control with a weak belief in the importance of students feeling supported or looked after. The person is in authority because someone *has* to be and kids need that from adults. This person has to be the boss, always has the final say and inflicts a powerful sting on anyone daring enough to step out of line or challenge him or her. Such a person sees students as objects to be managed (Vandeering 2010, p.8). If you think of the traditional, strict teacher of the nineteenth century, dressed in black gown and mortarboard, you have a good image of this leadership style. (The music group Pink Floyd's film *The Wall* springs to mind for many when thinking of this kind of teacher.)

In this zone, the practice is likely to be described by students as punitive and authoritarian. The person with authority 'does things' to people which might make them comment to others as follows:

- 'She's overly harsh – kids are really scared and the bad kids rebel.'

- 'He likes the smart and good kids and hates the kids who don't get it or go wrong.'

- 'She just won't listen – she just makes her mind up and that's it.'

- 'He holds grudges; go wrong once and you're a marked man.'

- 'As soon as there's a fight, kids are getting suspended left, right and centre – kids have been suspended for just watching!'

In this corner of the social control window, the person with authority is interested in getting students to do what he or she wants, in exactly the *way* he or she wants, and if they don't, such a person exercises their authority through intimidation and punishment: 'After all, this is good for them and will prepare them for life in the real world.' The management language is infected with phrases like 'You must, you will, they had better...', 'You won't', 'I want' and 'Do it now!' Mistakes are not okay and are seen primarily as the result of a moral failing on the part of students.

When wrongdoing or conflict causes disruption to school life, the person with authority gets angry and immediately concerns themselves with restoring order by finding out which of *their* rules have been broken and how the miscreants should be punished. Justice is about retribution, and rule-breaking is seen as a violation of the moral code. In the haste to apply swift and efficient justice, the person with authority gets it awfully wrong, missing important details and leaving those involved feeling at best unheard, and at worst diminished, angry, resentful and even vengeful. This is, of course, all because the person with authority had already made up their mind or guessed what happened – 'who did what' – based on students' reputations and past behaviour. Such a person then metes out punishments without dignity or compassion. Prejudices dominate the person's thinking and he or she believes that 'leopards never change their spots'. This person genuinely believes that if the rest of the teachers worked like they did, and if the school leadership stopped being so weak with the naughty kids, order would be quickly restored to the anarchy. The person despairs and yearns for the 'good ol' days' when kids knew who was in charge and showed respect to adults. Deep down the person believes that young people must be kept on a short leash, because if given enough rope, they will behave irresponsibly and selfishly. Underlying this is a dim view of human nature.

In this environment, students are in self-protection mode. With fear and shame being the dominant emotional forces, many students stop taking risks in their learning. When mistakes are made, or people cause harm to one another, the default response is for students to bunker down and deny involvement or responsibility. Out of a desire to protect themselves from being harshly punished and/or being seen as a bad person, young people are far more likely to focus on their own interests and will struggle to think empathically about the needs of others. A 'look out for number one' culture grows and students become highly punitive in their dealings with one another. After all, this is what is being modelled to them by the person with authority. In schools where students behave severely and retributively towards one another, you will almost always find a set of disciplinary processes that are both the cause and the misguided response to this state of affairs.

How might Tristan and Jason be handled punitively?

Going back to the story of Jason and Tristan (see Chapter 1), as soon as problems begin between Jason and Tristan, the person with authority starts dealing out detentions and suspensions to whomever he or she believes started any of the many incidents along the way. Often such a person guesses who did what and closes their mind to the possibility that perhaps this time it was a different set of circumstances. This person has made up their mind about who was most likely the culprit and has developed an unconscious bias towards one of the boys, creating situations where one of them can easily get away with murder while the other becomes extremely vulnerable to this.

The methods for getting to the truth may involve police-style interrogations, the use of witness accounts and even CCTV footage. The person with authority is not the slightest bit interested in the root causes of the issues between the boys, or how they have been affected by their own decisions. Such a person believes that stories of woe from the past and emotions just muddy the waters. The idea of brokering peace between Tristan and Jason is far from his or her mind due to an unconscious belief that the boys don't want peace – they just want to bicker, because this is what naughty boys do! What he or she is interested in is being seen by others (colleagues, students or parents) as being in control of the situation through swift, decisive and severe responses to the litany of escalating incidents. In this vein, such a person is mostly focused on making sure the wrongdoer gets their just deserts without any engagement of the harmed party. He or she makes the decisions about what will bring justice on the harmed boy's behalf.

When the boys' parents express concern about how the person with authority has dealt with matters, the person quickly dismisses them as overprotective 'helicopter' parents and politely (or not so politely) suggests that they mind their own business and not ask questions that breach confidentiality. (Oh yes, a veil of secrecy over what the person in authority has done saves him or her from having to justify the processes used to deal with such matters!) Student confidentiality is the reason for a lack of transparency and accountability. The boys' parents feel as though they have been kept in the dark, and their suspicion, mistrust and resentment grow daily.

Tristan and Jason become increasingly emotionally detached from one another and increasingly self-involved, thinking only about how they are being affected and how hard this is on them. They also don't spare a thought to the collateral damage their constant bickering is causing to the classroom environment. The ways the boys punish and pay each other back become increasingly inventive and damaging as a tit-for-tat cycle firmly embeds itself.

Being permissive

This section explains the 'FOR' quadrant shown in Figure 3.1. This permissive style lies in stark contrast to teachers who rely on heavy-handed punitive tactics. When the leadership style occupies the 'FOR' space in the social control window, students really know that the person in authority cares about them because this person does things *for* them. Such a person sees young people as helpless objects of need (Vandeering 2010). The person provides high levels of support to young people, who typically view him or her as nurturing, warm, understanding and 'soft'.

The problem is that such a person is not asking for anything in return from young people in the way of appropriate and considerate behaviour or academic performance. He or she fails to provide controls through setting boundaries and limits for behaviour. This person also lacks the willingness to confront young people when their behaviour is disrespectful. He or she thinks the best road to results is to serve students in an easy-going, friendly way, and the person has blurred the line between 'relationship' and 'friendship'. Under this style of leadership students' behaviour quickly unravels, and true to form, the person in authority minimises and downplays this inappropriate behaviour by making excuses for it. The person is deeply concerned about being seen as a nice teacher and genuinely wants students to like him or her. What might young people say about such a person? Here are some examples:

- 'She's really friendly and stuff, but kids run over her because nobody ever gets in trouble.'

- 'You can talk your way out of anything.'

- 'People just run amok – it's really funny, but nobody learns anything!'

- 'Some kids have done some really serious stuff, like really bad bullying, and nothing's been done about it. Heaps of kids have left the school, but the bullies have stayed.'

- 'Even the good kids go wrong in his class.'

- 'When kids are going wrong, they get counselling, but that's all.'

Despite the fact that the person in authority is blind to the effect that their over-indulgent style is having on young people, he or she often feels frustrated with the behaviour of the students and also despairs that not much learning is happening. His or her first reflex is to blame themselves – and even perhaps make apologies to students for their inadequacies as a teacher!

What's missing is a basic understanding that young people need to experience boundaries; otherwise, they will continue to test the waters. When students finally push too far, they experience the grey arrow that runs diagonally across the social control window (see Figure 3.1). The person in authority finally snaps, and out of the blue he or she becomes vengeful and punitive: this person has reached their breaking point, and students experience a Jekyll and Hyde routine, as all of a sudden the person becomes nasty and vengeful in dealing out sanctions. Students' responses range from shocked compliance to defiant protestations about the unfairness of the sudden change in expectations. (After all, the person has jumped quadrants and has become the punitive teacher!) Not long after this spectacular change in mood, the person in authority feels awful for turning so quickly on the kids, and his or her feelings of shame motivate him or her to make up with them again. How does such a person make amends? Of course, by becoming overly friendly, easy-going, undemanding and even apologetic. In other words, the person has moved back down the grey arrow right back to where they started: in the permissive quadrant (see Figure 3.1).

In this unstable environment, young people become confused. The influence of having the person in authority jump between the 'FOR' and 'TO' quadrants disorients them and they lose trust. Students begin to look to *each other* for leadership, and the socially powerful students begin to call the shots.

How might Tristan and Jason be handled permissively?

A permissive response is characterised by a high tolerance to the behaviours that are causing conflict between Tristan and Jason. The person in authority finds themselves making excuses for the teasing, theft and fighting, perhaps saying things like 'That's just this age' or 'Boys will be boys'. Believing that the boys may be experiencing some challenges in their home life, the person might minimise some of the awful behaviours by saying 'Poor Tristan is having a tough time because he's not seen his father in a while' or 'Jason's mother says he's not been sleeping well lately – that's why he snapped and pushed Tristan today'. Because of this, we run the risk of only supporting the wrongdoer when poor behaviour causes harm, and ignoring the needs of the student who was harmed.

Being high on understanding and nurturance, the person with authority wants the boys to feel looked after, but the person is not really holding the boys accountable to the school's code of conduct. Yes, in this zone, the school rules don't really get mentioned because the person is so focused on the people involved that he or she loses sight of the bigger picture around norms for conduct. There might not even *be* a code of conduct of which students and staff are aware. As a result, the person with authority floats from one crisis to the next with little talk about expected behaviour.

In this quadrant, the person is also reluctant to challenge the boys' behaviour because they don't want the parents to be upset with them. Consumed with a desire to please everybody all of the time, the person makes relationships the reason not to do or say anything that might make someone feel bad. He or she is missing the point that good relationships are a two-way street where tough conversations about expectations need to take place from time to time. Instead, the person avoids these conversations because they want to avoid the uncomfortable feelings involved.

When the frequency and intensity of the incidents between the boys gets to a point that causes an intolerable level of distress, the person decides that enough is enough and snaps into punitive mode, imposing a severe consequence. This really upsets Tristan, Jason and their parents, Galina and especially Louise, as the severe sanction comes as a bolt from the blue for whichever boy did the wrong thing this time. They question the fairness of the response and wonder why this didn't happen last time.

Being neglectful

This section explains the 'NOT' quadrant shown in Figure 3.1. When working from the neglectful quadrant, there's not much of anything happening at all. The person with authority fails to set and communicate expectations of behaviour, and of course, he or she doesn't respond when things go wrong (or mention it when behaviour is good). The person offers very limited support, encouragement, understanding or nurturance to young people. This creates a feedback void for students, which is obviously very bad for learning.

The person with authority is largely indifferent to the emotional needs of students and gets involved only when absolutely necessary. He or she may behave this way because of exhaustion (i.e. being under immense stress from another aspect of work) or may have the wildly mistaken belief that not responding will toughen kids up and prepare them to handle life's tough moments. The person might believe that this 'emotional-connection nonsense' has nothing to do with teaching, and might be described by students in these ways:

- 'He just lets people do whatever – it gets crazy.'

- 'Every lesson she's late – people are running amok by the time she shows up.'

- 'He doesn't see what goes on in lessons – I reckon he's lost it, had a meltdown.'

- 'Some of the language in the hallways has been really disgusting! Teachers just walk past like they didn't hear it.'

- 'One lesson he just worked at his desk on the computer like we weren't there. A fight broke out between two of the girls and he just looked up, yelled at the girls to stop it and went back to it – and one of the girls left the room in tears.'

- 'She just ignores fighting and bullying in the yard. When kids complain, she just tells them to go somewhere else, like it's too hard.'

The message that students receive loud and clear is that they are not cared about, they don't matter and the teacher doesn't expect anything from them. Young people are seen as 'objects to be ignored' (Vandeering 2010). The only possible emotional response from young people in this environment is to feel bad. Soon, they begin to defend against the awful feelings stemming from the teacher's disinterest by minimising their interest in whatever the teacher or the school is interested in, and this often comes in the form of rebellion. Classrooms become truly chaotic in this space, as the powerful students assume the leadership void left vacant by the teacher. A *Lord of the Flies* culture of 'might is right' may evolve. Widespread harm and disruption is normally the end result.

How might a neglectful teacher or leader deal with the Tristan and Jason situation?

In this zone, there's no response to the incidents between the boys. The person with authority turns a blind eye to what's happening and hopes that it will take care of itself. The person leaves the situation to escalate. Tristan and Jason receive no feedback whatsoever about how their behaviour is affecting the two of them as well as the other students who have to share a classroom and schoolyard with them. As a result, the boys eventually stop reporting any of the issues to the person with authority and go about taking care of the problem themselves with their limited conflict-resolution skills. This probably won't end well, as the boys involve more and more of the other students in the situation and things spiral wildly out of control.

Being restorative

This section explains the 'WITH' quadrant shown in Figure 3.1. This zone is the most effective way to develop emotionally intelligent, resilient, kind and compassionate young people. This zone has people in authority doing more asking and less telling.

Some describe this quadrant as democratic leadership. Although the restorative quadrant, characterised by high levels of control and support, is the closest thing of the four quadrants to what might be considered democracy, I believe that this environment is perhaps better thought of as a benevolent dictatorship. In a school setting, benevolence might be described as a desire to share power with young people and involve them, as much as possible, in the decisions that affect them. Allowing young people a sense of agency is indeed a key principle of restorative practice, but we must never lose sight of the fact that those in authority (teachers and leaders) have been placed in a position of power for a good reason. We have more highly developed brains, more experience and more wisdom than young people. At the end of the day, the person with authority has a duty of care and will be held morally and legally accountable for the well-being of young people. In contrast to operating in an authoritarian mode, when this person is in the restorative quadrant, young people experience their leadership as authoritative.

Teachers and leaders in this zone accept that conflict and wrongdoing are a completely normal part of life within school communities. There is an acceptance that young people (and not-so-young people) will conflict with one another and that good people will sometimes make horrible mistakes in judgement – or just do bad things! What emerges is an environment that is conflict positive where conflict and wrongdoing is addressed head on, not swept under the carpet (neglectful), minimised and excused (permissive), or reacted to through a sense of panic and impending doom (punitive). How might this practice be explained by young people? Well, on a good day it might be something like this:

- 'She's nice but can be tough when she has to be.'

- 'They talk about the rules a lot in this school.'

- 'A teacher actually apologised to me for accusing me of something that I didn't do. That must have been hard for him!'

- 'You know where you stand and what's expected of you – the rules are up in every classroom.'

- 'Most of the teachers here don't scream at kids in front of the class, they just ask questions or wait till later.'

- 'She'll always catch up with you if you have a bad lesson. She gets you in the end and always asks for *your* side of things, even if it's a day later.'

- 'You get a chance to fix things up – that's really important because everyone makes mistakes.'

- 'He doesn't hold grudges – he's respectful.'

- 'When there's arguments or fights, we get to sit down and work it out with each other.'

- 'Kids here have learned how to keep problems small by talking about them before things get out of hand.'

In the restorative quadrant, teachers and school leaders try to avoid assuming the roles of judge and executioner, and deciding who gets which punishment (a punitive response). Instead, it is the adult's role to provide all involved with a highly rigorous process whereby people are encouraged to talk with each other about what happened, what they feel and think, how they have been affected and what those involved in the problem think needs to happen to make things better. There is a strong belief that young people – even small children – can work together to create solutions to problems when taught the skills to do so. Restorative practice is seen by those who work in this quadrant as a way of thinking that can be taught to children and developed as *they* develop. In other words, restorative practice is seen as a pedagogy rather than a quick fix we try when nothing else has worked.

Good teachers and school leaders have always known intuitively that young people feel better and do better in schools where the adults work *with* them in an open, honest and transparent way. Young people's feelings and opinions are listened to and validated, even if they are not necessarily agreed with. When there are differences of opinion, young people are not held in contempt for how they feel. Teachers and leaders act based on a positive sense of self that allows them to permit dialogue with those involved when wrongdoing or mistakes happen. They can tolerate being a bit unpopular with students from time to time. Instead of building walls and defending their own positions, such teachers and leaders are secure enough to listen more and talk less in an effort to understand others' points of view – and calmly state theirs without falling into the trap of trying to make themselves right by making others wrong. This ability to treat wrongdoing and mistakes as opportunities for personal growth works because of the dominant view that problematic or 'bad' behaviour is not the *essence* of the person. In other words, when someone does a bad thing, this does not mean that they are a bad person (Kelly and Thorsborne 2014, p.65). The problem is the problem – the person isn't the problem.

From the student comments above, you can see that schools operating in the restorative quadrant use processes to engage students in decisions that directly affect them. One such opportunity is working with entire class groups to discuss what types of behaviours students and teachers expect from one another. Often the catalyst for these types of processes are when disruption and conflict have significantly impacted learning, but as schools become more confident with restorative practice, they begin to use creative approaches such as proactive classroom conferencing (Thorsborne and Vinegrad 2004, p.16) to help students and teachers clarify expectations and make plans for how teachers and students will respond when things go well or don't go well.

Until people have been inside these processes, it's perfectly normal for them to dismiss restorative practice as soft processes that are lenient on students who have done the wrong thing. In fact, most systems of accountability around the world, whether it be schools or the broader community, still largely operate in the punitive quadrant. Despite the spectacular failures of punitive-discipline systems to make schools safer and raise educational standards, and criminal justice systems to rehabilitate inmates, the popular rhetoric of policymakers is still largely punitive. One politician in my home state, when asked about overcrowded prisons as he talked tough on crime during an election campaign, famously responded that his government would 'rack 'em, pack 'em and stack 'em'.

Those with experience in the restorative quadrant will tell you that it is anything but a soft option. Restorative teachers and systems are big on accountability and responsibility-taking, but they recognise at the same time that students need high levels of support to work through incidents of harm. With this approach, teachers are vigilant in ensuring that all students are given opportunities to talk and that the conversation remains respectful. If students fail to take responsibility for their actions (e.g. don't admit their part in a problem or incident), fail to listen and fail to wait their turn to speak (or show deliberate disrespect to others, use put-downs, shout or act violently), the teacher respectfully instructs the student to leave the conversation (conference) and ensures that accountability comes to that student in other, more traditional – perhaps punitive – ways. Restorative practice works best in an environment of 'tough love', one that offers students high levels of control and support at the same time. A restorative approach firmly rejects harmful behaviour but does endeavour to understand it and repair the harm based on what those harmed and others involved agree needs to happen to make things better.

This is where a restorative notion of what is fair and just makes a critical split from traditional ideas of how to deal with inappropriate and harmful behaviour. The needs of those who have been harmed are considered central in these decisions. As Wachtel and McCold (2004) state:

> The fundamental unifying hypothesis of restorative practice is disarmingly simple: that human beings are happier, more cooperative and productive, and more likely to make positive changes in their behavior when those in positions of authority do things with them, rather than to them or for them. This hypothesis maintains that the punitive and authoritarian 'to' mode and the permissive and paternalistic 'for' mode are not as effective as the restorative, participatory, engaging 'with' mode. (pp.1–2)

Having explained the restorative 'WITH' quadrant, the task of the next chapter is to explore what a restorative approach looked like in addressing the situation between Jason and Tristan, which had spiralled out of control – distressing parents, teachers and the principal – and was looking likely to become a legal matter.

Chapter 4

Restorative Practice in Action
The Case of Tristan and Jason

Remember Tristan and Jason from Chapter 1? The story of how this issue was resolved restoratively is not a clear-cut one of preparation leading to a one-off restorative meeting (conference) with the boys and their parents where everything was sorted out. It was more complicated than this, because these sorts of issues are rarely clear-cut. These types of situations involve the combined complexity of feelings, thoughts and motivations. Things rarely go in the direction we hope they will when we embark on a restorative process to address a long-term conflict. What this case study will hopefully demonstrate is how a restorative compass keeps us pointing in the 'WITH' direction. Zehr (2002, p.10) says: 'Restorative justice is not a map, but the principles of restorative justice can be seen as a compass pointing in a direction. At a minimum, restorative justice is an invitation for dialogue and exploration.'

The case in detail
Planning with Mr Barker
I met with Mr Barker, the principal, took copious notes about the history of the conflict and talked with him about what he saw as a possible way forward. We agreed that I would interview each of the boys separately, with Mr Barker present. We wanted to see what each of them was feeling and thinking. We also wanted to see whether Jason and Tristan were interested in making the situation better and if they would be able to take responsibility. Would they be able to imagine the experience from one another's perspective? Would bringing the boys together into a restorative conference work, or would both boys dig in and deny any responsibility or, worse, exchange insults – and even blows?

I suggested to Mr Barker that in initial conversations with the boys, we'd skip the first three typical restorative questions (which you will learn more about in Part 3):

- 'What's been happening?'

- 'What have you been thinking?'

- 'What do you think now about what's been happening?'

Instead, we would focus on the fourth question typically asked to those who've made mistakes: who they thought was being affected by their arguing and how. Both boys had been given plenty of opportunities over the series of incidents (and in their wake) to talk and think about the effect this was having on them, and it was time to help the boys to shift their gaze to others. (When wrapped up in conflict we get so caught up in our own negative emotions that we become preoccupied with thinking about ourselves and lose perspective and the ability to think about others.) I also suggested to Mr Barker that we involve two other boys from the class in the conference between Tristan and Jason so they could talk about how the arguing and harassment had affected them and others. Mr Barker knew two boys, Adam and Aston, who were well respected and would do this job well.

Preparing the boys for the conference

Mr Barker and I sat down with the boys separately, Jason first and Tristan immediately afterwards. Mr Barker introduced me and my line of work. I told the boys that what had been happening sounded awful and that it mustn't have been easy for anyone involved, especially them. This show of empathy towards each of the boys, and the others involved, was important in communicating that what we were going to do wouldn't involve blaming them. This was an announcement that I thought the *problem* was the problem and that Jason and Tristan *weren't* the problem. This seemed to relax both of the boys and was important in building rapport and lessening their defensiveness. We needed Tristan and Jason in a space where they would be able to see past their own worries and look at the issues more through the eyes of others.

I explained that Mr Barker and I had a meeting in mind – something called a restorative conference – with the other boy, perhaps some other students from their class (who were good problem-solvers), Mr Barker and myself as the facilitator. In their separate meetings, both Tristan and Jason mentioned that there had been times when they had been friendly towards one another in the past. I asked each boy directly if they thought there was something worth restoring or whether things were too far gone. Both boys said there was still hope.

I explained that the goal of this conference, if they chose to take part, would be to talk about how the problems between them had affected people and to come up with an agreement about how the situation could be improved. I shared that this wasn't about trying to make the boys into best friends, but to decide on a way forward that would bring an end to the upset and nastiness.

Both Tristan and Jason expressed that they were interested in being part of a conference. In each of the initial interviews with the boys, I loosely followed this order of questioning:

- 'What's been the saddest part about this?'

- 'Who, besides you, has been affected by the arguing and fighting?'

- 'In what ways do you think other people have been affected by what's been happening?'

- 'How do you think it has been for [other boy]?'

- 'Do you want to stay fighting?'

- 'What needs to happen to make things better?'

In their separate meetings, both Tristan and Jason reflected deeply on these questions and shared with me that they believed that many people had been affected. They both talked about their mothers and the impact on them. Both boys reflected carefully on the 'What's been the saddest part about this?' question. I deliberately used the word 'saddest' to give both boys permission to see this situation as sad. Being a man and using a word like 'sad' with adolescent boys is quite powerful, and in my experience, this opens the door for reflection on feelings – something society doesn't encourage enough with boys and young men.

English was Jason's second language, and his responses to the questions weren't as detailed as Tristan's, but the emotions beneath were almost identical. Jason reflected that the saddest part had been the fact that he and Tristan had stopped talking to one another and had stopped playing together. When asked who he thought had been affected, Jason immediately talked about his mother, Galina, and Tristan's mother, Louise. He was concerned that it would get much worse with the mothers involved if the situation wasn't fixed. When asked if he wanted to stay fighting, he answered that the fighting definitely had to stop.

When I asked Tristan about the saddest part, he talked about how he and Jason had never had an actual friendship, but they had been sometimes put together for group work or sports and there had been plenty of times when he had felt friendly towards Jason. Tristan mentioned that Jason sometimes made jokes about him, and that he could take a bit of it, but that he would get silly too and begin retaliating with put-downs of his own. He said that Jason would sometimes then give him a friendly punch in the arm and call him a 'dumb ass' or 'idiot'. Tristan said that even though the punch in the arm had been meant to be friendly, it often hurt and would then be the beginning of bigger problems because he didn't know how to tell Jason that the punch was too hard – other than to retaliate by calling him a name.

Tristan reflected that he had made it worse at times: when trying to be funny, his remarks had been over the line and had been sometimes offensive to Jason. Tristan said, 'It's hard to make me laugh, but Jason finds everything funny.' He also said, 'I haven't done anything really offensive to Jason, just mildly offensive, but there have been times when we've got mad and the insults have got pretty serious.'

Tristan then said something that really got my attention: 'I've got no power.' When I asked him to tell me more about what that meant, he thought for a while and then said that Jason was physically bigger and that words were all he had to use against him. Tristan was also referring to how his mother had become so involved in the problems and how it felt like it was all spinning out of control.

When I asked Tristan if he wanted to stay fighting with Jason, he said that he had never wanted to be in a fight with Jason.

In these initial meetings, both Tristan and Jason were asked to share how they thought this would have been for the other boy and the boy's mother. The boys used their own experience of how this had affected their own mother to guess how it might be for the other's mother. This was very powerful because both boys felt a strong sense of loyalty and protectiveness towards their own mothers, and they were able to extend this instinct to the other's mother. This was very important, and both Mr Barker and I pointed out to each boy that they were demonstrating a mature understanding of the impact on the other boy and his mother. In the meeting with Tristan (which was after the meeting with Jason), I mentioned the similarities between what he and Jason had said: 'Jason thought that you and your mother might have been feeling that way too.' This was, of course, true, and mentioning it built good will between the boys that would help when they were later brought together for the conference.

Both boys in their meetings shared that Mrs Jansen, their classroom teacher, had been affected because of the disruption and the stress involved in having to constantly keep an eye on them. Tristan reflected on the time his mother came into the classroom and confronted Jason. He said that he was embarrassed by this and wished that she hadn't done it. Mr Barker immediately told Tristan that, being a parent himself, he understood how worried Louise was at the time. Hearing Mr Barker defend his mother was important to Tristan, as he was well aware that relations between Mr Barker and his mother were strained. Tristan softened towards Mr Barker in that moment. Mr Barker, who had been asked by Mrs Jansen to speak on her behalf, was able to confirm to both boys that their instincts about the impact this had had on Mrs Jansen were correct. (Ideally, Mrs Jansen should have been there to speak for herself, and in hindsight, I would have insisted on this. On that day, however, it didn't happen.)

Both boys said in their meetings that they knew that the problems had taken up a great deal of Mr Barker's time, and Mr Barker confirmed this. Mr Barker added that it had been awful seeing the boys, their mothers and Mrs Jansen so worried.

When asked about the impact on other students in their class, neither Jason nor Tristan could easily answer. Mr Barker suggested that two well-respected boys from their class be part of the conference to talk about the effect on them and the class. Jason and Tristan said they would be happy for Adam and Aston to be part of the conference.

At the conclusion of the conference preparation meetings with Jason and Tristan, Mr Barker and I had a couple of pages of scribbled notes from the boys' responses and were confident that bringing the boys together with Adam and Aston had a good chance of making a difference.

Preparing Adam and Aston

Mr Barker and I met with Adam and Aston together straight after the meetings with Tristan and Jason. We shared the idea of a conference and asked them how the problem between Jason and Tristan had impacted them and others in the class. The boys reflected on how things had become tense at times and how they felt like 'the meat in the sandwich' at times when their loyalties were divided. I asked them if they would be able to help Jason and Tristan by talking about this in the conference and then help Tristan and Jason come up with a plan (an agreement) about how things could be improved. Both boys agreed eagerly.

Tristan, Jason, Aston and Adam met briefly with Mr Barker and myself, and we shared the news that the conference was going ahead as soon as it could be arranged. We explained that we could go ahead because Tristan and Jason both wanted to put an end to the fighting and that both boys had taken responsibility for their part of the problem. It was also important for Jason and Tristan to hear that there was a high level of agreement between them about who had been affected (and how) by the problems.

Mr Barker and I talked with the boys about how the restorative conference would run and who would be involved. I talked about how the conference would end in everyone reaching agreement about how things could move forward. I explained that this restorative conference agreement would be signed by everybody in the conference and that Mr Barker would meet with the boys regularly after the conference to check how the agreement was going.

'Will our mothers be there?' asked a concerned-looking Tristan. I explained that if we could arrange it, both mothers would be there. 'I don't think that's a good idea,' Tristan said.

'Do you want to chat with us in private about your worries?' Mr Barker asked. Tristan nodded.

Both boys were enthusiastic about the conference going ahead, and it was clear that relations between them had already begun to improve. I said to the boys, 'I will arrange times to talk with your mothers and prepare them for the conference, just like we have with you today. I'm looking forward to telling them how mature you've both been in taking responsibility for your part of the problem and also understanding how others have been affected.'

Jason asked when the conference would take place. We explained that after talking to Louise and Galina, we'd have to look for a time that suited everybody. Both boys were happy with this. I asked, 'Tristan and Jason, how can we make sure that you guys keep it peaceful between now and then?'

'We will,' said Jason.

'If there's a problem, we will just leave it alone,' added Tristan.

'That's easier said than done boys,' added Mr Barker. I looked at Aston and Adam: 'Can you guys help these two to keep things steady between now and the conference?'

Adam replied with a grin, 'We'll help keep them out of trouble!' The room erupted in laughter.

When Mr Barker and I spoke with Tristan after the other boys had gone back to class, Tristan said he was worried that his mother, Louise, would get upset in the conference and say things that would make it worse. I explained to Tristan that those types of things tended to happen only when people didn't understand what the conference was about, or if they heard something upsetting that they hadn't heard before and it caught them off guard. I explained that it was my job to meet with everyone before the conference to get them ready and make sure there were no nasty surprises. I added that it was normal for everyone to feel pretty awful in the beginning stages of conferences. I explained that everyone catching these feelings from one another needed to happen so everyone could understand how others felt, and that this would make it easier for everyone to work together to fix things. Tristan seemed to understand and looked happier.

An obstacle and a clever solution

Unfortunately, we couldn't find a time when I was available to facilitate the conference when both Galina and Louise were free of work and study commitments. The idea was proposed by one of the boys that their mothers could be invited to the school as soon as possible after the conference, so the boys could report to their mothers, together, about how the conference went and present the draft written agreement to them for their opinion and approval. This was a master stroke! I could still explore the harm with the boys' mothers in a way that the boys could hear it, and Galina and Louise would be active participants in deciding the way forward – a critical step since Louise held deep reservations about the current plan the school had in place for the boys.

Preparing the mothers

A few days later, after meeting with the boys, I met with Louise at her home, and then Galina at the school. Both mothers were relieved to hear that Tristan and Jason had shown interest in improving the situation, and that the boys were able to understand the upset their bickering and harassment of each other had caused others. It was important that Louise and Galina knew that the boys had stepped up and shown maturity, as this helped them to feel better about the situation and lowered their anxiety.

Both mothers were also pleased with the boys' plan to be part of a restorative conference at school and then to have a second meeting with them to report on the outcomes of the conference for final approval, given that they couldn't be at the conference.

Louise had become heavily invested in (and affected by) the conflict between the boys. She was most concerned about what she called the end-of-day stuff, verbal slanging matches between Jason and Tristan at the school gates after school that she had witnessed on a couple of occasions. In Louise's eyes, Mr Barker and the school had failed in their duty of care to provide Tristan with a safe learning environment. Louise felt that Tristan was powerless and that the decision by Mr Barker to separate the boys at break times had impacted Tristan significantly. She felt that Mr Barker had a bee in his bonnet about Tristan and was favouring Jason.

It was important to just listen to Louise as she shared her frustrations and worries. To try to prompt her to view the situation differently at that stage would have only invited defensiveness. I encouraged Louise to keep talking. The depth of her distress, fear, anger and disgust about the situation needed exploring. The horrible feelings had to be aired before she could begin to open up her thinking to the impact on others, in particular the impact of *her* actions – the legally intimidating emails to Mr Barker and the day when she walked into Mrs Jansen's classroom without permission and told Jason she was watching him. Louise talked for a half hour about her feelings and the differences she had seen in Tristan. I knew my job was to encourage her to tell me more and to listen empathically, showing her that I understood how tough this had been for her and Tristan. Being a parent myself, I could certainly relate to Louise's worries.

Then things changed direction. 'I know Tristan is no angel,' Louise said. 'I have been hard towards Mr Barker – this has become personal and I didn't want it to be like this. It's been terrible.' Louise had just put it out there. I stayed quiet. She was seeing whether I was going to make this moment of vulnerability more shameful for her by agreeing with what she had just said. Experience had taught me that the best thing to do in such moments is to stay quiet, or speak in defence of the person's actions: 'Louise, you were a parent deeply worried about your little boy. I might have done the same thing if I were you in that moment.' That was true: if I had been Louise, seeing what she had seen and feeling how she felt, I would have acted as she had! Louise continued: 'I shouldn't have marched into the school like I did that day – that put Mr Barker in a tough position, not to mention how it would have been for Mrs Jansen.' Louise had taken my defence of her as emotional permission to take even more responsibility for her actions.

I talked to Louise about the boys' plan to meet with Mr Barker, Adam, Aston and myself to have a restorative conference to talk about the problem, how people had been affected and to make a draft formal written restorative conference agreement about how this situation could be resolved. I explained that as the next step, after their conference, the boys hoped to meet with her and Galina to present their formal agreement to them and seek their input and put the final touches to the agreement before it was formalised. Louise was pleased with this plan.

Directly after saying goodbye to Louise, I drove to the school to meet Galina. Galina had a contagious air of calm about her. Her take on the ongoing conflict between the boys was somewhat different from Louise's perspective. Galina, like Jason, spoke with a heavy accent. She spoke of her concern for both of the boys, but Galina saw the situation more as a normal conflict between two adolescent boys that had gotten out of hand because of the over-involvement of a parent. Galina acknowledged that Jason had certainly done and said things that he shouldn't have that had made the situation worse. She talked about how she had talked with Jason on many occasions about responding peacefully when Tristan did or said something that he didn't like. She had reminded Jason that he was bigger and stronger than Tristan and that he needed to stay mindful of this. Galina, like Louise, was encouraged by the plans to run a restorative conference with the boys.

Galina said, 'Louise must understand that this is just how kids behave. They take small things from school and sometimes make them big at home, and their parents then become upset and get too involved.' Galina mentioned that she understood that this situation had been stressful for Louise and that she would like to talk with her about what was happening with the boys and help her understand that this was just what kids did sometimes. Galina, however, also shared her concern about how this might be interpreted by Louise: 'Because I'm the mother of the boy that Tristan is having problems with, this might sound hard coming from me. It may sound like I'm making excuses for my son's behaviour.' I told Galina that certainly wasn't how it was coming across to me and that I didn't think Louise would interpret it that way either.

Community taking care of itself

A couple of days after the meetings with Louise and Galina, and a few days before the scheduled conference with the boys, I received a phone call from Mr Barker. He told me that he had received a call the day before from Galina saying that Louise and Tristan had followed Jason home from school and she didn't know what to do. My blood ran cold.

Mr Barker continued with the story. He explained that as Galina was speaking to him on the phone, she could see Louise and Tristan walking behind Jason, down the street, as he was approaching the front gate. Mr Barker at that point told Galina to hang up and that he was going to call the police. When the police arrived at Galina's home, they were met with a calm scene with Louise, Galina and the boys talking in the living room. Galina assured the officers that everything was alright and that the call had been a false alarm. (After ending the call with Mr Barker, Galina had bravely walked outside, greeted Tristan and Louise and invited them inside.)

Mr Barker and I talked about how a situation that had looked like it was about to turn out horribly and completely derail the process we had planned with the boys was, in fact, the best thing that could have happened. It was an example of two mothers taking the lead and showing their sons how restorative work is done.

Conference day

Before the boys entered the room on the day of the conference, Mr Barker and I had arranged six seats in a small circle. I had a clipboard with my notes and the questions I was going to ask of each boy. Mr Barker had a clipboard and paper on which to record the draft restorative conference agreement.

The boys entered and I showed them to their allocated seats in the Circle – Tristan and Jason sitting opposite each other. Tristan was flanked by Mr Barker on his left and Adam on his right. Jason had Aston to his left and me to his right. I began by welcoming everyone to the conference:

> Thank you all for being here. We are here to deal with a problem that has caused a great deal of upset to all of you here today, as well as some people who couldn't be with us. This problem has involved several incidents of teasing, insults, and sometimes stealing and damage of property between Tristan and Jason. The great news is that both boys have admitted their part in these problems and have both agreed that these behaviours need to stop immediately because of the harm they are causing themselves as well as other people.
>
> Aston and Adam, you have kindly agreed to join us to represent yourselves and others in your class, to share the effect the problems between Jason and Tristan have had on you and others.

Mr Barker, you are here as the principal of the school and someone affected by the problems as well. You are also representing Mrs Jansen, who is unable to be with us due to teaching commitments.

Louise, Tristan's mother, and Galina, Jason's mother, couldn't make it because of work and study commitments, so the plan is that Jason and Tristan will present what we come up with to them in another meeting as soon as we can arrange it.

Tristan and Jason, you know that we are not here to decide if you are good or bad people; we know you are both great boys. We are here to talk about what's been happening, how people have been affected and what we can do to begin repairing the harm.

I want to run some rules by you all that work well to make sure that everyone gets heard and that this meeting seems fair to everyone: One person speaks at a time (no interruptions), and we speak respectfully at all times. How does that sound to everybody?

If at any time anyone needs a break, let me know. Let's begin.

From here, I asked the boys the same questions I had asked them in the preparation meetings. The only difference was that everyone now had the opportunity to listen to others explain this problem and the effect from their perspective.

The questions below derive from the restorative practice conference script. They were, of course, modified to meet the needs of our situation. (You will see these types of questions and scripts, in different forms, throughout this book, and you will notice a common intention in them.)

Questions asked to participants during the conference

TRISTAN AND JASON

I asked Tristan and Jason the following questions:

- 'What's been happening that has brought us here today?'

- 'What's been the saddest part about what's been happening?'

- 'Who, besides you, has been affected by the arguing and fighting?'

- 'In what ways do you think other people have been affected by what's been happening?'

- 'How do you think it has been for [other boy] and his mother?'

- 'Do you want to stay fighting?'

- 'What needs to happen to make this better?'

MR BARKER
I asked Mr Barker the following questions:

- 'How have these problems affected you?'

- 'How have these problems affected others?'

- 'How has this been for Mrs Jansen?'

- 'What needs to happen to make this better?'

ASTON AND ADAM
I asked Aston and Adam the following questions:

- 'How have these problems affected you as the boys' friends?'

- 'How has the class been affected by these problems?'

- 'What needs to happen to make this better?'

Like most carefully prepared restorative conferences, the meeting between the boys, Mr Barker, Aston and Adam went according to plan. Everyone responded genuinely and thoughtfully to the questions, giving the sorts of responses they had shared with me in the preparation meetings – only now, many of the responses were better articulated. Because of the time between the preparation meetings and the conference, everyone had had time to process and refine what they wanted to say. (Mr Barker had met with Mrs Jansen and she had told him what she wanted said on her behalf.)

The agreement
The formal record of what was agreed during the conference is on the following page. This agreement ensured that the remainder of the boys' time together at the school remained peaceful. From reading the conference agreement you can see the insightful conversations that took place between the boys about what it would take for them to work together and manage the inevitable ups and downs that would come.

FORMAL RESTORATIVE CONFERENCE AGREEMENT BETWEEN TRISTAN, JASON, ADAM, ASTON AND MR BARKER – TO BE PRESENTED TO LOUISE AND GALINA AT THE NEXT MEETING

Conference date: 12/6/16

Conference participants:

Tristan and Jason, Mr Barker, Adam and Aston (as support people for both boys and representatives of the class), Bill Hansberry (facilitator)

What's been happening (the problem that brought us to conference)?

Jason and Tristan have been using teasing, put-downs, name-calling and awful comments about each other's families. This has sometimes escalated into defacing one another's school books, deliberately hiding belongings from one another and physical fights at times.

We have agreed that:

- Tristan and Jason agree that many people have been affected by their bickering – themselves, students in their class, their class teacher and Mr Barker, and both boys said that this has been very difficult for their parents.

- Both boys have agreed that the aggression needs to stop.

- Both boys have agreed to keep their words with one another respectful and clean.

- Jason and Tristan have agreed that even though Jason's punching in the arm was friendly, it has hurt Tristan, and it breaks the school's rule and it will stop.

- Both boys have agreed that if Tristan says something that is 'over the line' (as Tristan says can sometimes happen), Jason will calmly say to Tristan, 'Stop, don't say that again.' Tristan at that point will stop and apologise.

- Both boys agreed that it can make you feel small and weak to make an apology, so if one of them apologises, the other will gracefully say, 'Thanks for your apology.'

- We discussed what a sincere apology looks and sounds like.

- It was agreed that even though both boys would like to trial having the play restrictions lifted, this decision needs to be made with their parents and Mr Barker in a meeting with the boys' mothers.

- Bill and Mr Barker will arrange the meeting with Tristan and Jason's mothers, where the boys can present this agreement to their parents and the entire group can plan a way forward.

This agreement will be monitored by:

Jason and Tristan, Adam and Aston, and Mr Barker.

Mr Barker will check in with Jason and Tristan each day for a few minutes for five school days following this conference. If there are no problems, these check-in meetings will be weekly.

In each of these catch-ups (review meetings), Mr Barker will write a few notes on the back of the agreement original about what's been happening, and the boys will sign these notes.

If this agreement is broken/how we will handle it if this happens again (or conditions are not met):

- Another conference may be called so the person who broke our agreement can explain their reasons for breaking it to everybody.

- Those who broke the agreement may be asked to repair the harm.

- A formal school consequence may be decided upon by Mr Barker.

Signed:

The agreement was signed by all present in the conference as well as teachers of students (if applicable), parents of students (if required) and the conference facilitator.

SHARING THE AGREEMENT WITH THEIR MOTHERS

Two weeks later, I joined Tristan and Jason in the same meeting room where the conference took place. This time we were to plan what they wanted to tell their mothers about the conference and their agreement. Of course, Galina and Louise already knew about the agreement, as a draft had been sent home to them after the conference, with the understanding that it would be finalised with their input.

The meeting was going to be an important ceremony in healing for Galina and Louise, and a chance for Tristan and Jason to show their mothers how they had stepped up and taken care of the conflict.

Tristan and Jason were excited because, since the conference, they had both worked hard to stick to the agreement and had met with Mr Barker at the times specified. If there had been an incident between the boys in the time between the conference and the present, it would have been handled restoratively in accordance with the agreement. As frustrating as that would have been, it would have been dealt with. Thankfully, there had been no further problems.

We set up six seats in a circle, one for each of the mothers, one for Mr Barker and myself, and a seat for each of the boys. This time, however, Tristan and Jason decided they would be sitting next to one another.

The boys agreed that they would start the meeting by thanking their mothers for joining them to help finalise the agreement. Jason would say that part. Next would be my part when I would ask Louise and Galina the questions I would have asked if they had been able to attend the conference. After that, Tristan would hand a photocopy of the agreement to everyone in the Circle and then begin to read through it, point by point. Each boy would take turns reading, asking their mothers for comments or suggestions for each point. Mr Barker would have his laptop with the agreement on it and make the agreed changes.

Mr Barker stuck his head through the door and announced to the boys that their mothers had arrived and were waiting in the reception area. The boys went out to bring Louise and Galina into the room. The mothers were shown to their seats. We all took our places and Jason began the proceedings by thanking Galina and Louise for joining us.

I then began with the questions that I had emailed to both Louise and Galina before that day:

- 'How have you been affected by the fighting between the boys?'

- 'Who else do you think was affected?'

- 'When the fighting was happening, what changes did you notice in your son?'

- 'What was the worst of it for you?'

- 'What would you like to see happen as a result of the conference and today's meeting?'

Louise and Galina responded thoughtfully to the questions, sometimes individually and sometimes together, reiterating and adding to one another's responses. The boys listened intently. They saw their mothers united! When asked who else the problems had affected, Louise was quick to make the point of saying that Mr Barker had put a great deal of his time, energy and worry into the issues. This olive branch was an important gesture for Tristan to see.

Galina and Louise spoke of how encouraged they were to hear that the conference had gone well and that the boys had managed to get along in the time since. Jason and Tristan sat taller in their seats when both mothers said that they were proud of the boys for acting like men by taking responsibility for their actions.

When it came to discussing the draft agreement, Louise and Galina agreed that since the agreement had held well since the conference, nothing needed to be changed. The boys were stirring in their seats. They had the restricted play arrangement on their minds. Both were very eager for this restriction to be lifted so that they could return to normal play arrangements. It was agreed that there would be a trial of normal play arrangements. But at the first sign of trouble, all agreed that the boys would go back to separated play and the issues would then be addressed as laid out in the agreement. Galina and Louise were very comfortable with this idea, and all of the adults agreed that it was important that the boys understood that the normal break-time arrangements were something they would need to earn.

Mr Barker read out the agreement as it stood, and everyone agreed it was a good record of what had been agreed.

The meeting was brought to a close and the boys again thanked their mothers for coming to conclude the process. Galina and Louise thanked Mr Barker for his time and effort involved in this process. The boys and parents had a glass of orange juice and a biscuit while Mr Barker left the room to print copies of the conference agreement for everybody.

The next chapter will look at some of the essential principles and understandings for working restoratively. In doing this we will explore the importance of accountability for one's actions and how being accountable within a restorative framework differs from more traditional (punitive) models of discipline.

Chapter 5

Different Questions,
Different Outcomes

The definition of insanity is doing the same thing over and over again, but expecting different results.

— Attributed to Albert Einstein

Howard Zehr, often referred to as the father of the modern restorative justice movement, contrasts the main questions that restorative systems ask with the questions that traditional (retributive) systems of justice ask when people have behaved badly and harm has resulted. The two contrasting sets of questions shown in Table 5.1 create vastly different outcomes for people who have been involved in an incident of harm or conflict.

Table 5.1 Contrasting questions in traditional and restorative systems of school discipline

Traditional systems of school discipline (punitive: doing things 'TO' people)	Restorative systems of school discipline (restorative: doing things 'WITH' people)
What rules have been broken?	Who has been harmed (and how)?
Who broke them?	What do they need?
What consequence (punishment) do they deserve?	Who is responsible for meeting these needs?
	How do we ensure these needs are met and reduce the chance of these harms happening again?

Adapted from Stutzman Amstutz and Zehr (1998, pp.40–41)

The conflict between Jason and Tristan had us asking the boys to consider who had been harmed by their continued fighting with one another and what would need to happen to bring an end to that harm and repair some of the upset caused. When we ask these types of questions more, we end up with more restorative systems of school discipline. In these systems, students are held accountable to each other, not just to those in authority. Young people are asked to step up and take an active role in cleaning up the mess that their actions have caused. What does this look like in schools? The Tristan and Jason case study was just one illustration of restorative practice in action where an ongoing conflict between two boys had run too hot for too long and had become disruptive to the lives of the boys, their parents, their class and teacher, and the school principal, and was possibly about to spill over into civil action.

Of course, things don't need to get this bad before we call on restorative practice! In other forms of restorative work, small groups or entire grades of students may be found sitting in Circles, discussing various topics or a particular issue. Restorative interactions in all their forms bring students face to face to clarify connections between what happened and how people have been affected. Adults or trained peer facilitators (aka restorative peer mediators) guide these interactions by helping young people to think about and respond to a series of scripted questions, similar to the types of questions that were asked to those involved in the conflict between Tristan and Jason. (See Part 3 for different examples of restorative scripts.)

Restorative values

Examples of restorative values are as follows (Hendry 2009, pp.26–27):

- respecting individuals' rights

- taking responsibility for our own behaviour

- believing that people can change

- being open to supporting others who wish to change their behaviours

- believing that restorative responses are more helpful than retributive ones.

The restorative style of questioning engages entirely different neural pathways and guides young people through a process where an issue or incident is explored, intent is uncovered, stories of harm are shared and the needs of the harmed are discussed. Those who've been harmed are asked about what needs to happen so they can feel better, and those who've caused harm are asked to take responsibility for their behaviour by making efforts to meet these needs. When schools get these processes right, and work with the right intent and principles, those who've been harmed experience a fair and just process more often, and those who've caused harm (far more often than not) express genuine remorse for their actions and become interested in repairing the harm and accepting help to change their behaviour. When schools get it wrong and try to use restorative practice to force pre-determined, short-sighted outcomes (outside of the principles of restorative practice), they run into a lot of resistance and have poor outcomes.

What emerges from asking these restorative questions are systems of school discipline where students are held accountable to each other – not just to those in authority. (Accountability is essential, no matter which package it comes in!)

Wouldn't it be lovely if all of us were prepared to stop, listen, understand and acknowledge when our behaviour caused problems for others? But this isn't reality. For many reasons, there are many times when young people struggle with the emotions involved with taking responsibility for their mistakes and misdeeds. Not surprisingly, it's almost always the students with these difficulties who keep us the busiest. If we are really honest with ourselves, we realise that the stuff of owning up, admitting mistakes or poor judgement and taking responsibility is truly hard work for all of us. We all feel awfully exposed and vulnerable (ashamed) when facing feedback from those around us that we have fallen short, disappointed them or caused offence. Feelings of fear, anger and even a touch of self-disgust are characteristic of this moment and easily overwhelm us. In this moment it can feel as though we are wholly defective and that the stakes are just too high to admit our wrongs. (Chapter 9 goes into this experience that we call shame in greater detail.)

Restorative practice, being high on accountability (control) and high on support, demands that when harm is caused there be some form of accountability. In other words, something has to be done about the harm caused and it's someone's job to do this. In this sense, restorative and retributive principles agree with one another. Letting people get away with harmful or inappropriate behaviour would be permissive, even neglectful, if viewed through the social control window. There simply has to be accountability.

In a restorative framework, we invite people to be accountable, one way or the other. They can be part of a process where the focus is on truth telling, acknowledging, listening to one another and taking responsibility, where decisions are made 'WITH' them. Alternatively, they can be part of a process where all the decisions about how they will be held accountable will be made on their behalf. In other words, the process will be done 'TO' them.

Schools which are introducing restorative approaches may find that these new processes are viewed with some suspicion by some students. I've found this to be especially true in complex schools where students have become accustomed to a more punitive 'TO' style of discipline. The combination of teachers' inexperience with restorative processes and students who are new to this way of dealing with problems can make early restorative attempts interesting, to say the least.

At worst, students who've found themselves in conflict, or have caused harm or upset, may choose not to take up the invitation for responsibility-taking and restoration. There will be times when young people are not able to do the business of listening to others' viewpoints, opening their heart and mind to others or being interested in repairing the harm their actions have caused and changing their ways. At these times, teachers and leaders will choose to use more traditional 'TO' disciplinary approaches. When working with young people, I often talk about how things can be handled the new (restorative) way, or the old way; but either way, things must be dealt with!

There's no doubt which of these two ways delivers the outcomes we are looking for in terms of developing considerate and empathic responses. We always hope that students will be able to travel the restorative route with us because that's where the best learning happens. If they don't choose this road this time, we do what we must – what we don't want to do – to ensure accountability. The next time this same young person falls foul of others and our systems, we again begin with the intention to address the matter restoratively. If the young person can step up and take responsibility, then we have a preferred outcome. If not, we again achieve accountability through more punitive means. Eventually, as we keep offering a restorative way to right wrongs, that young person begins to realise that, although it is extremely tough, the restorative route is the best way to deal with things, stay connected to others and feel better. They also become less fearful of the emotions (manly shame) involved with doing business this way.

A young person said the following after a restorative conference:

> Listening to other kids tell me how my behaviour had harmed them is the hardest thing I've ever had to do. At the end, though, everybody felt better and I learned about how what I'd done had been for other people. We all got to fix the problem.

Below are students' reflections after a No-Blame Classroom Conference (see Chapter 18; Thorsborne and Vinegrad 2004). These responses are from students aged 11–13 years old:

> 'I think people realised what they're actually doing to people...they know how much it hurts now...how much it really affects us... It helped people clear the air with other people, so they can get on with them.'

> 'I reckon it changed a couple of people...I mean, how they think.'

> 'It's gotten into people's heads about how it's bad to harass and that sort of thing.'

> 'In the conference, Shiree started to cry, and I think Kiara really knew that she had hurt Shiree's feelings.'

> 'I think that once they really realised that people were getting upset, they were just like, "Oh, this is real stuff." They seemed to understand it, that it's not just a game.'

> 'I didn't expect people to open up as much as they did about what they've been doing.'

Exclusionary discipline: How well is it working for us?

In the context of accountability being critical, whether it be restorative accountability or punitive accountability, the stage is set for an examination of the more extreme disciplinary measures available to schools: external suspension and exclusion. I call these types of measures 'extreme' because, by their very nature, they exclude young people from the herd; they push them to the extremities of their learning community. As exclusionary measures are the consequence for high-level and persistent misbehaviour, this implies that to not belong is the ultimate deterrent for young people. Suspension can be a very necessary and powerful part of a larger strategic behavioural intervention for a young person, but as a community of educators, we need to stop kidding ourselves that suspensions on their own create any positive outcomes for the young people who concern us the most.

With this at the forefront of our minds, the question we need to ask is, 'What if the student excluded never belonged in the first place – would suspension or exclusion be a deterrent for them?'

If we critically reflect on students who are regularly dealt with through exclusionary processes, we can identify a shared characteristic: these students usually have little or no affiliation to the school, other people within the dominant culture in the school, or the values of the institution. These students often feel little to no social connection to the school and experience feelings of social exclusion. The research of Baumeister, Twenge and Nuss (2002) found that strong feelings of social inclusion are important in enabling individuals to regulate their own behaviour. These studies also showed that feelings of social exclusion and rejection reduce intelligent thought, increase aggressive behaviour and reduce prosocial behaviour. If exclusionary discipline processes trigger feelings of social rejection in young people, then are these processes compounding the problem by reducing a young person's capacity for intelligent thought, peaceful conduct and prosocial behaviour? Is using exclusionary practices as a main approach like treating a burn with a red-hot poker, thinking this will make things better?

Criminologist John Braithwaite makes a startling observation that is more poignant now than ever as extremist groups, on the fringes of their religions, actively target, radicalise and recruit young people who have drifted to the fringes of their communities (Braithwaite 1989):

> Having failed in the status system of the school, the student has a status problem and is in the market for a solution. He solves it collectively with other students who have been similarly rejected by the school. The outcasts band together and set up their own status system with values which are the exact inverse of those of the school; contempt for property and authority instead of respect for property and authority, immediate impulse gratification instead of impulse control, apathy instead of ambition, toughness instead of control of aggression. The delinquent's behaviour is right by the standards of the subculture precisely because it is wrong by the standards of his school. By participating in the subculture the poor academic performer can enhance his self-image by rejecting his rejecters. The boy's status problem is solved by the collective creation of a new status system in which he is guaranteed of some success. (p.22)

Figure 5.1 shows an image of disenchanted youth.

Figure 5.1 Disenchanted youth

The usual response to the behaviour of students with a status problem, as Braithwaite puts it, is suspension or exclusion. Although these measures can be necessary in the short term, if these are the only cards we have to play with young people, we push these groups of students further to the fringes, when what most of these young people desire is to belong; to be accepted, valued and respected. And so goes the cycle. The student becomes more distant from the school community with each suspension or exclusion. These are the young people who are most vulnerable to falling into the outstretched arms of gangs and terrorist organisations.

How do we interrupt this cycle? We could try a different approach and connect with them, giving them someone to care about, or alternatively, we could do what we have always done, and get what we always got.

Many enlightened educators have realised that exclusionary practices alone make no positive change in student behaviour but instead continue to justify these processes by saying that it is all they can do to keep the school community safe. Recent research is now indicating that this, too, is an errant belief. For example, Morrison (2007) states:

> … schools now argue that suspensions are used to keep the school community safe, rather than shift behaviour. The evidence is now clear that they do not shift behaviour in a positive direction; however, these punitive measures may shift behaviour in the opposite direction, thereby increasing the risk

to school communities. Schools, through capitalizing on approaches that developed out of law and order concerns, have compounded the biggest mistake (misconception) of the justice and penal system – that punishment keeps communities safe. (p.61)

Zero tolerance – Zero evidence

When examining exclusionary school discipline approaches, the term 'zero tolerance' inevitably comes up. Suspension, exclusion and expulsion are typically the instruments of zero tolerance in schools. The above heading is taken from Skiba (2000), where the effectiveness of policies that aim to deter inappropriate student behaviour by punishing both minor and major misconduct severely (i.e. zero tolerance) is analysed. Zero-tolerance approaches in schools have been historically applied to school violence as well as drug possession and use, but they have also found a home in any form of misconduct that school staff (or the wider school community) consider to be getting out of control. I once worked with an elementary school where the staff agreed that any verbal harassment involving sexualised language, no matter how minor, would result in immediate suspension from school. This is a perfect example of a zero-tolerance approach. Not surprisingly, it had little effect on the rates of reported sexualised language; in fact, there was more of it.

Zero tolerance is enticing for schools which find their ever-diminishing resources stretched by the increasing frequency and intensity of student misconduct. 'The idea of zero tolerance is powerfully symbolic, reassuring staff, students and the community that something is being done' (Noguera 1995, cited in Skiba 2000, p.16). In the current political climate, where schools are, more than ever, concerned with issues of accountability, being seen to be doing something straight away about unruly student behaviour is understandably attractive.

Skiba's (2000) research points out that there is next to no evidence that links zero tolerance to increased school safety. Data from the United States on exclusionary discipline processes – suspension and exclusion – are extensive but even less supportive of the effectiveness of zero-tolerance approaches. Zero tolerance, among other things, aims to send clear messages to the larger student body that certain behaviours, often only exhibited by a few students, will not be tolerated and will result in severe penalties. The accepted logic is that unless certain behaviours from certain students are dealt with severely, these behaviours will escalate in their seriousness and be adopted by other normally rule-abiding students. What the data strongly indicate is that, regardless of the nature of the discipline policies in place, a very small proportion of any student population (5–10%) is usually responsible for 80 per cent or more of the disruption and violent behaviour in any school.

For the aforementioned kind of student – at-risk, feeling disconnected from school – Skiba (2000, p.15) points out that the most consistently documented outcome of exclusionary discipline practices – suspension, exclusion and expulsion – appears to be further suspension, exclusion and expulsion, not an improvement in school behaviour.

Convincing the hardliners in schools of the merits of this research is no mean feat! The way we work with young people to challenge and get them to think about maladaptive behaviour is also what works best with staff who have not yet let go of the romantic notion that kicking kids out of school improves their behaviour. We need to engage in respectful dialogue, and most importantly, we need to listen carefully to the fears and concerns of our colleagues who are grappling with the many questions that come up as a school starts to examine a more restorative approach. Below are some points of discussion to promote dialogue with your staff about this very contentious issue of suspension and exclusion:

- When is suspension appropriate in a restorative school?

- At what age should we begin to use suspension?

- What is the purpose of suspension?

- How do we make suspension a procedure that enables success rather than disables it?

- What are the implications when re-admitting students following suspension? How do we reconnect them with the school community?

- What do we believe about zero-tolerance approaches and what data support these beliefs?

When young people feel that they do not belong, there is a sense of disempowerment and shame. In these instances, students create circumstances where they are empowered. Invariably these incidents wind up being destructive and unacceptable, much to the detriment of themselves and others. These students, feeling rejected by the 'law-abiding' members of the system, float to the fringes and form communities with others like them. These negative subcultures or shadow school communities become a big problem for the school. Through a range of antisocial behaviours they become further alienated when schools label them as 'gangs'. These are the young people who run the greatest risk of involvement in the criminal justice system and/or falling into the waiting arms of gangs or extremist groups. The task of restorative school communities is to hold such students accountable in a highly personal way that brings them back into the fold.

Bringing the educative agenda back to school discipline

Behaviour management can be an educative system, just like all other modes of learning that occur in schools. Discipline can be described as having three broad goals:

- to keep young people safe

- to teach young people to become socially competent

- to teach young people to take responsibility for their actions.

So often, the emotions that are stirred in teachers when students' behaviour causes the teacher harm, interferes with the right to teach, harms others or disrupts the learning environment muddy the waters. In their highly disgusted state, teachers can forget that behaviour management works best when it teaches young people something about the effect of their actions on others, rather than merely attempting to scare them into compliance. The instinctive response to any actions from students that interrupt the teacher's ability to enjoy or remain interested in their work triggers negative emotions like shame and anger, and sometimes fear, and the teacher is then motivated to do something about the problem. The gut response to this can cause the teacher to respond to wrongdoing in retributive ways, where the prime objective is to ensure that the student receives their 'just deserts' for their misdeeds. When this is the modus operandi, discipline practices end up being thinly disguised systems of 'an eye for an eye'.

If you've ever felt like 'teaching that kid a lesson', don't be too hard on yourself. To seek revenge when we feel angry about a student's behaviour can be linked to a cluster of neurons in the centre of the brain called the caudate nucleus. Modern brain-scanning techniques have shown that the caudate nucleus becomes highly activated when we have thoughts of revenge. There vengeful thoughts, in turn, activate the reward centres of the brain – making us feel good! (The caudate nucleus also lights up with activity when we think of something we like to eat, like chocolate cake. So revenge *is* sweet after all! Of course, I'm simplifying a very complex system of unconscious neural systems, but it is interesting to consider nevertheless.)

Knowing that revenge-centred discipline feels good in the short term, but never brings the long-term outcomes we want, our task becomes clear. First, we have to acknowledge this hardwired retributive urge, and then use our frontal lobes to override our innate desire for revenge when students do the wrong thing ('tit-for-tat' impulses). We also need to work in a way with young people that teaches them how to handle their own revenge reflex in the same way. The educative (teaching) component of discipline is very quickly lost in schools and classrooms where tit-for-tat cycles of revenge dominate student interactions and disciplinary processes.

Teaching young people how to engage in respectful discussions in the most provocative of situations is at the heart of creating emotionally literate citizens with the resilient thought processes they need to handle (and recover from) the ups and downs of sharing a planet with other people. We also have to remember that teachers are pressed for time, and that the rush of classroom life can make it difficult to get students together for conversations, to listen intently to all sides of an issue and to allow students to work towards resolution. It is much faster to do the process 'TO' students and make assumptions and inferences – to arbitrate an outcome and move on. (I still have to stop myself from doing this with students when the pressure is on.)

School rules and the restorative framework

School rules (or codes of conduct) are crucial for any school wishing to create a safe and productive learning environment. Many have a problem with the term 'rules' (I don't), believing that it smacks of traditional images of discipline. Rules are a statement of what a school values and how these values are expected to play out in people's day-to-day interactions and behaviour. All communities have norms of behaviour that serve the function of keeping that community connected and moving it in a common direction. Rules are the explicit expression of these norms and an important teaching tool.

The introduction of restorative practice should never mean a reduced focus on school rules. In fact, quite the opposite should be the case: implementing restorative practice is often a catalyst for schools to re-examine their rules.

Questions for schools

When a school approaches me or my colleagues in Australia to work with them to develop a restorative system of discipline, our first questions to these schools often go something like this:

- Can you articulate your school's values?

- How well can your staff and students articulate them, and how do you know?

- What kind of a fit do you see between your school's values and the values of restorative justice?

- What are your school rules (or code of conduct) and how up to date are they?

- Can you articulate them?

- How well can your staff and students articulate them, and how do you know?

- In what way do you see restorative practice supporting the communication of your values and school rules to your students and the wider school community?

These are thought-provoking questions that require that a school's personnel examine their beliefs and think about their values, rules and restorative practice. They always spark interesting conversations, and people quickly realise that there's six months of work in just developing reliable answers to some of these questions.

These questions clearly communicate that restorative schools are communities that are clear with one another about expectations of behaviour. Part of developing a restorative culture is helping everyone become clearer about what we expect from one another so we can go about our business in a way that doesn't cause harm. Harm is often the result when we fail to communicate our communities' expectations and fail to hold one another personally and communally accountable for harm caused when these rules are not followed. (Throughout this book you will read many case studies about how this accountability process looks in restorative schools.)

Rules protect rights and relationships

When schools go restorative, there is often a re-framing about the role that rules play. We want young people to understand that rules are not in place so adults can push young people around and limit their fun. Rules are put in place to protect rights and relationships. A school without rules is an environment without boundaries, and young people struggle terribly in environments without boundaries. Young people become disoriented and feel unsafe without steady, well-communicated expectations of behaviour from adults.

School Wide Positive Behaviour Support

School Wide Positive Behaviour Support (SWPBS) is an incredibly rich resource to be mined for research-supported approaches for developing school rules that are well articulated, well communicated and, most importantly, well taught to young people. The data-keeping and analysis methods within SWPBS are breathtaking and support restorative work in any school. The New Zealand Ministry of Education (2014) has done stunning work in bringing restorative practice and SWPBS together into a system and training package for schools called PB4L.[1]

We now move to the next part of this book, 'Feeling Restoratively', which explores the emotional side of working restoratively. It is my task in the chapters that follow to either convince you or remind you that work in schools is essentially emotional work, and that learning and emotion are indivisible. If you are thinking of skipping straight to what you may feel are the more practical matters of Part 3, I strongly urge you to resist. If you can't resist, then I challenge you to read Part 2 straight after Part 3. Trying to work restoratively without a grasp of the psychology underneath will seriously limit your ability to mine the riches of a restorative approach.

---

1   This can be found at http://pb4l.tki.org.nz/PB4L-Restorative-Practice. I highly recommend this resource for schools.

PART 2

Feeling Restoratively

A Psychological Framework for Restorative Practice

Chapter 6

Silvan Tomkins and Humans as Emotional Beings

Restorative practice has far more to do with how people feel than what they think. People don't really change their minds before changing their ways, and their feelings change (towards themselves and others) depending on how they believe they are being treated by others. Their minds change afterward. People's problematic attitudes and behaviours towards others start to shift in positive directions when they feel as though others are interested in them – when they feel cared for.

The realisation that working restoratively is more about understanding and acknowledging people's feelings than anything else has made me a far better restorative practitioner than when I started out. This realisation has motivated me to learn more about emotion and to change how I train schools in restorative practice. My working hypothesis is that schools where initial training is focused on teaching the theory of emotion that explains restorative practice – affect script psychology (ASP), which is Silvan Tomkins' theory of human emotion and motivation – will have greater success in implementing restorative practice than schools where the initial focus is on restorative questioning and the logistics of using restorative practice.

So far, feedback has been overwhelming: teachers, leaders and other staff have enjoyed learning about ASP, and this has placed all further learning into a powerful context. There's something about the stuff of our shared emotions that speaks to people's hearts and their deeply held values about what it is to be an emotional, social and moral being. Looking at restorative practice by starting at the level of feelings reminds us that we are all, first and foremost, emotional beings. As George (2015) states:

> Teaching is moral work that is attempted by fallible and very human people as a
> service to other fallible and human people still developing fully into the adults

they will become. Teachers have hopes, dreams, fears and disappointments, and so do their students. They are emotional beings. Teachers who are able to understand themselves, their colleagues and their students can help ensure that the mini-society that is their classroom, will flourish. Affect Script Psychology provides teachers with a theoretical framework for developing these understandings.

According to American psychologist Silvan Tomkins, all of us, no matter our age or cultural background, share a basic biology of emotion that is explained through ASP, which describes how restorative practice weaves the emotional magic that it does, as well as what's going on, on an emotional level, when restorative efforts don't deliver the desired outcomes.

How we feel about ourselves, how we feel about others and how we believe others feel about us drives most of our behaviour in families, workplaces or schools. Feelings can cause people to spin terribly out of control, so when working restoratively, we find ourselves in the affective domain, whereas traditionally, perhaps we'd rather think of schools as places where the best learning happens when we take emotion out of the picture and act rationally. ASP renders that notion an impossibility.

About Silvan Tomkins

Silvan Tomkins was quite a character. (Figure 6.1 shows an image of him.) Described by some as America's Einstein, Tomkins was a deeply insightful and intelligent man who would hold groups of people spellbound at cocktail parties as he talked about topics from horseracing to comic books to his theories on emotion and personality development. Among other distinguished awards, Tomkins was the first scientist to receive a Career Scientist Award from the National Institute of Mental Health. In 1947, after earning his PhD, Tomkins began an 18-year tenure in Princeton University's Department of Psychology, where his interest in the relationship between emotion (which he came to call 'affect') and personality formation became the defining theme of his career. Tomkins published a great deal about affect, personality and emotion, but his best-known work is the four-volume *Affect Imagery Consciousness* (Tomkins 1963), which divides its readers evenly 'between those who understood it and thought it was brilliant and those who did not understand it and thought it was brilliant' (Gladwell 2005, p.202).

Figure 6.1 Silvan Tomkins

Tomkins didn't know about restorative practice when he developed ASP. He died six days after his eightieth birthday in 1991 and never lived to see how his life's work would find a home in this growing field of peace building, dispute resolution, community building and criminal justice we call restorative justice or, more broadly, restorative practice. According to Abramson (2014):

> …Tomkins would be in awe of restorative practices. They not only allow but encourage human beings to be fully human – which, for him, meant being deeply emotional, mindful, and social. This is built into our biology. And restorative processes create, by design, such a safe and inviting space – sometimes more like an alchemist's cauldron – to be human in these precise ways. (p.85)

In the year of Tomkins' death, the Wagga Wagga police in Australia, led by community sergeant Terry O'Connell, were beginning to adapt a process from New Zealand called family group conferencing, to bring juvenile offenders face to face with those harmed by their actions, to explore the harm caused by the offence, to help all affected individuals identify their needs and bring restoration and healing. This highly emotional process was something vastly different from the traditionally formal and emotionally distant processes that characterised Australia's legal system. Some believe O'Connell's work with the Wagga Wagga police to be one of the symbolic birthplaces of restorative practice as we know them today, as this important work was well documented and taught widely. As it turns out, O'Connell's work was one part of a broader movement that was gaining momentum in different parts of the world. These isolated programmes that spanned fields, such as justice, education and community development all had an important common thread – they sought to empower the voices of people involved in conflict and harm (particularly victims) and valued restitution over retribution. Although these programmes were isolated from one another by distance and jurisdiction, and largely unaware of one another's existence, they were all restorative.

Tomkins, like his hero Charles Darwin, believed that the face held valuable clues to people's inner emotional states and motivations. Like Darwin, Tomkins believed that regardless of where humans came from, regardless of creed or culture, we all display nine basic emotions – distress, fear, anger, joy, excitement, surprise, disgust, interest and shame – the same way on the face and the body. Tomkins built himself a reputation as a legendary face reader who, as legend has it, could look at the face of a wanted felon on a poster and say with amazing accuracy for what crimes that individual was wanted. This wasn't a fluke. This ability had been developed by Tomkins through his tireless study of how affect presented and originated on the face. Tomkins' face-reading abilities went on to inspire the work of many others, including Paul Ekman and his incredible work on the Facial Action Coding System that is taught to people who wish to better identify others' emotional states.

The next chapter explores this list of nine basic, hardwired emotions that Tomkins proposed motivate us all, and explains how these basic building blocks of emotion keep us alive and cause us to care for one another.

Chapter 7

Affect
What Makes Humans Tick?

Silvan Tomkins' work teaches us that all humans are born with nine hardwired biological affect programmes that operate continually in us from birth until death. Tomkins called these the nine innate affects. How could Tomkins know that we are born with these preprogrammed affects? He studied infants, including his own son, Mark, and noticed that there were nine sets of responses to situations, each characterised by a particular set of facial, vocal and bodily reactions that was similar for all infants. 'Observing his infant son, Tomkins marvelled at the amount of information an infant, fresh from the womb, could communicate.'[1] From this, Tomkins concluded that all of us are born with nine, preprogrammed affects that are the biological foundations of all human emotion. Tomkins gave most of these affects two-word names to indicate the range of intensity with which they can be experienced.

The nine innate affects

The nine innate affects are shown in Table 7.1. Two of these affects, interest and enjoyment, are the biological programmes that are at work underneath anything that feels good – anything of which we want more. There are six other affects that underlie anything that feels bad – anything of which we want to experience less. Another affect, which Tomkins called surprise-startle, feels neither good nor bad, it merely acts as a reset button for the entire affect system after a sudden and dense stimulus (like a thunder clap) and causes us to pay attention to what's about to come next.

Affect script psychology (ASP) teaches us that we can only consciously notice something (a stimulus) if it first triggers one of these nine affect programmes. In other words, nothing makes its way into our conscious awareness until it

---

1   This quote is from the Tomkins Institute website (www.tomkins.org).

triggers one of these affect programmes. People can only *feel* if an affect has been triggered. Tomkins taught us that affects are the biological programmes that lie underneath every possible human emotion.

Table 7.1 The nine innate affects

Positive affect[a]	Neutral affect[b]	Negative affect[c]
Interest–excitement Enjoyment–joy	Surprise–startle	Anger–rage Fear–terror Distress–anguish Disgust 'Dissmell'[d] Shame–humiliation

a　*These affects feel good (inherently rewarding) and we are programmed to do more of anything that triggers these affects.*
b　*This affect on its own neither feels good nor bad; it merely resets the affect system and motivates us to pay complete attention to what will come next.*
c　*These affects feel bad (inherently punishing) and we are programmed to do less of whatever triggers these affects.*
d　*'Dissmell' is a term coined by Tomkins.*

Affect is the innate and biological basis of emotion. Each affect is triggered by a particular pattern and density of neural firing. 'Affects are the inborn protocols that, when triggered, bring things to our attention and motivate us to act.'[2] Each affect has particular to it a specific set of facial and bodily responses that are directed towards our survival. For instance, the affect programme for fear–terror displays itself as a widening of the eyes, lower eyelids tensed, eyebrows raised and drawn together and the hair standing on end.

> Affect = biology (the basic biological programme for a particular profile of neural firing).

Feelings are our awareness that an affect has been triggered as we feel our body's programmed physiological responses to an affect. For example, the affect shame–humiliation causes us to blush, slump forward, hang our head and even feel sick in the stomach. When we feel ourselves do these things, we come to know this as the feeling of being ashamed.

> Feeling = biology (affect) + physiology (the body's response to that affect).

2　This quote is from the Tomkins Institute website (www.tomkins.org).

Emotions comprise an affect plus a feeling plus associations to previous memories of historical experiences of that affect. The triggering of an affect begins a search through memory for other times this affect was triggered.

Emotion = affect + feeling + biography (memory of past times that affect was triggered).

Scripts

From birth, without realising it, our brains store and *bolt* our memories (or scenes) onto each of the nine affects. Even a small child will have a multitude of scenes of times they felt interested, joyful, excited, surprised, angry, fearful, distressed, disgusted, dissmelled or ashamed. These memories of what we did that worked (helped us to feel good) or didn't work (made us feel worse) become sets of instructions or rules about what to say and do in new moments to get more positive affect (good feelings) and less negative affect (bad feelings). Tomkins called these rules scripts. We are continually building, reorganising or trying to fit new experiences into our existing scripts, which distort our perception of reality. This is like the young person who immediately thinks that someone meant to hurt them when they are accidentally bumped in a game because of their established scripted reponses to the surprise-startle affect. The pattern of scripts that we use to try to experience more *positive affect* and limit *negative affect* become our personality.

How affects keep us alive

Tomkins' work teaches us that affect is the biological part of emotion that calls our attention to anything in our environment that has changed and may require action from us. This system of nine affects has evolved to keep us alive by working with other parts of our central nervous system to decide, from one moment to the next, which stimuli require our attention and which do not. Each of these affects evolved to motivate our behaviour in a direction that will maximise survival.

Without such a system to make these important decisions, we'd be overwhelmed by the millions of signals our bodies receive every second through our senses. Humans have a limited channel of consciousness. In other words, our brain has limited information-processing capacity; we can only pay attention to, and act on a small number of, stimuli at one time. Without a well-functioning affect system, our ancestors would have been eaten by the first predator that happened to pass by whilst overwhelmed by trying to make sense of, and act on millions of, pieces of sensory input every second.

The Tomkins Institute website states:

> We are born into our human lives with the propensity to survive, and the nine innate affects kick in immediately to help us do so, moving us to cry, connect, and learn. There are nine affects, each containing its own unique experiential signature, each attaching a specific type of meaning to information as it is taken in, stored and recalled. Affects are the inborn protocols that, when triggered, bring things to our attention and motivate us to act. Affects are not the same as emotion. They are the biological system that underlies emotion.[3]

How affects motivate us to survive

Before Tomkins, the world of psychology was dominated by Sigmund Freud's thinking that all human behaviour is motivated by primal drives (e.g. sex, hunger, sleep). Tomkins believed that drives alone were not enough to motivate humans to do the things they do. Tomkins challenged the idea that drives were the only motivators of behaviour with questions like 'What wins out if you bring fear to the bedroom?' or 'If a mathematician is completely absorbed with solving a math problem, how much will s/he sleep and eat?' (Abramson 2014, p.87). Tomkins' theory of a biological system of nine innate affects that combine with drives to motivate behaviour filled large gaps in our understanding of what makes people tick (Table 7.2).

Interest–excitement, the first of two positive affects, is the affect that motivates the drive to learn – to master something in our environment. The second of the two positive affects, enjoyment–joy, signals to us that all is well. Surprise–startle orients our attention to a sudden, extreme stimulus (like the lion pouncing from the bushes). The negative affect of anger–rage motivates us to act to fix something quickly (fight), and fear–terror motivates us to run, or be very still. Distress-anguish signals that all is not well and motivates us to seek relief from attentive others. Disgust evolved to make us expel anything we may have ingested that turned out to be toxic, and dissmell is an avoidance signal to keep away from bad (smelly) food that may be poisonous. (I won't mention shame–humiliation for the moment.)

---

3   See www.tomkins.org/what-tomkins-said/introduction/nine-affects-present-at-birth-combine-to-
     form-emotion-mood-and-personality.

Table 7.2 Affects, emotions and motivations

Affect	Associated feelings	How it motivates us
Interest–excitement	Fun, in the zone, tuned in, engaged, switched on, focused, on task, astonished, bouncy, chipper and so forth	Motivates us to engage, to learn more about someone or something. It is the affect that drives all new learning and the push towards mastery.
Enjoyment–joy	Contented, chilled, happy, fabulous, warm, joyous and so forth	Motivates us to want to be social, to share enjoyment with others, to affiliate. It is the affect that motivates us to share good news with others.
Surprise–startle	Shocked, freaked out and so forth	Motivates us to pay complete attention (stop, look, listen) to something in our environment that just changed quickly and could be a threat to our safety.
Fear–terror	Scared, frightened, jumpy, freaked out and so forth	Motivates us to run or freeze to be safe. It is the signal to become occupied with our survival and it dominates our attention until the perceived threat has passed.
Anger–rage	Mad, aggravated, cranky, grumpy and so forth	Motivates us to act quickly to stop something happening that might harm us – we attack. It is the signal to immediately deal with a state of stimulus that is way too much for us to handle.
Distress–anguish	Stressed, sad, cranky, nervy, grumpy, listless, rushed and so forth	Distress signals to those around us that all is not well, something is amiss and we need help. It motivates us to seek relief (comfort) from others or to offer comfort to others who are distressed, so we can relieve our own distress by relieving theirs (the empathic response). Our earliest attachment scripts teach us that other people are the best relief from negative affect.
Disgust	Disgusted, put off and so forth	Motivates us to spit it out and get it (or them) away from us. Disgust is a dominant affect in the breakdown of relationships (e.g. 'I once found that person tasteful, but now I want to expel them from my life').
Dissmell	Wary, stand-offish, grossed out and so forth	Motivates us to keep away from it – to avoid it (or them). It is essentially rejection of food, people or ideas without sampling them. Dissmell is the affect underneath prejudice that drives all forms of social segregation and racism.

Shame–humiliation	Confused, embarrassed, exposed, mortified, ashamed, guilty and so forth	Signals an interruption of the good feelings of interest and enjoyment, and motivates us to seek to restore positive affect. Because most positive affect is experienced in the company of others, shame has become a mainly social affect, motivating us to reconnect (after a disconnection), so important relationships can be restored and positive affect resumed.

Why restorative practice works

Kelly (2014) states:

> Restorative interventions work because human beings care. Amongst other things: people care about what others feel and think about them; they care that others have been harmed and are in need of repair; they care that they may have harmed others and don't know how to fix it; they care that others care for them; they care if others act as if they don't care for them; and they sometimes care to act as if they don't care because they have been harmed. Furthermore, all human behaviour is motivated by what we care about. (p.26)

Being social and emotional beings, humans are built to *transmit to*, and receive *affects from*, one another. In other words, affects are highly contagious. Our bodies are built to broadcast affect and emotion to the world. We have faces that are purpose-built with highly complex networks of nerves and muscles to show our affective state through our expressions. We have bodies that give our emotional states away to others through odour, sweat, skin colour (e.g. blushing), movement and posture. We are constantly broadcasting the affects we are experiencing to other members of our herd, and each member of our herd is individually equipped to resonate with these affects (i.e. to feel what we are feeling).

This is what makes restorative practice work. Being around interested or joyous people tends to be interesting and joyful because those affects are triggered in us when we see them. When others laugh, it's hard not to start to giggle as well, or at least smile, even though we may not know what was funny. Merely seeing and hearing others laugh triggers our laughter. A child roaring in full-throated rage can trigger anger in those around them. If you've ever travelled on a plane with a distressed infant, you know all too well how his or her cries of distress spread distress throughout the cabin like wildfire, triggering distress in everyone within earshot. A massive amplification of distress results. Caregivers who look after multiple infants see affective resonance at work all day long.[4]

This *affective resonance*, also known as emotional contagion, is what motivates us to care about one another. Because seeing and hearing distress in you triggers distress in me, I become motivated to put an end to your distress in order to ease my own distress. My attempts at this may range from me comforting you right through to yelling at you to 'stop your stupid crying' or even threatening to hurt you if you don't stop, as my distress changes to the affect anger, which now motivates me to quickly fix the problem of you making me feel distressed. Whether I comfort you with kind words or scold you, both are my attempt to get you to stop displaying your distress so it no longer makes *me* feel distressed.

O'Connell, Wachtel and Wachtel (1999, p.25) explain affective resonance in the context of restorative conferencing: 'People recognize the affects seen on others' faces and tend to respond with the same affect. When one is angry, others become angry. When one feels better and smiles, so do others. Tomkins calls this Affective Resonance or empathy.'

The fact that humans catch emotion or, more correctly, affect from one another is the biological mechanism behind caring, and caring is what makes restorative practice work.

In the next chapter we look at a blueprint for emotion, or a set of rules for affect, that if followed in a balanced way makes for mentally healthy individuals and communities. We then consider the role of restorative practice in helping school communities adhere to this blueprint for emotion.

---

4   You may have seen the viral YouTube clip of a mother with her laughing quadruplets (https://www.youtube.com/watch?v=CQo2FJPLeQk). This is a stunning illustration of the contagious nature of affect.

Chapter 8

A Blueprint for Mentally Healthy Schools

Tomkins' Central Blueprint for 'well' individuals and communities

Because all humans have evolved with an affect system with some affects that feel good and some that feel bad, Silvan Tomkins proposed that each of us runs by an inbuilt, hardwired set of instructions for affect (Table 8.1).

Table 8.1 Tomkins' Central Blueprint for individuals

We do better when we:	In other words:
1. Maximise (increase) the positive affects of interest and enjoyment.	Do more of what feels good.
2. Minimise (reduce) the negative affects of anger, fear, distress, disgust, dissmell and shame.	Do less of what feels bad.
3. Minimise the inhibition of affect.	Don't bottle up your emotions or try to fake an emotion – if you feel it, show it.
4. Maximise the ability to achieve goals 1–3.	Achieving goals 1–3 is good for a healthy life, and anything that interferes is bad for the individual.

Adapted from Kelly (2012)

This blueprint for what makes an emotionally well individual naturally extends to a blueprint for healthy communities (Table 8.2).

Table 8.2 Tomkins' Central Blueprint for communities

We do better when we:	In other words:
1. Share and maximise the positive affects.	Show others when we are feeling good.
2. Share and minimise the negative affects.	Negative affect dissipates when we make it mutual (i.e. share) with others what we feel bad about (within the accepted rules of our community).
3. Create opportunities for the public expression of affect.	Make it okay within our community to talk together about what feels great and what feels awful.
4. Maximise the ability to achieve goals 1–3.	Anything that helps to achieve goals 1–3 is good for the community, and anything that hinders this makes the community emotionally unwell.

Adapted from Kelly (2012)

Tomkins taught us that this blueprint, made up of four imperatives, is how we are wired, and this is how humans come to *want*. Tomkins' Central Blueprint is at the heart of affect script psychology. When individuals and communities achieve these four imperatives in a balanced way, they simply do better. This is, of course, no different for the individuals that make up schools (students, teachers, support staff and leaders) and the communities within schools (class groups, pastoral care groups, sports teams, special interest groups).

Nathanson (2004) states:

> Just as together this lets the good times roll, we're willing to make mutual each other's negative affects and to do our best to make them hurt less. A good relationship serves as an emotional heat sink that absorbs much of the pain that life can hand out. What works for each of us as individuals and for the relationship is anything we can do to maximise the two positive affects and minimise the six negative affects. In every sense the community process we propose is an extension to a larger group of this blueprint for a successful one-on-one relationship. It encourages all members of the community to share what feels pleasant and to sympathise with what might go badly for us. After all, what do we mean by sense of community? Yes, we share excitement and laughter as a group, but together we also feel the pain of each other's tragedies. As a group, we try to improve life for everyone.

The Central Blueprint at work in restorative schools

Young people and adults are happier and more productive in schools where the positive affects are maximised, negative affects minimised, where there is sharing with one another of what feels good and bad, and when people always look for new ways to help one another feel good.

Whether they know it or not, restorative schools respond to situations that feel bad in accordance with the Central Blueprint. Restorative processes (such as restorative conferencing, which you will read about in Part 3) are designed to bring those involved in a situation that feels bad back to positive affect so they can all feel better again. This takes place through the minimising of negative affect and the maximising of positive affect. Restorative schools lessen their reliance on practices that are designed to make people, particularly wrongdoers, feel worse in the wake of harmful acts. Punishment is one such practice. Just punishing young people for their misdeeds makes them feel worse and gives them no road back into the good graces of others. Punishment alone often also makes those who've been harmed feel worse, because they know that soon they will be together in a classroom again with the person who made them feel bad.

According to Deppe (2008, cited in George 2015):

A Restorative Process…helps meet the Central Blueprint for Community by:

- Bringing people together in a safe place (blueprint goal 4)

- Asking people to express their feelings about an incident (blueprint goal 3)

- To share and maximize positive affect and shame and minimize negative affect (blueprint goals 1 and 2).

As you read later chapters in Part 3, you will be introduced to many different versions of the restorative conference script, otherwise known as restorative questions. You already saw these questions at work in the case study involving Jason and Tristan. As well as dealing with incidents of harm restoratively, restorative schools are always looking for interesting and enjoyable ways to bring students and adults together so that positive feelings can be maximised. Circles, also known as Circle Time, is one highly effective pedagogy that the micro communities in schools, such as class groups or pastoral care groups, can live by the Central Blueprint that is enjoyed by students and adults regardless of their age or grade level. (Circles are covered in Chapter 22.)

The next chapter introduces the affect that lies beneath anything we might call 'hurt feelings'. This affect can work as a helper or a hinderer to positive behaviour change, depending on how well it is understood and managed in schools and communities. This affect is shame–humiliation.

Chapter 9

Affect Shame
Our Inbuilt Social Alarm Bell

If distress is the affect of suffering, shame is the affect of indignity, of defeat, of transgression and of alienation. Though terror speaks to life and death and distress makes of the world a vale of tears, yet shame strikes deepest into the heart of man... Shame is felt as an inner torment, a sickness of the soul. It does not matter whether the humiliated one has been shamed by derisive laughter or whether he mocks himself. In either event he feels himself naked, defeated, alienated, lacking in dignity or worth.

– Silvan Tomkins

Now we turn our attention to the affect Tomkins called shame–humiliation. Of the nine innate affects, the shame–humiliation affect and the family of emotions that fall within what we know as shame are of particular importance to understanding the psychology of restoration.

To understand how the shame–humiliation affect has evolved to motivate our behaviour, we need to put aside all preconceptions about the word 'shame' and remember that, when we talk about affect, we are at the purely biological level of emotion (Figure 9.1).

Figure 9.1 A young lad with angry people behind

According to Tomkins, affect shame was the last of the affect programmes to evolve in humans. The purpose of this affect programme is to signal to us when anything partially interrupts the two positive affects of interest or enjoyment. In other words, affect shame signals when something has gotten in the way of our ability to stay interested in, or to enjoy, someone or something. Shame then motivates us to search for what that impediment might be, and to do something about it, so we can return again to the positive affects of interest and enjoyment. This is important because Tomkins' Central Blueprint is constantly directing us to:

- maximise positive affect

- minimise negative affect

- maximise the expression affect

- maximise our ability to carry out these three goals.

Anything that partially interrupts the first imperative of Tomkins' emotional blueprint must be noticed and dealt with so we can return to positive affect. Signalling this interruption is the task of the affect that Tomkins named shame–humiliation.

Affect shame in more detail

Let me give an example that illustrates a social moment where interest and enjoyment have become impeded. Imagine yourself in a coffee shop with a friend. It's a nice morning; the coffee is good and so is the conversation. Interest and enjoyment are the affects being continually triggered in both you and your friend in this moment of connection.

You are interested in the conversation: You are interested in what your friend has to say and you are interested in what you have to say to them. You are also interested in how interested they are in what *you* have to say. When you say something to your friend, you wait in anticipation for their reaction. When they nod, agree or smile (signalling interest or enjoyment), you, in turn, resonate their enjoyment and become interested in what they have to say next, or a thought that just popped into your head that you want to share with them. This affective exchange goes back and forth between you and your friend.

Imagine that while you are in mid-sentence, telling your friend something that you think is very interesting, your friend suddenly breaks eye contact and looks away. You feel confused and dreadful for a brief moment. That dreadful feeling is affect shame telling you that something just interrupted the good feelings you were sharing with your friend a moment earlier.

After the brief moment of awfulness triggered by your friend's sudden glance away, Donald Nathanson tells us that we begin an inner search. This begins what is known as the cognitive phase of shame and involves a brief inner search: 'Did I say something to offend? Did I spit? Is my breath bad?' In this fleeting moment there have also been physiological responses that go along with affect shame. Your eyes have likely looked down and away (probably only briefly) from your friend. Your head may have slumped slightly as your neck muscles lost tone. A slight blush may have even stained your cheeks or neck. These are all physiological components of affect shame.

How shame signals a loss of connection

Affect shame has signalled to you a momentary loss of connection with your friend and has begun recruiting your cognitive processes, including your memories, to search for a reason for this partial impediment to the interest and enjoyment that you were experiencing just a few seconds earlier.

What did I just say that may have upset my friend? Why does affect shame trigger this inner search? Tomkins believed this happens so you can learn from this moment about how to avoid such a loss of positive affect in the future. So, what was it that caused your friend to look away, to disconnect? You want to know, but actually asking them 'Why did you look away while I was talking?' seems difficult. It might seem rude to ask. Although it's possible that it might have been something you said that caused your friend discomfort, confirming this suspicion risks triggering even more shame. Instead of asking, you just keep talking as if nothing happened.

In this moment with your friend, affect shame first directed your attention to the fact that they looked away and then motivated you to check yourself, to analyse the brief interruption to emotional connection with your friend. You concluded from your analysis of the moment that it can't have been anything you said or did. Perhaps your friend remembered something important they had to do as you were talking. Maybe they felt a jab of pain from an old knee injury. There's every chance that their glance away had nothing to do with you, but affect shame did the very important job of signalling the brief emotional disconnection when your friend first looked away.

Within a second of glancing away, your friend has looked back at you again and positive affect returns to replace the dreadful feeling of affect shame that had just briefly signalled the problem. This all happened very quickly.

How shame tries to keep us connected

Thorsborne (2005) states:

> We are all warm blooded hairy mammals, albeit with large frontal lobes and lots of grey matter to be clever with, but are animals all the same. Here's the thing; we are herd animals. We live in small and larger groups – families, tribes, communities – defined sometimes by geography, sometimes by our work, sometimes by our faith and interest groups. We survive best when the connections between us are strong and healthy...

What followed in that fraction of a second after your friend in the coffee shop broke eye contact with you is absolutely vital to our survival as a species. Tomkins said, 'Shame affect exists to help us foster our sense of belonging and mastery by asking us to make sense of and overcome what might get in the way.'[1]

If we fail to stop and pay attention to what just got in the way of feeling good with others, our emotional connections to those we depend on are at risk. This is the reason that affect shame is thought of mainly as a social affect. It is mostly in the company of others that we experience the positive affects of interest and enjoyment, so it follows that most of the times these are impeded will be during our social interactions with others.

Shame as a social regulator

Shame is a powerful regulator of social behaviour. In every moment, we make decisions about our behaviour to try to feel good more of the time (interest and enjoyment) and to avoid the sting of shame. Just the thought of feeling shame is punishing enough to make most of us think carefully about what we will do or say next. We want to avoid the awful thoughts and feelings that accompany a moment of shame, so we try to conduct ourselves in ways that will keep others interested in us and enjoying our company. Our primitive brain knows that our survival depends on our ability to sustain this interest and enjoyment in, and with, others.

Thorsborne (2005) states: 'Shame can be triggered by a wide range of events but most often occurs when the experience of being connected with another is interrupted, [initiating] a sequence of thoughts, feelings and reactions.'

---

1   This quote is from the Tomkins Institute website (www.tomkins.org).

There is, of course, an infinite number of possible scenarios where our good feelings towards others and their good feelings towards us might be impeded and affect shame triggered. In each possible instance, what makes the experience of affect shame feel so awful is a sudden awareness of something about the self that we didn't really want to know. In the coffee shop, your friend's sudden glance in another direction caused you to ask some important questions about the possible reasons for their apparent loss of interest in you. It is awful to think that something you may have done or said (or not done or said) might have caused your friend hurt feelings. Affect shame asks us to delve into our memories of past shame experiences and question ourselves. It asks us to examine the possibility that we might not have been as interesting, clever, competent, charismatic or even attractive as we would like to believe we were.

We are all extremely interested in any information that affirms that we possess these desirable personal qualities, but as soon as any impediment – any disconnection with another – is signalled by affect shame, we are motivated, by affect shame, to re-examine our view of ourselves and search for what it was about us that might have just caused the problem. (As you have read this, your thoughts may have wandered to the faces of students, or perhaps family members, who seem incapable of the navel gazing that affect shame wants them to do.)

The next chapter looks at, in more depth, shame's motivation to trigger self-examination and why so many of us seem incapable of this task.

Chapter 10

Grasping the Nettle
Shame's Difficult Demand

This is an example of how I sometimes talk with young people when trying to help them to make sense of their feelings when their behaviour has seen them fall foul of others:

> I can see you feel awful. That feeling you're getting is called shame, and it has a really important job. It's telling you to do the brave work of owning up to what you did and fix it. You might feel like running and hiding, pretending it didn't happen or blaming someone else for what happened. I feel like that, too, when I make mistakes. What you're about to do will be hard, but when you do the brave fixing work, you and everyone else will feel a lot better.

This example explains how difficult the task of acknowledging wrongdoing can be and how brave we have to be to face up to our mistakes and do the job of fixing that shame asks us to do. One of the main tasks of preparing people for a restorative encounter is helping them make sense of the emotions that course through them in anticipation of a restorative conference.

A large body of empirical evidence, including Donald Nathanson's work as well as a host of others (e.g. Ahmed and Braithwaite 2004; Morrison 2007; Nathanson 1992, 1994, 1996, 2000, 2004; Retzinger and Scheff 1996), tells us that what people do with the terrible thoughts and feelings that come with affect shame can mean the difference between what might be considered well-adjusted responses that reconnect them with others or, alternatively, a range of unhealthy patterns of behaviour that try to make shame go away. Unhealthy responses to shame can range from simply withdrawing from the company of others right through to explosions of murderous violence (as seen in high school and college shootings in recent years).

The shame experience leaves all of us feeling confused, hurt, diminished, exposed and vulnerable. It becomes the task of authoritative communities to teach young people how to deal constructively with shame so they can do the important work that this affect demands of them.

Why it's so hard to listen to shame

Now that we understand affect shame's social purpose – first, to signal an interruption to our connections to others, and second, to motivate us to examine and deal with the causes of that interruption – the solution to the shame problem seems obvious. We simply need to do the self-scrutiny and, if we conclude that we have caused the problem, take steps to deal with it and reconnect. But unfortunately, for most of us, in many situations it's not that simple. If most of us could do this very brave work with shame immediately – 'You looked away, are you okay? Did I say something wrong?' – the world would be a far safer place.

The problem is that the self-scrutiny stage of the shame experience triggers a second wave of shame, which adds to our shame pain. For us to hang in there with the moment of shame, and then follow through with self-reflection and social reconnection, we must feel as though we are loved and accepted by others. We have to be at our best. The problem is that in the moment of shame we may feel so terribly exposed, so utterly defective, that it is easy to forget that there is anything good about us – anything worthy of pride.

Nathanson (2004) states:

> The most mature way of responding to a moment of shame starts with an inner search after which we realise it is okay to love ourselves. From this search, we remember the loving support of those who have truly cared about us. And it is from this solid sense of a good and lovable self that we then respond to and accept whatever has been exposed about ourselves, no matter how awful it may have seemed a moment earlier. At best, shame leads us to an acceptance and deeper truths. Sadly, for most of us, this is rarely so.

To deal with shame in a healthy manner, we need to be able to remind ourselves of the loving support of others. 'I am okay because there are other people who know that I am okay.' When we can remind ourselves of our loving bonds with others, we are more likely to regain a stable sense of self. When standing on this stable ground, I am able to accept that even though this moment of shame feels awful, and something shameful about me has been exposed, I can handle shame and take care of whatever caused this impediment.

When shame strikes and we don't feel loved and accepted, we are completely helpless to do anything constructive with shame.

Why only the loved and connected can meet shame's demands

For people who have strong connections with others and the accompanying feeling of belonging, once the initial shock wave of shame passes, these individuals are able to remind themselves of good attributes that make up a lovable and worthwhile self. They recognise that they are still worthwhile people and worthy of pride. Those familiar with cognitive behavioural therapy may refer to this as the ability to 'talk sense with one's self' after a moment of shame.

Patterns of thought associated with shame

The fictional scenarios in Table 10.1 demonstrate contrasting ways that four young people deal with a moment when affect shame signals to them an interruption to good feelings about other people and/or an interruption to good feelings about themselves. On the left side are healthy responses that we might see from young people who are feeling self-assured (loved and connected) in the moment that shame strikes. The responses on the right side are typical of what young people might think and do when shame strikes and they cannot remind themselves that they are okay and that they are loved and accepted.

Table 10.1 Healthy and unhealthy thought patterns regarding shame

Young person	Thoughts that show a person is feeling stable and connected (can deal honestly and bravely with a moment of shame)	Thoughts that show a person is *not* feeling stable and connected (is unable to deal honestly and bravely with a moment of shame)
Alexandria	Jess saying that she doesn't want to hang out with me feels like a rejection, but I know I'm a good friend. Maybe I upset her when I didn't ask about her dad yesterday. She's been pretty worried about his health. I'll ask her how he is when I see her in lesson three. She might still be angry, so guess I'll apologise for not asking earlier.	Jess saying that she doesn't want to hang out with me feels like a rejection. She's probably mad because I didn't ask about her dad. Oh no, that's what I did wrong. She's probably really hurt and thinks I'm insensitive. I suppose she hates me now. I'm going to keep away from her from now on. She'll just hate me more if she sees me.

Nicky	Being told off by Mrs Stewart for talking in class was embarrassing. What must she think of me? Usually I don't get in trouble, I'm normally pretty good in class and get along well with teachers. This wasn't like me. I'll make sure I don't talk while she's talking next time. Perhaps I'll sit away from Claudia and Eliza. They love to chat! I could apologise to Mrs Stewart next time I see her. I'm sure she'll be okay about it.	Being told off by Mrs Stewart for talking in class was really embarrassing. What must she think of me? It's so typical of me to do stupid stuff like that, I just can't help it. This is twice this week. Ms Donaldson glared at me for being too chatty on Monday (at least that's what I think her look meant). Does this mean I'm one of the bad kids? Perhaps I'll just sit with the bad kids next lesson.
George	I can't believe I failed the algebra test. What went wrong? Usually I do pretty well in maths when I study. I guess this time I slacked off a bit. I should have studied for the test instead of playing basketball Monday night. I'll study next time and try to make up the lost marks. Dad will just give me that look and ask, 'What's this taught you?' I know, I know…if you want the results, you have to put in the effort. I hate it when he does that, but he's usually right.	I can't believe I failed the algebra test. I've probably dropped to a 'C' from an 'A' now. Dad will go nuts when he sees the test. I'll hide it from him. Who cares about maths anyway? Where in my life will I ever *use* algebra? I'd rather stay longer at soccer training than study for stupid algebra tests because I'm the best soccer player in the school, and I won't need algebra when I'm a star striker.
Ben	The boys are ignoring me. They just do this sometimes. I think they feel powerful when they exclude people. They might be mad because I didn't make that catch yesterday in softball. That's so petty if it's true. I know I'm a friendly guy; the kids at Scouts like me. I'll hang around with some other kids today, but if I see the boys, I'll still be friendly.	The boys are ignoring me. What did I do? They are such losers. They get their kicks from being mean to people. They do this all the time. I can't stand them. Who'd want to be in their stupid gang anyway? I'll get Josh, Simon and Peter together and we'll bash them after school.

In all of the situations in Table 10.1, the difference in these young people's responses to the situation that triggered shame depends on whether or not they could remind themselves of their positive and pride-worthy attributes, and their loving connection to others during their moment of shame. Only from a stable sense of self, which comes from solid connection with others, could they bravely examine what they might have done to cause the problem and make plans to either restore a relationship or remedy the problem.

Analysis of the thought patterns presented in Table 10.1
Thoughts that show a person is feeling stable and connected

In the first situation with Alexandria and her upset friend Jess, and the second situation with Nicky and Mrs Stewart, her teacher, both young people experienced an interruption to their interest in themselves as good people. They faced a moment that challenged their view of themselves and impeded the enjoyment they usually receive from thinking of themselves as good, kind and considerate people.

In their moment of shame both girls were able to do the hard work of examining what they may have done to cause the interruption to the good feelings between them and the others involved. Alexandria reminded herself that she is still a good friend (and a good person) but also accepted that she had not shown enough interest in how Jess was feeling about her sick father. Nicky was able to remind herself that she's normally polite in class and that her recent behaviour isn't normal for her. From this stable sense of a good and lovable self, both Alexandria and Nicky were strong enough to do the brave work of trying to repair their relationship with Jess and Mrs Stewart, respectively, and in the process restore their own positive view of themselves. This repair work (i.e. reconnection) would give Alexandria and Nicky the best chance of ending the interruption to the positive feelings of interest and joy.

In the third scenario, George's interest in himself as a competent mathematician was interrupted by a poor test result. This moment made it hard for George to feel good about his abilities in maths. In spite of this, George was able to do the honest and brave work of putting himself as the cause for bombing out in his algebra test. From a stable sense of self and his abilities, he examined the reasons that he did so poorly on the test and came to the realisation that his lack of effort was the problem. This helped George conclude that he didn't fail the test because he was dumb. George also predicted that his father's reaction to his failing the test would be calm but would challenge him to think about what he's learned from this experience. This would be shameful as well, but George would be able to handle it.

In the final situation, Ben's interest in himself as a popular and likeable person, and his enjoyment (usually gained from spending time with the boys), was interrupted when the boys ignored him. Although this felt awful (shameful), Ben was able to quickly recover from the initial shock and use a thought process that allowed him to accept that even though the behaviour of the other boys wasn't fair, sometimes people act unfairly, and he could handle it. This wasn't the end of the world. Ben could only think this way because, in the moment of shame, he was feeling connected to others and self-accepting. Because of this, he didn't catastrophise this event; rather, he saw it as a glitch, where normally nice people (the other boys) were acting badly. Ben speculated as to what he may have done to upset the boys and reasoned that it might have been because he dropped the catch in softball. From a stable sense of self, Ben was able to remind himself that he was still a friendly person who had other people in his life who accepted and liked him.

Thoughts that show a person is *not* feeling stable and connected

The right side of Table 10.1 contains contrasting reactions to the moments when interest and joy were interrupted and affect shame was triggered. In these situations, the initiating events were identical for Alexandria, Nicky, George and Ben. What was different in these moments of shame was that, for whatever reason, the young people involved weren't feeling centred, self-assured or connected when shame struck. They just weren't strong enough in that moment to do the brave work demanded by shame. Each of them drew on a range of defensive strategies to try to make shame go away without dealing directly with the problem.

In the first scenario, Alexandria's rejection by Jess was painful, but her response was different. Alexandria began the task of dealing honestly with shame by searching her memory for what she may have done to invite Jess's rejection. From this inner search she realised that it may have been bad of her not to have asked Jess about her father's health. This realisation triggered a second wave of affect shame, but in that moment, Alexandria just wasn't up to the task of dealing authentically with it. Instead of accepting the information that shame wanted her to consider, Alexandria told herself that Jess probably hated her now and that any further contact with Jess would only give Jess more reasons to despise her. Alexandria then planned a withdrawal from the relationship: 'I'm going to keep away from her from now on. She'll just hate me more if she sees me.' This deliberate pulling away from Jess is a self-defence mechanism to limit the damage to her own self-esteem. The problem now is that unless Alexandria can find the strength to deal with this shame, she will damage a friendship that is important to her.

In the second situation, Nicky felt ashamed about her behaviour in class but wasn't in a space to deal with the awful thoughts and feelings that accompanied the triggering of affect shame. Shame was accompanied by self-disgust. Nicky immediately accepted a reduced status, a diminished opinion of herself, as if she was wholly defective and that this behaviour was normal for her (because she is a bad person). Nicky's self-talk took on an attack-self flavour, and by talking to herself in this way, Nicky was able to let herself out of taking responsibility for her behaviour: 'It's so typical of me to do stupid stuff like that, I just can't help it.' The problem for Nicky is the acceptance of a reduced status in life that comes along with this type of response to shame. Nicky allowed a small indiscretion in class to begin to redefine her as one of the 'bad kids'. If she takes this view of self on permanently, she will behave in accordance with it.

In the third scenario, George failing the algebra test caused an impediment to his interest in himself as a competent mathematician. Affect shame signalled this impediment and created an uncomfortable moment for him. In this moment, George's self-esteem took a hit and he couldn't remind himself that he is okay, loved, smart and competent. George also worried that his father would be angry (which would be his father's response to his own shame associated with his son failing at maths). This thought triggered more shame as well as distress and fear. George panicked and was unable to deal honestly with the reasons for his failure. Like with Alexandria, Ben and Nicky, George was motivated by the Central Blueprint to return to positive affect – and feel good again. He decided to evade the terrible thoughts and feelings of shame. He planned to keep the test from his father and distracted himself by thinking about something (soccer) that gave him feelings of pride. This avoidance of shame caused George to over-exaggerate his soccer abilities, but at least he didn't have to think about algebra any more. He avoided the task of shame by focusing on an aspect of the self that brought him feelings of pride and, in the process, exaggerated those qualities.

In the final scenario, Ben's problem with the other boys ignoring him carried the sharp sting of shame that always accompanies social rejection. This time, though, instead of self-forgiveness, we found Ben in a very different state when shame struck: He turned the tables and went on the attack. Feeling desperate and hurt about the unfairness of his mistreatment by the other boys, Ben decided to deal with his feelings of vulnerability (shame) by converting these feelings into anger towards the boys (i.e. the desire to bash them). Turning shame into anger and directing it towards the other boys helped Ben to feel stronger in this moment of vulnerability. ('Anger is shame lying to you' is something I say to young men in Ben's position when I talk with them about their feelings in such moments.) Ben could also choose to take his shame pain out on somebody else besides the boys who rejected him. He could tease a weaker student or pick an argument with a teacher. When people use attack-other responses to shame, the targets of their attacking behaviours can be many and varying. They usually involve a weaker person who will accept their taunts and mistreatment. Either way, Ben's attack-other response to shame will not end well for anybody.

In all of the situations, when a stable sense of self couldn't be found by the four young people, their responses to shame involved a series of strategies that brought them some short-term relief from shame. Alexandria decided to withdraw from her friendship with Jess so as to limit damage to her already fragile sense of self. Nicky turned her shame inward and attacked herself with thoughts that she was a bad kid, based on a single indiscretion. George avoided the hard work of shame by focusing on and exaggerating an aspect of the self that brought him feelings of pride. Ben converted his feelings of hurt and vulnerability into anger and planned an attack on those who were the source of his humiliation. These four strategies that Alexandria, Nicky, George and Ben employed to try to make shame go away are arranged in an amazingly insightful model called the Compass of Shame.

The next chapter uncovers this amazingly insightful model for human behaviour and explains how restorative practice gives young people an effective way to meet shame's demand honestly and authentically.

Chapter 11

The Compass of Shame

Don't you hate it when the world gives you feedback that you're not as nice, smart, adored, clever, strong, attractive, amazing, competent or cool as you'd like to think you are?

– Bill Hansberry

Donald L. Nathanson, who was a student of Silvan Tomkins, is the founding executive director emeritus of the Tomkins Institute and has spent a large part of his career studying the shame–humiliation affect. He is a well-respected psychiatrist and the author of *Shame and Pride: Affect, Sex and the Birth of the Self* (1994) and *Knowing Feeling: Affect, Script, and Psychotherapy* (1996). Nathanson's decades-long research has shone a revealing light on the experience of affect shame and has helped us to understand the emotional conditions required for people to confront shame, and what happens when we can't deal honestly with shame.

The Compass of Shame describes four universal but unhealthy sets of behaviours that people employ when an event (or experience) triggers the shame–humiliation affect and they don't know how to deal with the information (Figure 11.1). Our four young people – Alexandria, Nicky, George and Ben – showed us what responses to shame at the levels of withdrawal, attack self, avoidance and attack other might look like, albeit in their less-extreme forms. Actions people take at each pole of the Compass of Shame vary over a range from mild and quite ordinary (like in the case of our four young people) to severe (pathological and/or dangerous). The more skill an individual develops in the techniques associated with any of these libraries of defensive behaviour, the more they will be limited in their emotional growth (Nathanson 2000).

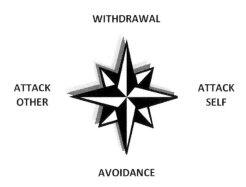

Figure 11.1 Compass of Shame

According to Nathanson (2000), there are generally eight categories of shame triggers:

1. matters of size, strength, ability, skill

2. dependence/independence

3. competition

4. sense of self

5. personal attractiveness

6. sexuality

7. issues of seeing and being seen

8. wishes and fears about closeness.

When life points out that we might not be as clever, kind, competent, strong, interesting or attractive as we'd like to think, and we can't draw on a stable and connected sense of self to reassure ourselves of our pride-worthy qualities, we are not able to gather the strength to deal authentically with the awful feelings of shame. The Compass of Shame explains sets of behaviours we all sometimes use to try to defend our threatened ego when we are unable to grasp the nettle of shame. Let's look at these four sets of ways that we respond to shame when we are not feeling okay with ourselves.

Exploring the Compass of Shame

Withdrawal

Withdrawal concerns behaviours that involve withdrawing from social contact with others. Like with Alexandria's response when she realised she had upset her friend Jess (on the right side of Table 10.1), retreating from the gaze of others (to save face) is a defensive strategy when one feels shamefully exposed and fears that staying with others will give them even more reasons to hold one in contempt.

At the mild end, withdrawal responses may involve socially acceptable behaviours like going quiet after being contradicted or interrupted (a shame-triggering event). Shyness in children and adults is a form of withdrawal. Any attempt to hide one's face is a withdrawal response to shame. Extreme withdrawal involves any long-term, self-imposed loss of contact with others through deliberate self-isolation. It's true that from time to time we all withdraw from the company of others to give ourselves time to be alone and process a situation. This needs to be allowed within the rules of any relationship. However, it's important to know when withdrawal is a response to a shameful or humiliating situation with which one needs help.

Attack self

Attack self involves behaviours where people engage in mindsets that involve accepting a diminished way of being that says, 'I am lesser than you, and you can treat me as such because I deserve it. I don't believe I'm good enough, so I don't deserve respect or kindness from others.' People who use attack-self scripts know that withdrawal feels awful, so they keep themselves connected to others through accepting a reduced social status. Nicky's reaction to getting in trouble with Mrs Stewart (see the right side of Table 10.1) involved low-level attack self when she began to convince herself that this indiscretion was typical of her and that she always did stupid stuff like that. Nicky began accepting a reduced view of herself as one of the 'bad kids'.

At the mild end, attack-self strategies involve moments of negative self-talk, either as internal dialogue or said aloud for others to hear. Mild self-deprecation, such as 'I'm such an idiot sometimes' or 'I've done it again, silly me', is a socially acceptable form of attack self, and in many situations this can rescue a social situation with humour before everybody feels bad. Many of us have mildly attacked self before to deny someone else the opportunity of attacking us. A self-admonishment is far less shameful than a rebuke from another person. The extreme end of attack-self responses to shame involve self-harming behaviour, self-loathing (as often seen in young people with attachment disorders) and, ultimately, the belief that 'the world would be better off without me' – the tragic consequences of suicide.

Avoidance

Avoidance contains inventive behaviours that are designed to call others' attention to attributes of the self that create feelings of pride. When we use avoidance, we try desperately to present a proud, competent, unashamed and happy self to anyone who may be looking. Unfortunately, those who witness these attempts soon see them for what they really are: insincere. George's response to the shame of failing an algebra test was to avoid thinking about the implications by distracting himself by thinking about what a fantastic soccer player he was and how, when he was a top-level player, algebra wouldn't matter. George was cheating at the task of cultivating healthy self-esteem.

Avoidant responses to shame at the mild end involve the tendency to parade in front of others what we can do well, or what we have (that others don't). It might involve trying to look like the smartest one in the crowd, the funniest, the strongest, the wealthiest or just the most invulnerable and arrogant. We all know people who constantly post images and information on social media that cry to the world 'Look what I have', 'Check out the amazing friends I'm with' or 'Notice the incredible things I'm doing'.

At the extreme end of avoidant responses to shame are chronic behaviours designed to make shame go away like substance abuse – behaviours which disrupt the affect system at a neurochemical level, switching off shame and artificially inducing positive-mood states by triggering positive affect.

Attack other

Attack other contains behaviours directed at causing harm to others in an attempt to make them feel just as bad as (shameful), or worse than, the person delivering the attack. When there is nothing we can do to raise our own self-esteem in the moment of feeling diminished, our only short-term relief from our shame pain will come from reducing the self-esteem of another through words and actions aimed at making them feel shameful. Behaviours at this last pole on the Compass of Shame are reserved for moments when we feel truly helpless in the face of shame and have no other strategy to make shame go away. Ben's planned response to the humiliation of being ignored by the other boys was an attack-other strategy.

In schools, young people who have developed habits of teasing and harassing others, cyber bullying or trolling, violent attacks on others or persistent bullying are often dealing with moments of shame at the attack-other pole of the Compass of Shame. Sadly, as an individual hones the skills associated with attack-other behaviour, they fail to develop the ability to negotiate, moderate, love and nurture (Nathanson 2000).

> Nathanson (1994) argues that shame is at the heart of all violent behaviour. He suggests that when we better understand the role of shame in our lives, we are better able to appreciate that violence, as expressed in anger, is an emotion that is masking the trigger for this anger: shame. (Real Justice nd)

Mild attack-other behaviours involve friendly put-downs and banter that are acceptable within the bounds of trusting relationships. Those working with teenage boys watch them struggle as they learn the social rules about employing banter, sometimes going too far and then living with the social consequences of their error. At the extreme end of the attack-other pole are behaviours aimed at dismantling another's self-esteem or sense of safety. The most extreme attack-other behaviour involves deliberately taking another's life.

What the Compass of Shame teaches us

What the Compass of Shame teaches us about the ways people handle, or fail to handle, shame has particular significance for those working with the intellectual, emotional and social development of young people. This information also compels us to look for ways in which we can help young people engage with us, and each other, in a manner that will facilitate the development of emotionally safe and healthy school communities.

Discharging shame: How to let it go and reintegrate back into the community

Deliberate acts to harm others can be both an attack-other behaviour and a cause of further shame. Those who have worked with young people caught in cycles of harming others with their words and actions intuitively see through the bravado and know that they are dealing with highly insecure people who are struggling to accept themselves and to feel a stable connection with others at school. There are many reasons that some young people find themselves in this bind. At the more extreme end are young people who have abused or neglected others, or are the victims of abuse or neglect, or who are living with attachment disorder. At the lower end, we find young people who, from time to time in their development, use attack-other scripts but, when held accountable in a restorative way, learn how to handle moments of shame in more adaptive ways.

A great many researchers and thinkers have contributed a great deal to our understanding of the importance of responses to wrongdoing that support young people to acknowledge their shame over wrongdoing instead of allowing shame to be bypassed. As social bonds with others are restored (or created) through the process of making amends, feelings of shame in wrongdoers, and the victims of their misdeeds are reduced to manageable levels. As Ahmed and Braithwaite (2004) state:

> Indeed, some have conceded the possibility that shame acknowledgment plays a central role in maintaining adaptive interpersonal relationships. In acknowledging shame, [a young person] accepts that they feel shame, comes to terms with their responsibility for what has happened, and takes steps to make amends for the harm done. Once these three elements combine together within the [young person's] belief system, they create an internal sanctioning mechanism helping the individual discharge shame. (p.2)

Restorative practice focuses heavily on the restoration of these relationship connections, and restorative processes help young people deal honestly and authentically with their feelings of shame that are triggered by relationship breakdown, or acts of wrongdoing, thus helping them to discharge the shame.

Why shame is not a dirty word

Shame has inherited a bad name as a toxic emotion, and many experts shout from the rooftops about the negative effect of shaming young people. These people are missing some key points: First, all of our emotions have information for us to help maximise survival. Young people need to know this so they can make sense of their feelings. Shame's vital task is to keep us close to our community by becoming an internal sanctioning mechanism to regulate our behaviour. It is also the affect that signals, loud and clear, when our emotional connections with others have become threatened, and it motivates us towards action to repair and restore these social bonds.

There is shaming, and then there is *shaming*

Communities and families have always used shaming as a tool to socialise young people to deal with misbehaviour and promote prosocial behaviour. Asking Tristan and Jason who they thought had been affected by their behaviour (see Chapter 4) was a question that was always going to trigger shame. This, of course, was intentional. Triggering shame about their deeds was an important step to motivate the boys towards behaving differently and restoring themselves to their previous place in the community. As you read the case studies in Part 3, you will be exposed to many types of restorative language that are designed to trigger affect shame (negative affect) in young people and motivate them to restore so that they can return to feeling good (positive affect) again about themselves and others. There's no way around it – restorative practice is a ritual in reintegrative shaming.

So what is reintegrative shaming and how does it differ from its opposite, stigmatising shaming? John Braithwaite, a noted criminologist and researcher, has dedicated his work to understanding shame and how different cultures employ shame to socialise their young and respond to wrongdoing. It is beyond the scope of this book to explore the very complex issues surrounding shaming processes, but I do want the reader to get a clear understanding of the difference between stigmatising and reintegrative shame as Braithwaite (1989) explains it.

When we use reintegrative shaming processes such as restorative practice, our message to young people is:

> You are considered a good and worthy person but your behaviour was not good. Your actions have caused harm and we expect you to repair this harm. When this has happened, you will be restored in our eyes, reintegrated into the community and life will go on as before. (Braithwaite 1989, p.22)

The phrase 'The problem is the problem, the person isn't the problem' is mentioned several times in this book and ties in closely with the reintegrative shaming theory. In effect, reintegrative shaming encourages us to work in ways that are highly confronting of wrongdoing but at the same time supports the intrinsic worth of the people being called to account. The saying 'Hate the sin but love the sinner' comes immediately to mind when thinking about this mode of shaming.

In stark contrast to reintegrative shaming, stigmatising shaming sends a very different message to people who have wronged. Driven mainly by affect disgust, the message to young people who've wronged is: 'Your behaviour has been bad; therefore, you are a bad person and deserve to be treated as such by your community.' When young people receive these messages, there is no way back for them, no way to restore themselves in the eyes of others and there is a negative label that will stay with them. The problem here is that this approach doesn't allow young people to use shame adaptively. Their only option is to resort to Compass of Shame defences to defend themselves and to gravitate towards the open arms of other, similarly stigmatised young people to meet their need for connection. (This process is mentioned in Chapter 5.) This brand of shaming is characteristic of the punitive ('TO') quadrant of the social control window discussed in Chapter 3.

Children who have been abused and neglected

Schools are dealing more and more with young people from backgrounds of trauma associated with abuse or neglect. These young people live with chronic levels of shame that severely affect their ability to emotionally self-regulate. This must be understood by schools if these young people are to have any chance of improving their behaviour and their connections to those around them, on which their self-regulation hinges. Children from backgrounds of abuse and neglect often have far more intense shame responses, than their peers, to perceived failures, insults or to the experience of being disciplined. These reactions can come from all four points of the Compass of Shame but typically reside in the avoidance and attack-other poles, and manifest as acting out or externalising behaviours. 'People who live with toxic shame feel fundamentally disgraced, intrinsically worthless, and profoundly humiliated in their own skin, just for being themselves... [T]oxic shame arises when an individual's inner core is tormented through rejection' (Garbarino 1999, p.58).

Whenever affect shame is triggered for these young people, their response is as if the humiliation of the abuse is being relived in that moment. These children are sometimes referred to as shame phobic. This explains their extreme Compass of Shame responses to any situation where they may perceive themselves as being wrong or failing. They are left in these moments feeling intrinsically bad and worthless, without the capacity to remind themselves of the loving support of others. Because of their history of tenuous and inconsistent care and love from significant adults, they are unable to deal with the moment of shame – they cannot grasp the nettle. Being overwhelmed by shame increases affect dysregulation and can often lead to aggressive (i.e. attack-other) outbursts. Traumatised children can try very hard to control their environments to avoid the experience of paralysing shame. 'Michael experiences extreme…shame when he can't do something or does not succeed in front of his peers. He becomes very silly [avoidance] or aggressive [attack other] at these times' (Queensland Government Department of Communities, Child Safety and Disability Services and Department of Education, Training and Employment 2013, p.16).

Restorative approaches appear to be about the only truly effective response to misconduct of young people with trauma, because restorative approaches allow discharge of shame and incorporate ceremonies of reintegration back into the very community that is so important to their ability to regulate their emotions. Punishment alone further isolates these young people, increasing their feelings of worthlessness. Punitive environments make life much worse for traumatised people and those around them.

Teaching young people about shame

I have talked with hundreds of young people, both in class groups and in private counselling, about the shame experience and the Compass of Shame. Young people relate very easily to the shame experience when it is explained to them using this framework. There's much relief in just realising that all of us have to deal with moments of shame at times. The key message for young people is that shame has an important job: it keeps us connected to our community as long as we are able to listen to it and do the work it demands of us. In groups, young people talk in a Circle about a particular, but common, trigger of shame: the realisation that they may have upset somebody or caused harm. When restorative practitioners talk about the job shame is trying to get people to do, young people understand how hard it is to do the brave work of fixing the problem when one feels lonely and disconnected. Students as young as seven or eight years old are able to share with each other about how shame is a very isolating experience – how one feels isolated in that instant after discovering the problem and that one may have caused it.

When young people reflect with others on their own responses to shame, they reflect on how admitting that they've made a mistake and then doing the required fixing with others is easier to do when they have relationships that make them feel worthwhile. They talk about the importance of having a friend nearby to say something like 'You've made a mess of this but you're still okay – let's start the fixing', or to simply show that the friend still likes them.

Incredible relief comes from facing up to our misdeeds and fixing things with those we may have upset, as long as we trust that this will make things better and restore us in the eyes of others.

When we feel disliked, socially excluded or even held in contempt by others, the prospect of facing up to a social problem and admitting our mistakes to others is just a bridge too far. For young people in schools who are not experiencing stable and affirming connections with others, a moment of shame can be so painful that, to avoid the pain, they use Compass of Shame defences.

This is what makes a restorative approach so necessary in schools. From time to time, all of us need a way back from shame, back into positive affect and back into a community of care. Our most vulnerable young people need this more than others.

The next part explores the practical application of what the previous six chapters have taught us about affect, emotion, shame and reintegration.

PART 3

Working Restoratively

Restorative Approaches for Different Ages and Situations

Chapter 12

Continuums of Responses to Disruption and Wrongdoing

Now that we have explored thinking restoratively in Part 1 and feeling restoratively in Part 2, it is time to turn our attention to how these belief systems look in practice. Different schools respond to different levels of misbehaviour in different ways. Usually, the more severe incidents of misconduct attract more formal responses. This is true regardless of whether a school operates within a punitive or restorative philosophy, because both philosophies believe in justice and accountability for actions. What differs between these systems is how schools think about what needs to happen when students misbehave as well as their beliefs about the most effective ways to restore justice and deliver accountability.

Different systems

High control + low support (punitive) schools

In these settings, behaviour types and responses fall along a continuum (Figure 12.1). These schools usually work tirelessly to apply predetermined consequences to misbehaviours fairly and consistently.

The main questions in these schools are usually:

- What rules have been broken?

- Who broke them?

- What consequence (punishment) do they deserve?

(Adapted from Stutzman Amstutz and Zehr 1998)

The list of possible misbehaviours on a continuum like this will, of course, vary from school to school. What might be considered a high-level misbehaviour in one school would constitute mid-level misbehaviour in another school. When students misbehave in these more traditional or punitive schools, factors that might influence whether an incident is seen as severe and deserving higher-level sanctions include:

- how many school rules have been broken in the incident and the number of times they were breached

- the messages that the school wishes to send to the school community about this sort of behaviour

- the degree to which the teacher's authority was ignored or threatened

- the track record of the students involved – whether they have form or not

- the involved student's connection or their family's history with the school

- the profile of this type of misbehaviour in the school – is there a crackdown happening with this type of behaviour at the moment?

- the disciplinary philosophy of those making the decisions about consequences

- the level of distress, anger and/or injury of the victims of the misbehaviour and their status in the school community

- the skills and attitudes of staff members who were caught in the incident(s) of misconduct, or first on the scene (when skilled teachers can de-escalate situations, things don't get as serious).

(Thorsborne and Vinegrad 2009, p.61)

It's easy to see how schools get themselves in trouble when making decisions about what to do about an incident based on such a dynamic range of variables. Responses are inconsistent at best and corrupt at worst when you consider how some well-connected and well-resourced families can exert political pressure on school leaders to influence discipline outcomes for their children. The real difficulty with these systems, however, lies in their narrow focus on establishing guilt and determining appropriate sanctions. When preoccupied with these matters, schools completely forget about the needs of those involved (both the harmed and the wrongdoers). Decision-makers become bogged down with thinking about those who've broken the rules and what needs to be done 'TO' them. This preoccupation with establishing guilt and handing down appropriate consequences makes these systems largely offender focused, while the needs of those harmed are left unaddressed.

Having worked for many years trying to perfect these behaviour = consequence systems of school discipline, experience has shown me over and over that heartache, mess and confusion are the only result as politicking becomes a main focus of discipline policy, and schools lose sight of what's best for young people. In these systems student behaviour standards across the school often decline.

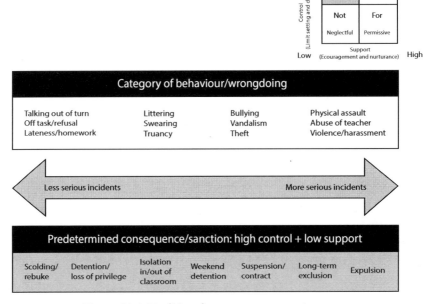

Figure 12.1 Traditional consequences continuum
(Adapted from Thorsborne and Vinegrad 2009)

High control + high support (restorative) schools

Restorative and punitive settings are similar in that behaviour types and responses fall along a continuum (Figure 12.2). However, instead of simply matching sanctions to incidents, restorative schools focus on matching the right process to an incident, so those involved (both the harmed and the wrongdoers) can work together ('WITH' students, staff and sometimes parents) towards an outcome that seems fair(er) to all affected and involves an appropriate level of accountability.

The main questions asked in restorative systems are:

- Who has been harmed (and how)?

- What do they need?

- Who is responsible for meeting these needs?

- How do we ensure these needs are met and reduce the chance of these harms happening again?

(Adapted from Stutzman Amstutz and Zehr 1998)

Those who have seen restorative processes used well will tell you that they are anything but soft on wrongdoing. Quite the opposite is true: Restorative practice demands much more of those who've caused harm than punitive systems could ever hope to achieve, but at the same time it offers a high level of support to all involved. Restorative processes are meant to make young people work much harder than punitive systems.

Thorsborne and Vinegrad (2009, p.62) list factors that influence how a disciplinary incident is viewed by a school in a restorative setting. These factors include:

- the depth and breadth of the harm done (material, relational, emotional)

- the readiness of all those involved (the wrongdoer(s), those harmed and others who might support them) to be part of a restorative process

- whether the wrongdoer(s) can admit their part in the problem and is willing to acknowledge this and work to restore the situation

- the outcomes that all parties involved want (including the school)

- the belief that holding someone accountable for harmful acts can be achieved by their facing up to those affected and taking responsibility (and that punishment doesn't provide the same level of accountability)

- the willingness to put the time and effort into achieving a lasting fix to a problem

- a willingness on the school's behalf to acknowledge how the system might have contributed to the problem (shared responsibility)

- a belief that those involved in the problem are the best people to decide how to fix the problem (when provided with a process and support)

- a belief that solving problems is best achieved by righting wrongs and repairing the harm

- an awareness of the risks involved if appropriate action is not taken.

When these are the key considerations, those in a school tasked with responding to an incident or ongoing issue can talk with all involved and ask some simple but highly respectful questions to gauge the extent of the harm. When they know what they are dealing with in terms of what's happened, who has been involved, who has been harmed and what their needs are, they can decide which process from the restorative practice continuum will be best suited to the issue (Thorsborne and Vinegrad 2009, p.62).

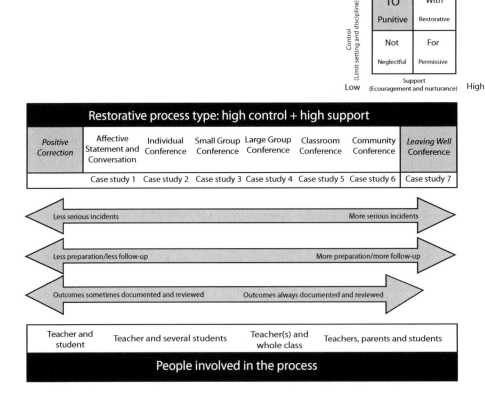

Figure 12.2 Restorative practice continuum
(Adapted from Thorsborne and Vinegrad 2009)

Working up the restorative practice continuum

Chapters 13–20 look at some of the different processes on the restorative practice continuum and examine each intervention type, covering the different ways the restorative script is used at each point as well as the preparation and follow-up that gives us the best chance of lasting outcomes. Depending on what you read, you will see different versions of the restorative practice continuum, and processes will have different names. (The continuum I propose is from my own experience working restoratively in schools.)

Chapter 21 offers deeper insights into using restorative questions (the restorative script), and Chapter 22 looks at Circles (aka Circle Time).

Chapter 13

Positive Behaviour Correction[1]

After years of training teachers in restorative practice, I've realised that people sometimes mistakenly believe that using restorative practice means that every problem behaviour will need to be addressed with scripted restorative questioning that will be introduced in Chapter 15. These teachers say, 'We haven't got the time to ask all of these restorative questions every time a student does something wrong. Can't we just tell them to stop it?', and of course they are right. In the cut and thrust of school life there are many times when we do give brief and direct feedback to kids about their behaviour because that's all we have time for and asking a set of restorative questions just isn't appropriate in that moment. All of us know, however, that what we say and how we look to students in these brief corrective moments makes all the difference.

Whenever we address behaviour positively – in a way that aims to take care of a young person's dignity and give them a way back into the good graces of those around them – we are being restorative. Alternatively, if we scold, humiliate, insult or intimidate, we are being anything but restorative – in fact we are bringing further harm to the situation.

We need a place on the restorative practice continuum that acknowledges a range of brief corrective approaches that teachers use from moment to moment literally hundreds of times a day. Positive behaviour correction or positive correction encompasses a wide range of these strategies that are brief and not overly intrusive on the student (Rogers 2006). These approaches aim to assertively and quickly correct problematic behaviour before it brings undue disruption or harm. These positive strategies minimise negative affect (shame, distress, anger, disgust, fear, dissmell) in situations where an adult has to correct student behaviour.

Effective classroom teachers call on a repertoire of corrective approaches in their work with young people. As mentioned earlier, approaches don't involve

---

1   This chapter is heavily influenced by the wonderful work of Bill Rogers, a necessary staple in the behaviour management repertoire of any teacher.

asking the full script of restorative questions, but still intend to minimise defensive reactions and prompt students to consider what's happening in that moment and how this may be affecting themselves and others. Interventions further along the restorative continuum use the scripted restorative questions in their more complete form, like in a situation where a teacher decides to take a few moments (or longer) to take a young person aside to talk with them after a lesson about their behaviour.

Relationships between teachers and students matter the most when things go wrong. Restorative schools are in the game of helping young people learn how to accept responsibility, giving them experience in being held accountable for one's own choices, and learning how to put things right with those who share the problem (Hopkins 2011).

The ability to be able to positively correct behaviour that causes irritation – such as a student who refuses to begin a task or the young person who begins a conversation with a classmate while we are addressing the class – requires that we overcome the initial wave of shame triggered by the impediment to our interest and enjoyment, and the following urge to fix the problem quickly (anger). If we can't talk some sense to ourselves in this moment and calm our initial reactions, we will likely give ourselves and the young person trouble. Hopkins (2011) has devised a set of silent questions for teachers. When silently asked to ourselves (self-talk) in challenging moments, these become a habitual calming strategy, and a *ready reckoner* for 'How bad is this situation really?':

- What's happening from my own perspective?

- What am I seeing and hearing?

- What am I telling myself about this? What sense am I making of this student's behaviour?

- How is my interpretation affecting my own emotional response?

- How am I being affected?

- What do I need right now – is it appropriate to bring these needs into the equation right now?

- Will I invite the others here to consider my needs as well?

- Can I support them to find ways forward without my interference, or do I need extra support myself?

Unlike scolding or rebuke, which rely on the negative affects of fear, anger and so forth, the aim of positive correction is to help a young person bring their behaviour back into line without humiliating them. This helps maintain the dignity of the young person and avoids their resorting to Compass of Shame defences. What makes positive correction approaches *restorative* is that they are always used in a respectful way, so young people see that their *behaviour* is the problem, not them as a person. (The problem is the problem, the person isn't the problem.)

This helps keep the moment of shame for the student and the teacher as brief as possible, restoring both teacher and student to positive affect as quickly as possible. Below are just a few of my favourite positive correction approaches that are used by effective teachers.

Methods of positive behaviour correction
Tactical ignoring

Here a teacher chooses to pretend that they haven't noticed a particular behaviour and doesn't react or respond in any way. Life carries on as if the behaviour didn't happen. Teachers often tactically ignore young people who are calling out, or a younger student who crawls under tables while the rest of the class are sitting on the floor, because they know that the student may be seeking the attention of being told off.

Tactical ignoring can also be a lifesaver when speaking to a student about their behaviour and the student engages in a range of secondary (disrespectful) behaviours such as eye rolling, tongue clicking, scoffing, jaw dropping or speaking to the teacher in a rude tone. In these moments, clever teachers tactically ignore these behaviours that, although irritating, are secondary to the main issue. The teacher keeps the focus of the conversation on the main issue and doesn't become sidetracked ('Excuse me, don't roll your eyes when I'm speaking to you') from the main issue.

Non-verbal messages

These are a low-intrusive form of correction as they happen from a distance and involve a teacher catching the attention of a student for a moment and delivering a nonverbal signal.

Non-verbal messages might involve using eye contact, hand gestures, head movements or even bodily movements that initially indicate that you have noticed them, and then to gently indicate that something different needs to happen. To do this, look over to the young person and use your body language in a relaxed way to indicate that you are curious (not angry or disapproving) in what is happening with them. The aim is to register concern, not disapproval (Hopkins 2014). Jerky, aggressive movements that draw too much attention (head forward, chin out, eyes bulging with an intense glare) often have a negative affect and can cause an escalation in behaviour, particularly in young people with oppositional behaviours.

Teachers who use these non-verbal cues well often deliver non-verbal messages in a way that is humorous and even good fun. This helps to minimise negative shame responses from young people because it indicates that even though something they are doing needs changing, the teacher still regards them positively. The beauty of non-verbal messages is that they keep the behaviour correction discreet and avoid the public shame involved with being spoken to in front of others.

Proximity

Using proximity involves moving closer to a student or student(s) who might be off task or making poor decisions. This is not to be confused with walking over to a student or a group of students and glaring at them without speaking. A teacher using proximity might innocently go and stand next to a table of students who are talking too loudly and perhaps quietly check the work of a student nearby. Usually a student noticing that a teacher is nearby will act as a powerful cue to check themselves.

Quiet questioning

Quiet questioning involves having a quiet word with a student who may be off task or making other poor choices. Quiet questioning might sometimes be overheard by other students in the immediate area, but the goal is to keep this conversation as brief and private as possible.

This form of positive correction involves initially moving to the student in a relaxed way, saying hello and then saying in a relaxed but curious way what you've observed. For example:

'I see you've not started with the work.'

Rogers (2006) calls this a description of reality – no questions (yet), no accusations, just describing what you see.

Next, with a curious and friendly tone ask:

'What's up?'

or

'What's happening for you right now?'

or

'Is there anything I can help you with to get you started?'

or

'What might you do to make a start?'

Once the question is asked, the teacher (importantly) gives the young person time to respond. At the very least, this strategy gives the teacher more of an idea about what is happening for the young person and, at best, helps the young person to make better decisions in that moment.

Pause direction

This involves a teacher first gaining a student's attention by saying their name (sometimes more than once), pausing a moment after the student has given the teacher their attention, and then delivering direction in a calm and friendly tone of voice: 'Jonah, Michael [pause; boys don't hear the teacher]… Jonah, Michael [pause; boys look at teacher]… Get on with your work. Thanks.' Notice that the teacher ends the direction with 'thanks' to indicate an expectation of compliance. (The fact that this is just good manners is also important, especially if we demand good manners from students!)

Rule reminders

Sometimes a teacher will quietly move to a student and give a direct rule reminder or ask a question about the rule: 'Skye, the rule about mobile phones is that they stay in bags or on my desk. Pop it in your bag or on my desk. Thanks.' Alternatively: 'Skye, do you remember our rule about mobile phones?' In the second instance, the teacher will wait for Skye's response, as cranky as it may be (tactically ignoring Skye's tone), and then calmly remind Skye of the rule and then give her some take-up time to comply.

Take-up time

This is perhaps the most important skill a teacher can use after issuing a direction to a young person. Simply put, take-up time is moving away from a student after redirecting them, so they have some time to respond to the redirection and save face. Few of us want to comply with a direction we've been given immediately. After all, our pride is at stake. Most of us need some time to convince ourselves that we are deciding to do it! Take-up time preserves the dignity (pride) of both student and teacher and often avoids unnecessary power struggles, which often see teacher and student using attack-other Compass of Shame defences. Putting pride aside for the moment, there are also more cognitive considerations. Take-up time allows young people to process a teacher's redirection. Many students who need regular behavioural redirection have slow language-processing abilities, so it takes them longer to work out what was said by the teacher and longer to respond.

Returning to the example given earlier, after using pause direction and asking Jonah and Michael to return to their work, the teacher deliberately diverts her attention elsewhere, perhaps even moves away from the boys to give them take-up time to follow the instruction. This way the boys can choose a different behaviour without feeling as though the teacher is standing over them demanding immediate compliance. Standing and waiting for a student to comply (e.g. hands on hips, foot tapping) can trigger Compass of Shame defences (giving cheek, even abusing the teacher) in some students. The simple act of moving away from Jonah and Michael after giving the direction conveys an expectation that they will, in fact, follow the instruction and get on with their work. A few moments later, the teacher will glance at the boys to check if they have gotten back on task.

Acknowledgement of feeling and deflection

This is an approach used by clever teachers who find themselves in a situation with a distressed or angry student. In this moment the teacher acknowledges the student's feelings. Following on from the example given earlier, the teacher says to Skye: 'Skye, I can see you're uptight about this…' This permits Skye to share her negative affect, and perhaps the teacher even resonates the affect: '…and I don't like to see you uptight.' The teacher then deflects the strong feelings and says: 'We will chat about this a bit later, but right now, I need you to make a decision about where your mobile phone is going to go. Thanks, Skye.' Next, the teacher moves away, allowing Skye some much-needed take-up time.

Choice direction

This is used when a student has not responded to other (less intrusive) forms of positive correction (see earlier). The teacher might say, 'Caitlyn, I know this is annoying [acknowledging affect], but I've asked you twice now to use the equipment safely. If you don't use the equipment safely, you and I will be having a chat in break time.' If Caitlyn doesn't respond, the teacher will make time later for an affective conversation or an Individual Conference with her (see Chapter 15).

This list of positive correction approaches isn't exhaustive, of course, and many of these approaches can come under different names depending on who you talk to or what you read. What they all have in common is a calm and dignified approach as well as being, whenever possible, minimally intrusive on the student (and only become more intrusive if necessary). These approaches are also solution focused in that they aim to manage emotion and give young people options rather than forcing instant compliance or dolling out immediate sanctions for breaches of rules.

The next chapter looks at the power of affective statements and conversations in helping young people take responsibility for misdeeds and putting things right.

Chapter 14

Affective Statements
and Conversations

Case study: Zack's BIG mouth!

During science 13-year-old Zack repeatedly calls out and makes jokes. Zack doesn't respond to a couple of non-verbal signals, nor does he stop after Mrs Stewart privately tells him that if he doesn't quieten down he'll be asked to leave the room. Eventually, Mrs Stewart quietly asks Zack to move to the time-out desk in the hall, and he complies. Later, as the class packs equipment away, Mrs Stewart invites Zack back into the room for a quick chat before break time. She begins with the following affective statement:

> Zack, you're a nice guy and I enjoy working with you in this class, and I didn't like asking you to leave the room, but you need to know that when you called out repeatedly, it was hard for me to teach. I was disappointed because you're normally much fairer than that.

Whether Zack is in actual fact usually fairer or not might be up for debate depending on which teacher you speak to, but building relationships with students who display challenging behaviour requires us to look for likable attributes in them. Good teachers give tricky students a reputation to live up to.

After the affective statement, the rest of the affective conversation follows as Mrs Stewart gives Zack the right of reply: 'Is there anything I need to know about your calling out?'

As soon as teachers give the right of reply like this, they have to be ready for the possibility that the young person may have some feedback for them! Teachers do best in these moments if they listen to what the young person has to say and resist the urge to defend themselves or interrupt the person. If it becomes clear that they've made a mistake, an emotionally intelligent response will be to acknowledge their error. This is fantastic modelling to young people.

Tips for tricky moments

Zack might make excuses for his calling out, such as 'I had my hand up but you didn't answer', or insist that other teachers don't mind his calling out. In either case, a good response will be to partially agree with Zack and then calmly and respectfully restate the expectations of the classroom and tell Zack how he can show these behaviours next time:

> Zack, I'm not those other teachers who don't mind people calling out. In our classroom I reckon people should be more respectful to each other than that. Next lesson, I just want you to relax, tune in and, if you have a great joke to tell, leave it until I've finished talking to the class. Does that sound fair?

Expectation clarity: follow-up

Mrs Stewart might go one step further and ask Zack what he thinks a fair way to deal with the behaviour will be if he persists with his calling out in the next lesson. Rarely do students give a cheeky retort or blow this type of question off. If Zack does reply with cheek, Mrs Stewart might say, 'You seem angry, Zack, what am I missing here?'

At the end of the chat, Mrs Stewart will ensure that she and Zack part amicably with a smile or handshake – or even a high five! She might say, 'Thanks for chatting with me about this, Zack, and listening to my side, I'm feeling better already. How are you feeling about things?'

Affective statements and conversations are used in situations where a teacher wishes to respectfully confront a student about something which caused offence or upset. Young people can also be taught to use affective statements with one another.

The recipe for affective statements and conversations

The affective statement has been extremely powerful in setting the conditions for a fair and respectful confrontation, which has a greater chance of helping Zack to take responsibility (stay off the Compass of Shame) for his calling out. Within this short but powerful interaction, Zack's intrinsic worth has been affirmed: 'You're a nice guy and I enjoy working with you...'

The problem behaviour and its effect have been clearly identified: 'When you called out repeatedly, it was hard for me to teach.'

A feeling word (affect) has been used to demonstrate how the teacher felt about that behaviour: 'I was disappointed.'

Zack is again affirmed as a person at the end of the affective statement: 'You're normally much fairer than that.'

After this affective statement, Mrs Stewart opens the door for a conversation by inviting Zack to reply: 'Is there anything I need to know about your calling out?'

Steps for the affective statement and conversation

Take the following steps for the affective statement and conversation:

1. Affirm the student.

2/3. Challenge the behaviour using an affect word.

4. Reaffirm the student.

5. Give right of reply.

Affective statements and conversations: Preparation and follow-up

At all levels of restorative practice, three 'keystone' phases must be in place to ensure that the process is robust. These phases are the preparation phase, the participation phase and the post-conference or follow-up phase (Figure 14.1).

The preparation phase is anything we do to prepare ourselves and young people to be involved in the restorative interaction. The participation phase is where the talking and listening take place between those involved in the issue or incident, and where resolution is sought. The follow-up phase is what takes place afterward to support students to understand the new expectations of behaviour and to make the agreed changes, or to follow through with agreed restitution.

These three phases come together to form a conceptual arch made up of three keystones. Like with architectural keystones, if one of these phases is neglected, cracks soon appear in the process and the entire restorative effort can crumble (Jansen and Matla 2011, p.92). At all stages of the restorative practice continuum these keystones will be used to illustrate the relative amount of time that needs to be put into each phase to give the best chance that a process be successful.

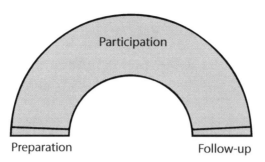

Figure 14.1 Keystones for affective statements and conversations
(Adapted from Jansen and Matla 2011)

The only preparation needed for the affective statement and conversation is for the teacher to prepare emotionally (calm themselves and remind themselves that no matter how the conversation goes, they are still a good teacher). Running through what you want to say to the student in your head is also advised.

Follow-up might involve, as it did with 13-year-old Zack, whatever teacher and student agree. For example, Mrs Stewart might say, 'What would be a fair way for me to deal with it if the calling out gets out of hand next time?' Mrs Stewart may quietly take Zack aside at the beginning of the next lesson and say with a friendly smile, 'Do you remember our deal about calling out?' This response, known as pre-correction, is a very effective follow-up strategy.

Affective statements and conversations are an extremely powerful tool with behaviourally challenged students, where it is especially necessary for teachers to challenge inappropriate behaviour but support their relationship with the student at the same time. If there's one restorative skill to master and then employ with creativity and conviction, this is the one. Well-used affective statements and conversations can transform the working relationship between teachers and students.

The next chapter moves us up the restorative practice continuum to an approach not unlike the one you have just read about in that it too involves an interaction between a teacher and a young person. The difference is that the approach, the Individual Conference, uses restorative questions.

Chapter 15

The Individual Conference

The Individual Conference, also known by some as the restorative chat, is the first point on the restorative practice continuum where an adaptation of the mistake-maker (aka the wrongdoer) questions from the restorative practice conference script is used.

Below is a shortened version of the foundation conference script with the questions that are asked to a student who has acted in a way that has either caused harm or has the potential to cause harm. As you will see in the script cards, these foundation questions have been modified for use in schools and gives teachers greater choice in the language they use:

- What happened?

- What were you thinking at the time?

- What do you think now?

- Who has been [could be] affected by what you did, and how?

- What needs to happen to fix this?

The Individual Conference is suited to lower-level incidents that haven't caused sufficient upset to anyone to warrant a conference involving others. The questions asked by the adult help a young person consider the impact of their choices on others and to make a plan to fix the problem.

If it becomes obvious that the incident will require bringing all of the young people affected together for a higher-level conference, the Individual Conference questions work well to prepare the wrongdoers before they sit down with others involved in an incident for a group conference.

The questions from the Individual Conference script help young people understand how their actions may have caused (or could potentially cause) harm to others. The question 'Who do you think could be upset by what you did?' or 'Who could be affected by that behaviour?' asks young people to do some empathic thinking about whom their actions may affect. The adult will already know the harm or potential harm of the behaviour and will prompt the child, using the scripted questions, to help them recognise and acknowledge this. Asking young people questions is also much more effective than telling them what they should be doing.

A restorative practice mantra: 'When at all possible, ask – don't tell'

Different ages, different questions

Below are examples of conference scripts that can be used for individual conferencing. The questions and format of the Early Years Individual Conference script works best with younger children (ages seven years and younger), or older students with special needs such as language disorders, intellectual delays or disabilities. Younger children usually haven't developed the language skills needed to engage with the Individual Conference script (Figure 15.1). They need shorter, more concrete questions. They also require explicit guidance from adults to understand what harm has resulted, how others are feeling and what might help fix the problem. The Early Years scripts combine the traditional Socratic questioning style, seen in standard restorative scripts, with explicit teaching of expected behaviours (Figure 15.2).[1]

In Chapter 16 you will find an Early Years Small Group Conference script. The Early Years script was first developed by Jane Langley, a teacher and restorative practice practitioner and trainer. Jane and I have refined and adapted these scripts.

---

1   Pocket-sized Early Years script cards are available from www.hansberryec.com.au.

Individual Conference script

Teacher respectfully challenging a student's behaviour

Show calm and friendliness, trigger surprise, interest and enjoyment

Say 'hi', introduce yourself, small talk, compliment, comment or question and then say:
'I noticed just before [*describe*]. I just wanted a quick chat with you about it.'

What were you thinking when you [*describe behaviour*]?

*Only ask **'what happened'** if you didn't see or hear it.*

What do you think about that now that we are chatting?

> *If student is struggling, ask kindly but firmly if it was:*
>
> - a good look or a bad look
> - fair or unfair
> - kind or unkind
> - helpful or unhelpful.
>
> *Kindly paraphrase 'so you think it was… I agree. That's a brave response…'*

Who gets affected by this kind of behaviour?

How does this affect people?

Which school rule does this affect? (Optional)

What will fix this?

How can I help?

What's a fair way to deal with it if this happens again?

Thank the student for the chat and, if appropriate, decide when follow-up will take place.

Figure 15.1 Individual Conference script

Early Years Individual Conference script

Teacher respectfully challenging a student's behaviour
Developed by Jane Langley and Bill Hansberry

What happened   **Or**   **We** need to talk about…

When you [*explicitly describe behaviour*] was that a good choice or a bad choice?

If student is struggling, gently ask if it was:

- kind or unkind
- friendly or unfriendly
- fair or unfair
- helpful or unhelpful

How do you think…felt when you…?

Or   **How** do you think…might be upset by [*explicitly describe the behaviour*]?

Or   I think that…has been/will be upset because…

At school it's not okay to… Next time I want you to…

What will make this better?

Or   **To fix this up** I want you to…

What can I do to help you?

Figure 15.2 Early Years Individual Conference script

Case study: Rubbish in the wrong place

During recess time Peter, a teacher, notices six-year-old Steph push a piece of rubbish into the metal cage surrounding an air conditioner unit. Peter had caught Steph doing the same thing yesterday and had asked her to take her rubbish to the bin, which she had done. Peter feels irritated and considers making Steph walk with him at lunch to pick up litter as a punishment. Instead, he decides to see if he can help Steph to learn about the effect of her behaviour on others. As soon as Peter approaches Steph, her eyes drop. She knows why Peter has approached her (i.e. affect shame has been triggered). Peter smiles knowingly.

Peter: Hi, Steph.

Steph sheepishly looks sideways at Peter.

Peter: Steph, is putting your rubbish into the air conditioner cage a good choice or bad choice?

Steph stares at the ground and doesn't reply. This is something Steph sometimes does when the moment is too much for her. Peter crouches beside Steph, so they are both looking at the air conditioner cage. Peter knows Steph is in a bad way and that he needs to proceed carefully to keep her engaged.

Peter (pointing to the cage): Sweetheart, is putting your rubbish in there helpful or unhelpful?

He waits quietly for 3–5 seconds. Steph then mumbles something.

Peter: What was that, Steph?

Steph: It was a bad choice.

Peter realises that this was Steph's response to his first question. (She has taken that long to process it!)

Peter: I think that too, Steph.

Steph's eyes shoot up for an instant and then quickly look down again. She is checking Peter's face to see if he looks angry.

Peter: Don't worry, Steph, I'm not angry. I'm just worried about that mess in the cage. Steph, who do you think would be upset by seeing all of that rubbish in the cage?

Steph: Mrs Fabian?

(Mrs Fabian is the principal.)

Peter: Yes, Steph, Mrs Fabian does like a tidy school. Who else might be upset to see the rubbish there and not in the bin?

Steph: The man who has to get it out and put it in the bin.

Peter: Do you mean Grumpy Joe, our grounds person?

Steph (looking up at the cage): Yeah.

Peter: Steph, at school, rubbish goes in the bin, doesn't it?

Steph nods.

Peter: How do we fix this?

Without answering, Steph goes and removes her wrapper as well as a few others from the air conditioner cage.

Peter (with delight): What a great idea!

He grabs a few crisp packets and banana peels. They both walk to the bin and deposit the rubbish.

Peter: Right, time to lick our hands clean.

Steph (giggling): Nooooo, silly – we've got to wash our hands, with soap at the taps.

Peter (smirking): Oh, I always forget that bit.

Peter: Hey, Steph.

He waits for her to look up.

Peter: Do you feel better now that it's fixed?

Steph (smirking): Yep.

Peter: Where's the bin, Steph?

Steph points to the bin.

Peter: Where isn't the bin, Steph?

Steph giggles and points to the air conditioner.

Peter: Good one, Steph.

They both wash their hands.

The beauty of the Individual Conference script is that it can be used at a moment's notice in virtually any location – wherever an adult and child can find a quiet spot to chat. The behaviour being addressed is quickly identified and resolved.

What if...? When things don't go so well

Some young people, whether they are Steph's age or much older, can become stuck in Compass of Shame responses when challenged about their behaviour and have great difficulty acknowledging their mistakes. Some young children refuse to talk, cry (attack self or withdrawal) or lie (withdrawal or avoidance) to make the problem go away. Some yell, curse and threaten (avoidance or attack other), and some young people just run away (withdrawal). We now know about the shame experience and understand that, in these moments, we are dealing with young people who are helpless to deal with shame of the situation. Although these behaviours could be called naughtiness, they also indicate a ship without a rudder when it comes to dealing with the awful thoughts and feelings that accompany affect shame.

Not having internal scripts (see Chapter 7) to deal well with the tricky feelings (shame) that are stirred when a teacher challenges their behaviour, some children lose their composure as fast feelings bubble over and a classic flight, fight or freeze response is triggered. In these moments, these children are completely reliant on the adult's class and composure, like how Steph relied on Peter to keep calm and carry on with the conversation even though she wasn't doing so well. As children become more anxious, agitated and upset about an incident, the less likely they are able to access their neocortex, the part of the brain they need to use to process and answer restorative questions. We need to be patient, friendly and use pauses.

As teachers it is tempting to try to fix tricky situations quickly, whereas young people might need between 10 and 30 minutes to come down from high levels of arousal. If Steph had panicked and run away when Peter first approached her, chasing her or yelling at her to stop and come back would have been disastrous. Instead, Peter would have kept a watchful eye on her and then approached her again a little later. After all, it was just some rubbish in an air conditioner cage – nothing worth a child running out of a schoolyard over.

On trying again with Steph a little later, Peter could try leading into the Individual Conference script questions by saying something like:

'Steph, talk with me for a minute and we will be able to fix this without you getting in trouble';

'Steph, you look worried about what happened. It's okay. Let's chat about how we can fix this'; or

'Steph, I think you are a nice person who wants to fix this. I'll help you.'

If, in spite of our best efforts to engage a young person in an Individual Conference, the young person still won't engage, then it's time to calmly say that we will give them some time to think. Tell them that the problem can be handled with a little chat, but if they decide not to chat with you, you will decide on a consequence. For example:

'We will talk about this a bit later, Steph';

'Steph, I will have to decide on a consequence if you won't help sort this out';

'I can see that you aren't ready to sort this out so I will have to...' (say what consequence is); or

'Steph, it's now my choice about how this will be sorted out and what happens next.'

If you decide to implement a non-restorative sanction, it is important to continue to be calm and respectful. Scolding a young person with 'I gave you a chance to fix this and you blew it, now you'll have a consequence to deal with' is completely unnecessary.

Individual Conference preparation

The only preparation an Individual Conference needs is for the teacher to prepare themselves emotionally, preparing to be friendly and calm and planning the questions they will ask the young person. This is called cognitive rehearsal.

Keystones for the Individual Conference are shown in Figure 15.3.

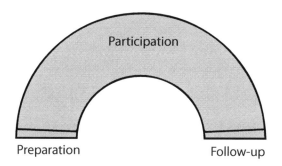

Figure 15.3 Keystones for the Individual Conference
(Adapted from Jansen and Matla 2011)

Individual Conference follow-up

Whether or not an Individual Conference requires follow-up is a case-by-case matter. Many teachers have asked me, 'What do we do about the kids who do the same thing again and again?' This is a good question, because for some young people, for many reasons, they may do the same thing again. Although Steph now understands the impact of putting her rubbish into the air conditioner cage (and because of this is far less likely to do it again), there is still a chance that she just might forget, fall victim to force of habit or be in a hurry one day and think nobody is watching. So what do we do in this situation?

The first part of the answer to this question lies in good record-keeping. In a non-restorative school, Peter may have sent six-year-old Steph straight to yard detention for her littering with no opportunity for her to understand who littering affects and no expectation to fix it. Typically, Peter or the staff member on duty in the yard detention room would have filled out some form of documentation regarding Steph's indiscretion. A permanent record of the offence would now exist for future reference. However, Steph is in a restorative school where teachers understand the limitations of this approach to low-level misconduct. The problem is that, in schools, we typically don't usually document conversations in the same way we would document a formal sanction like yard detention.

So let's imagine that Steph has been spoken to by three separate staff members this week for putting her litter in the air conditioner cage. It would seem that Steph has a chronic, low-level littering habit. Without communication between staff about the Individual Conferences they've run with students in the playground, Steph could go on having numerous Individual Conferences with different staff for weeks (if she was unlucky enough to get caught that often). In reality, Steph would have to be a pretty hardened litterbug, or actually want to be caught, to continue this behaviour in spite of having so many Individual Conferences about it. Either way, schools need a safety net that identifies repeat offenders who are not responding to Individual Conferences. It's worth thinking about a system where staff can share information about which students they've spoken to and about what. The main question is: How can this happen without creating more unnecessary paperwork for busy teachers?

Some ideas that clever schools have used to record Individual Conferences are the following:

- Creating a tick box for the Individual Conference on a generic yard-incident triplicate form that staff can tick as well as a behaviour-type tick box. Each week the person tasked with looking through these forms can identify particular behaviour hot spots and bring these to the attention of staff via a staff memo or during a staff meeting.

- Having a 'yard behaviour book' in the staff room where staff jot down a few notes about the restorative chats they had with students with what they think might need observing or follow-up. Other staff glance at the book before going on duty.

As you read these suggestions, you might be thinking, *Yeah right, as if my colleagues would use this system!* This needs gentle challenging because often the teachers who complain about the time it would take to jot a few notes down about a restorative chat are the same teachers who spend most of their yard duties completing detention slips for students.

'What's a fair way to deal with it if this happens again?' This is the final question in the restorative practice Individual Conference script, and although this question doesn't feature in the Early Years Individual Conference script, Peter could still ask Steph this question, or a version of it: 'Steph, what should happen if we see you put your rubbish in the cage again?'

Asking this question isn't always necessary, but it does create a second layer of accountability when we believe it might be needed. When asked this type of question, young people usually suggest a sanction of some sort: 'You should give me yard detention.' In this case, the teacher might reply: 'Yes, that's one option, but you'll also be asked to fix the problem.' Following this, the teacher might record that a sanction has been discussed with the student so that if the sanction is applied by another staff member, the young person involved may not be so surprised.

We now move along the restorative practice continuum to the first point where we bring students together to sort out their own issues and conflicts. This marks the point on the continuum where we switch over to working restoratively in groups with young people and our restorative processes begin to look more like they do in the bigger world of restorative justice.

Chapter 16

The Small Group Conference

The Small Group Conference, also known as the impromptu conference or mini conference, is the most frequently used point on the continuum in many schools because of its effectiveness in addressing low-level conflict between young people.

Many teachers are looking for alternatives to sanctioning young people with detentions or withdrawal (time out) as a way to address problematic student interactions. Small group conferencing can offer this.

Experienced teachers know that relying on punishment to address conflict between students causes more unrest. Young people become angrier and more resentful, and conflicts intensify. It is not unusual, particularly with boys, to feel that a teacher has taken sides when punishments are used to address conflict. Instead of looking for ways to compromise with each other, they become consumed by the perceived unfairness of the response. Consequently, the conflict flares up again.

When schools use sanctions exclusively to deal with inappropriate behaviours originating from student conflict and do not complete the process by bringing students face to face to resolve issues, some students will use their detentions or reflection rooms to plot revenge on those with whom they had the conflict, or on the teacher who sanctioned them. This isn't the style of thinking we are hoping to promote! Ian Lillico's 52nd recommendation from his 'The School Reforms Required to Engage Boys in Schooling' states:

> Schools need to review their pastoral care and disciplinary procedures so that the current pre-occupation with punishment changes to natural consequences for misbehaviour. Boys who are punished often have revenge fantasies that interrupt true remorse for what they have done. Boys who are quickly punished by our school systems are not given the opportunity to make amends for what they have done, as punishment clears the ledger and allows boys to re-offend in the future without attendant feelings of guilt. (Lillico 2000)

The Small Group Conference is the first point on the restorative practice continuum where the scripted restorative questions for those who caused the harm (wrongdoers) and those who were harmed are asked by the adult facilitating the conference (Figure 16.1). (See Chapter 21 for more information on these types of script.) We use both sides of the restorative script. In addition, there is a script for the Early Years Small Group Conference (Figure 16.2).

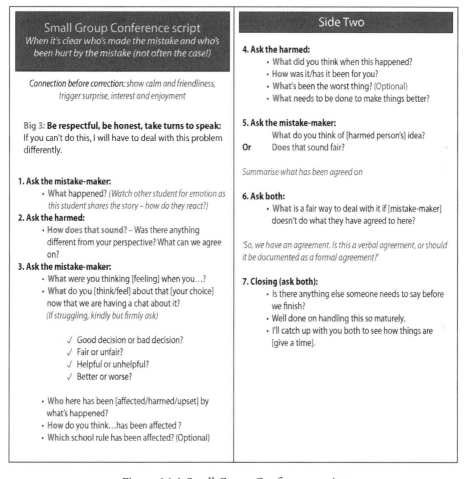

Figure 16.1 Small Group Conference script

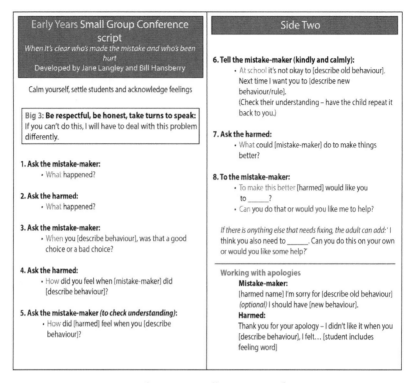

Figure 16.2 Early Years Small Group Conference script

The next case study illustrates how a clever teacher adapts this script for use with a group of teenage boys to address a potentially volatile conflict.

Typically, Small Group Conferences occur in the schoolyard or classroom when inappropriate behaviour has occurred and a teacher can bring those involved together without delay. These conferences are most manageable with roughly six or less students. If an issue involves more students, it pays to do a little more groundwork. Depending on the nature of the matter, a Large Group Conference (see Chapter 17) might be more suitable.

Case study: Turf wars

Jess is on yard duty when she overhears angry words between four 14-year-old students who seem to be arguing in the space between two makeshift soccer pitches. Jess can see two of the four boys, Domenic and Andrew, edge closer to one another with chests puffed out. Dale and Ryan move in behind them.

'It's going down for real!' yells a boy from a few metres away. The multitudes on the oval smell conflict and a crowd forms. Jess knows she has to get to the boys fast before Domenic or Andrew do something they don't want to do. She walks quickly and directly towards the four boys:

Jess: Hey, boys, can I see you for a moment, please?

The four boys look at Jess as she arrives.

Jess: Hi, boys, thanks for giving me a moment. I'm Miss McKay, I teach English and physical education here. What are your names?

The boys, looking surprised, begin to mutter their names. Domenic and Andrew don't take their eyes from one another for a few moments. Jess shakes each of their hands as they introduce themselves.

Jess: Thanks, boys. You'll need to help me because I'll be sure to get your names wrong at some point. Boys, I noticed what was happening over here. You all looked pretty uptight. I want to help you sort this problem out without anyone getting themselves in trouble. What's happened?

Domenic: Oh, no problem, miss, we were just talking about who might win the World Cup.

Jess (straightens as her face takes on a slightly more serious expression): Domenic, you and I both know that's not true. So please, what's happening?

Domenic: These jerks kicked our ball away when it rolled into their game.

Jess: Thanks, Domenic. You just reminded me of something important. The rules of this conversation are that we speak respectfully, one person speaks at a time and we tell the truth. If anyone can't follow these rules, I'll refer the problem to grade coordinators and it will get bigger than it needs to be. I think we can keep this problem small, though, boys, how about you?

Jess looks to the boys for a response. Andrew and Domenic look at each other through lowered eyes and both nod in acknowledgement. Jess knows that most boys this age, even the really tough ones, don't want to fight and only fight when they believe there is no other choice.

Jess: Do those rules make sense, boys?

Jess makes eye contact with each of the boys to check that they heard the rules.

Jess: So, Domenic, sorry for interrupting you. Can you start again but without any name-calling, please?

Domenic rolls his eyes and clicks his tongue (secondary behaviours to deal with his low-level embarrassment from Jess's mild rebuke).

Domenic: These fine young men kicked our ball in the opposite direction when it went onto their pitch. It was the second time today and we're growing rather tired of it. Was that respectful enough, miss?

Jess (grinning): That was on point. Thanks, Domenic. (She turns to Andrew.) Andrew, thanks for waiting. You've been patient. What's your take on this?

Andrew: Well, we're sick of their ball coming into our game. They need to learn to kick straight.

He turns and spits on the ground. Jess chooses to ignore that for the time being.

Jess: So, Andrew, you kicked their ball in the opposite direction when it came into your game?

Domenic (interrupting): Twice.

Jess (assertively): One at a time, please, Domenic.

Domenic grunts. Jess looks back at Andrew.

Dale: Can we just go back to the game, miss?

(He and Ryan have been slowly edging away from the conversation towards the game, which has resumed in the meantime.)

Jess (smiling): Boys, stay with us, please, you both seemed keen to stay when this looked as though it was about to turn into a fight. I'd like you to be part of the solution. You both look clever and I'd like your thoughts in a moment on what will fix this.

The compliment seems to work, as Dale and Ryan move closer.

Jess (turning back to Andrew): So, Andrew, you've been kicking the ball away instead of back to the boys in this game?

Andrew: It's not just me, miss, heaps of people have done it.

Jess: Andrew, seeing I've got you here, can you tell us what you were hoping would happen when you kicked these guys' ball away?

(Having realised that asking teenage boys what they are thinking is futile, Jess has found that the 'What were you hoping?' question generally gets more thoughtful answers. Andrew is quiet for a moment and then replies.)

Andrew: I don't know…that they'd be more careful with their kicks, maybe.

Jess: And now that we're having a chat about it, what do you think now about kicking their ball away?

Andrew (looking at the ground, muttering): I don't know.

Jess: Did it make things better or worse?

Andrew: Worse, I suppose.

Jess: Who has been affected by this?

Andrew (motioning towards Domenic and Dale): Probably those guys and their game.

Jess (loud enough so that everyone hears): So you think these guys and their game have been affected?

Andrew: Yeah.

Jess: That's a courageous admission, Andrew. I wish all the kids in this school could admit their mistakes as bravely as that. Which school rule has been affected?

Andrew (looking confused for a moment): The respect rule?

Jess: I'd say that's the one, Andrew. (She turns to Domenic and Dale.) How's your game been affected?

Dale: Well, we've had to go and get the ball every time they've booted it away. Some of the other boys are really pissed.

Domenic nods in agreement.

Jess (aware that the heat has gone out of the issue after Andrew's acknowledgement): So what will fix this?

Andrew: We'll just give them their ball back when it comes into our game.

Jess (turns to Domenic and Dale): Does that sound fair?

Domenic: Yes, and we'll do the same.

The four boys all look relieved and are keen to get back to their games.

Jess (motioning towards the students playing soccer on the separate pitches): Boys, who will tell the others about our plan?

Ryan (speaking for the first time): We'll tell everyone to just give it back.

The boys all nod in agreement.

Jess: So the agreement is that we give balls straight back?

Domenic (grinning): Yes, we all need our own balls.

The other boys snicker, while Jess ignores the comment.

Jess (to all of them): Boys, does this agreement need to be recorded or do we leave it as a verbal agreement?

Domenic: I think we'll be alright, we don't need it written down.

The others agree.

Jess: What's a fair way for a teacher to respond if this happens again?

The boys ponder this for a moment.

Andrew: Whoever does it gets yard detention.

Jess: Yard detention is certainly a possibility, but you'll also be asked to take part in a conference, perhaps a more formal one to deal with it. If you boys stick to what you've agreed here, hopefully it won't come to that.

The boys nod.

Jess: Thank you, boys. I'll make a note in the staff bulletin that you've agreed to be respectful of each other's balls from now on.

The boys are smirking. Jess looks deliberately confused. (Humour is a very good sign.)

Jess: Before we finish, is there anything else anyone needs to say?

The boys remain silent.

Jess: Thanks for sorting this one out like the sensible young men you are.

The boys return to their games.

Why this approach worked: Conferencing micro-skills

You might be thinking that Jess had a lucky run with a highly volatile situation. That could be true. We might also say that the cards were stacked against Jess. Being a young female teacher who was unknown to the boys, intervening in a testosterone-fuelled battle over territory, the task of bringing the boys to some form of restoration was huge. Many young teachers in this situation would have understandably called for backup from the 'alpha-male' physical education teacher who knew the boys and could maybe intimidate them into line.

Jess made her own luck by her highly skilled use of the Small Group Conference process. Most importantly, Jess was skilful in how she read and responded to the boys' emotions in this situation. Jess employed strategies that helped to settle the boys' highly excited amygdalas and allowed them to bring their neural activity back into their frontal lobes. In short, her response to the situation both soothed the boys and held them to account for the situation. Let's examine some of the conferencing micro-skills Jess used.

A surprising and friendly approach

Jess approached the boys in a calm, assertive and respectful manner. She didn't stand at a distance and demand that the boys come to her; she moved to them. Jess then triggered varying levels of affect surprise by introducing herself, asking the boys their names and shaking their hands. This would have been completely unexpected because the boys knew exactly why Jess had approached them. They may have been expecting her to use a raised voice or to be angry. You might recall that when the surprise–startle affect is triggered, all other affects cease. Jess began to take the heat out of the moment simply by how she approached the boys in a surprising way. She understood that the only authority she had in that situation was the authority the boys were prepared to 'give' her. She didn't assume she had any power; she instead worked hard to earn it.

Acknowledged feelings

It's easy to forget that teenage boys have very tender feelings they don't understand and struggle constantly to express appropriately. Jess made a point to let the boys know that she could see that they were uptight – a carefully chosen word and much more masculine than 'upset'! Jess also avoided using 'angry' (an overused word with boys, in my opinion). Acknowledging that young people are in distress is very important, because it makes it clear to them that the person with authority is concerned about them, not just angry or annoyed.

Helped, not chastised

Jess used some powerful language with the boys that clearly signalled her intentions. The boys saw that she was there to work 'WITH' them to handle the situation, not to exercise her authority as a teacher. Saying 'I want to help you sort this problem out without anyone getting themselves in trouble' signalled to the boys that Jess wanted to solve the problem peacefully, but if the boys didn't manage this themselves, the prospect of trouble was alive and well. The subtext was 'Do this well and nobody gets a detention'. In another situation, Jess may have said just that, but using the 'D' word may have triggered negative emotions.

Respectfully established rules of engagement

In restorative schools, we teach young people how to have respectful conversations in tough situations, and we then insist that it happen. This requires setting ground rules. Domenic's unhelpful use of a put-down (calling the other boys jerks) early in the conversation had the potential to derail the process. Jess seized on this moment to set the boundaries for the rest of the conversation by making it clear that name-calling wasn't going to be tolerated. After explaining the rules that I refer to as the 'big 3' of restorative conversations ('Be respectful, be honest, take turns to speak'; see Figures 16.1 and 16.2), Jess made it explicit that these rules needed to be followed; otherwise, the situation would be handled differently (non-restoratively). Jess then made a point of pausing and looking at each of the boys for acknowledgement that they had understood these rules.

Made it clear that it was about the problem, not about the teacher

Jess skilfully kept the focus of the conversation on the problem to be solved (the harm caused by the ball being kicked away, and restoring peace between the boys). Despite the fact that Jess was there to help the boys, she had to sidestep some low-level disrespect from Domenic (eye rolling and a snide comment: 'Was that respectful enough, miss?'). It's too easy in these moments to become caught up in these secondary behaviours – 'What did you say to me?' – and lose track of the original purpose, and engage the student in a power struggle.

Jess also maintained good manners throughout the conference with the boys by thanking them for their involvement and their accounts as they shared their stories. In heated moments when teachers are feeling stressed and anxious, it is easy to forget the little social nuances that make the big differences.

Used humour

Jess knew the power of humour as an antidote to negative emotion. Instead of shutting down Domenic's remark 'We all need our own balls', she ignored it and let the boys have their fun. When people laugh together in restorative processes, it is a strong indicator that the group has moved out of the negative affects into the positive affects and healing is taking place.

What if…? When things don't go so well

What if, in spite of Jess's best efforts, Andrew hadn't acknowledged the problem with his choice to kick the ball away? What if Domenic had continued insulting and provoking the other boys? What if it had become clear that neither of the boys were interested in restoration? Young people become resistant to a restorative approach for a range of reasons:

- They believe that there will be a punitive sanction added at the end of the conference and think, *Why bother with the restorative stuff?*

- The shame of the wrongdoer is so intense that they resort to Compass of Shame defences.

- Some of the students involved are fearful or have become anguished.

- There is an ongoing conflict between the students that has eroded trust and caused a high level of distress.

- Restorative practice is relatively new in the school and students are still using duck-and-cover or fight-and-argue self-defence techniques.

- The students don't trust the teacher trying to guide them through the restorative process – perhaps this teacher has behaved punitively in the past.

Regardless of the myriad of reasons that young people may not take the invitation to be part of a restorative process, the fact remains that there has to be accountability for the harm caused. Just walking away from a problem would make our practice permissive ('FOR') at best and neglectful ('NOT') at worst.

If Jess had decided the Small Group Conference was making the situation worse between the boys, she would have politely called the meeting to an end and referred the issue to a more senior colleague. If Andrew had showed no interest in acknowledging or fixing the problem, Jess might have issued him a detention for kicking the other group's ball away or asked him to leave the game. If Domenic had continued to provoke the other boys during the conference, Jess would have asked him to leave the conference and informed him that this behaviour would be dealt with later. None of these approaches would have healed the rift between the boys, but would have been necessary, however, to signal that the school was serious about students doing restorative business respectfully and holding people accountable for their actions.

Small group conferencing for general conflict

What about when there's no clear 'wrongdoer' and 'harmed' students?

The situation on the soccer pitch between the four boys was relatively straightforward to conference using the questions from the Small Group Conference script (see Figure 16.1), because it was clear who had done what to whom: Andrew had kicked away the ball from Domenic's game. It had only happened once, and Domenic hadn't done the same to Andrew's ball. There was a 'villain' and a 'victim'. Things are rarely this simple.

Analysis of the 'Turf wars' case study

Let's imagine for a moment that both groups had kicked each other's ball away in a tit-for-tat battle before the confrontation between Domenic and Andrew. How might the situation have changed? What would have been different with Jess's approach and the questions she asked? The answer is that not much would have changed at all. Jess would have made some very slight changes to which questions she asked to which boys.

The Small Group Conflict Conference script can help in these situations because it allows a little more flexibility and saves the teacher from getting caught up in determining who the wrongdoer and the harmed person(s) are. The Small Group Conflict Conference script varies slightly to the Small Group Conference script in that the 'wrongdoer' and 'harmed' questions are asked to people on both sides of the conflict. Teachers who are experienced with using restorative processes naturally switch between both scripts depending on the situation.

Figure 16.3 shows the pocket-card version of the Small Group Conflict Conference script. Following it is advice on the micro-skills that will increase the chance of a successful conference using this script.

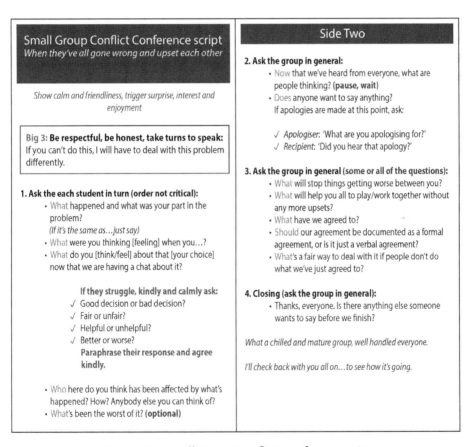

Figure 16.3 Small Group Conflict Conference script

Improving the success of a Small Group Conference to deal with conflict: Use of micro-skills

Below are some general guidelines for using the Small Group Conflict Conference script. Jess used these micro-skills to great effect in her encounter with the boys on the soccer pitch.

Showing calm and friendliness to trigger the positive affects

To be able to help young people with the tricky emotions (negative affects), teachers need to be calm and enter the situation in a poised way. Because people catch each other's affects (discussed in Chapter 7), teachers will catch the affects (anger, distress, fear) from the young people as they approach them and will likely just do as the young people do. This is the reason some teachers (on a bad day) enter conflict situations by trying to shout young people down in an attempt to subdue them. The teacher is trying to bring an end to their own negative affect by using anger to shut down the expression of negative affect from the students. This may work sometimes because of the surprise–startle affect involved, but often anger, fear and distress return at greater levels, and the chance of restoration is lost.

When teachers approach tricky situations in the right way, they share their frontal lobes with the students involved and help the students' frontal lobes do the work of suppressing difficult feelings so the students can reroute their neural activity to the neocortex (where planning and reason reside), and away from the more primitive hind-brain regions.

Upon entering a conflict situation with young people, it helps if teachers ask themselves:

- How am I feeling about approaching this situation? Can I calm myself enough to help these students with their own emotions?

- Can we start this discussion right now or does somebody (including me) need cool-off time first?

- Is this the right time or is it better to just help the students calm down and defer the conference for later when we have the time to do it properly?

- Am I ready to do this process 'WITH' the students, not 'TO' them or 'FOR' them?

Responding to feelings and setting boundaries

Part of settling down distressed brains is to respond to hurt feelings but then bring some boundaries to the situation that felt out of control, so the young people involved can start to feel that the situation is now more predictable. If there's been a physical scuffle, with a concerned but firm voice ask the involved students if anyone is hurt and needing to go to the sickroom. In addition, you can say the following:

> I can see that you're pretty upset. If we can keep ourselves calm, we might be able to sort this out now. You'll all get a chance to have your say, but for this to happen, there are some rules we need to follow:
>
> * We must be respectful to each other.
>
> * We must tell the truth.
>
> * We must not interrupt unless it is okay with the person whose turn it is to talk.
>
> Can we all do this? (Check for commitment from all students.) If we can't do this, or if I think this chat is making things worse, I'll stop our chat and this problem will be handled differently. Does everyone understand? Who goes first?

Normally, the teacher makes a judgement about which student is the most responsible for the problems, and first asks them what happened and what their part in the problem was. In conflict situations it's quite hard to work out who is most responsible for the problem, so the teacher should just go with their instinct about who might need to tell their story first and who is able to wait. When young people believe the teacher is going to help them – not blame, yell or get uptight – they won't be as concerned about who tells their story first.

Asking the students 'Who should go first?' gives an opportunity for one of the students to allow another to start. If this doesn't happen and one of the students says 'me first', the teacher can still check with the other student(s) by asking, 'Is it okay with you if they go first?' Often the response will be 'yes', which again creates some good feeling between the students.

The Small Group Conference Process

An effective process for this type of conference is explained below.

Asking each student the necessary questions

Ask each student in turn (the order isn't critical) the following questions:

1. What happened and what was your part in the problem? (When the second and third young person have their turn to respond, say to them, 'If your story is just the same as [another person's] story, let us know; if it is different, tell us how.' This avoids students giving identical accounts of the same incident if they all saw it the same way.)

2. What were you thinking [feeling] when you…?

3. What do you [think/feel] about your choice/decision now that we're having a chat about it?

When people get stuck

Sometimes young people get stuck at the 'What do you think now that…?' question and struggle to acknowledge the error in their decisions. At this point, teachers can gently help young people get past this impasse by gently but assertively asking one or more of the questions below, with deliberate pauses in between, until a young person feels safe enough to reflect on the problem with their behaviour:

- Was that a good decision or a bad decision?

- Was it a good or bad call?

- Was that fair or unfair?

- Did that make things better or worse?

- Was that kind or unkind?

- Was that a strong choice or a weak choice?

- Was that friendly or unfriendly?

- Was that a good look or a bad look?

These questions are often adapted by schools to suit the language being used across the school. For example, schools using 'The Way to A' programme (Manasco 2006) might ask the question 'Was that an "A" choice or a "B" choice?' to a young person on the autism spectrum.

If a young person is able to respond to one of these questions, acknowledge their brave response. When people admit the wrongness of their actions in front of others, they can be left feeling exposed (affect shame) and in need of support. Clever teachers might kindly show that they agree with the young person by nodding or saying, 'Yes, I agree with you. It wasn't a good decision to...' This isn't about making a young person feel worse, it's a supportive acknowledgement of their admission and leads into the next question(s):

- Who here do you think has been affected by what's happened?

- How do you think they might have been affected? (Optional)

- Is there anybody else who might have been affected? (Optional)

- What's been the worst thing about this? (Optional)

As young people respond to these questions and acknowledge the harm caused to one another, it is a good idea to paraphrase their responses to ensure that everybody hears when a young person acknowledges that somebody has been affected. Jess in the case study earlier quickly followed Andrew's acknowledgement by saying, loud enough so everyone could hear, 'So you think these guys and their game have been affected?'

Questions to ask the group in general

The first question is: 'Now that we have heard from everyone, what are people thinking?' Here we are inviting students to make amends with each other or to begin to make suggestions about repairing the harm. Sometimes students will want to make apologies to one another. If this happens, always follow up an apology by asking:

- What are you apologising for? (Directed to the person who apologised.)

- Did you hear that apology? (Directed to the person being apologised to.)

A forced or insincere apology feels wrong to everyone involved. Simply getting young people to apologise is not what restorative practice is about. Whether or not apologies are offered or accepted is up to the students involved. This is why the teacher asks 'Did you hear that apology?' instead of 'Do you accept that apology?' – which can put a young person in a position where they feel that they have to. Young people are usually quite forgiving, unless they are still distressed or there's a burning issue that hasn't yet been raised.

More questions to ask the group in general

In addition to the previous questions, the following questions should be asked:

- What will stop things getting worse between you?

- What will help you all to play/work together without any more upsets?

- What have we agreed to?

- Should our agreement be documented as a formal agreement, or is it just a verbal agreement?

- What's a fair way to deal with it if people don't do what we've just agreed to?

Closing the conference

You can close the conference by saying, 'Thanks, everyone. Is there anything else someone wants to say before we finish?'

This question is important because it reaffirms that the process (and the problem) belongs to the young people, not the teacher. Usually, nobody needs to say anything more, but occasionally one of the young people will take the opportunity to say something restorative like thanking the other students, apologising again or even thanking the teacher for taking the time to help them sort through the conflict. (Yes, that does happen sometimes!)

Keystones for the Small Group Conference are shown in Figure 16.4.

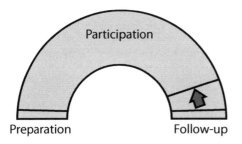

The amount of follow-up will depend on whether the conference agreement is made formal and recorded

Figure 16.4 Keystones for the Small Group Conference
(Adapted from Jansen and Matla 2011)

Analysis of the conference process

Preparation

Small Group Conferences don't need preparation, as they are impromptu. Teachers call students together and hold these conferences on the spot, either immediately after the incident or after the young people involved have had some time to calm down. Students and teacher might usually form a standing circle and get down to the business of dealing with the problem, like how Jess and the boys did.

The teacher makes a quick assessment about the readiness of the students to resolve the matter and whether or not the student(s) who appear to be responsible for the harm will be able to acknowledge this, at least in part. Like any restorative process, if there is no acknowledgement of wrongdoing on the part of the young people who caused the upset, the process will cause further distress to those involved and the incident should probably be deferred until later and/or investigated and handled differently.

The way a teacher enters the situation can't be underestimated. These first critical seconds determine whether the young people involved will be able to work restoratively with one another or whether they will become resistant. Jess skilfully and respectfully calmed the boys down in the beginning and paved the way for a respectful interaction. If Jess had approached the boys by aggressively calling out from across the oval, 'Hey, you four, come here now – I want a word with you!', the conversation would have gone very differently.

Being aware of possible trauma and attachment disorder

Be prepared to delay any restorative process for students with a history of trauma or those experiencing attachment disorders. The time needed between the incident and starting to deal with it restoratively can be anywhere up to, and even beyond, an hour. This of course means that the conference will no longer be impromptu. Working restoratively taxes the brain's neocortex, and young people need to be regulating their emotions to be able to do restorative work. The perceived threat from the problem or incident will cause some young people to emotionally dysregulate. Their endocrine system will produce far too much adrenaline and cortisol that stays in their system for much longer than normal, causing them to act as if their life is literally under threat (constant triggering of fear, anger and distress affects). The result of forcing a young person into a restorative conversation too soon will be an outburst.

Howard (2013, p.53) recommends that at least 30 minutes of low-stimulus activity for young students, and up to an hour or more for adolescents, is needed for adrenaline and cortisol levels to drop to a point where these young people can regulate themselves well enough to be part of any questioning or behavioural intervention. *The Red Beast* (Al-Ghani 2009) gives a wonderful example of how young people can be helped to regulate their emotions before dealing with the problem.

Small Group Conference follow-up

At the end of a Small Group Conference, the teacher sometimes asks the students involved, 'Is our agreement a verbal agreement, or do we need to make it formal and write it down?' In the case study earlier, the boys didn't feel that their agreement needed to be formally documented, so Jess informed the boys that a note of the incident would go into the staff bulletin so other staff would be aware of the agreement they had made. The reason for this was so that other staff could be watchful of the interactions between the boys.

Although asking the students involved to decide if their agreement should be formally recorded is a respectful act, there will be times when the teacher involved will decide to formally record the agreement so it can be communicated to other staff and reviewed with the students at a later date. Situations where this might be the case are the following:

- One or more of the students involved has been part of several incidents of this nature and may have a pattern of behaviours, despite having been part of restorative interventions.

- One or more of the students involved has not honoured verbal agreements or agreements recorded from previous yard-incident reports.

- The students involved have a history of conflict and will need added support to adhere to agreements made in conferences.

- There isn't unanimous agreement in the group about the need for the agreement to be recorded – some want it recorded and some do not.

Processes for formally recording and reviewing restorative conference agreements are covered more thoroughly in Part 4.

Teacher skill level

Although Small Group Conferences typically deal with less serious issues and are less formal, teachers need lots of practice to become as proficient as Jess was with the boys on the soccer pitch. All staff will be anxious about getting it right with students, and it should be openly acknowledged by everyone that not all Small Group Conferences go well.

Schools which make a regular commitment to practising Small Group Conferences with each other do best. These practice sessions need to be light-hearted and collegial. The leaders should be brave and put themselves out there first, showing a willingness to make mistakes. The importance of leaders telling their own stories of when conferences didn't go so well, and openly reflecting on why this may have been the case, cannot be underestimated. All staff look to leaders for the courage to take professional risks. The beauty of role-played restoratives is that the action can be paused, rewound and played back as several different possibilities and potential student responses are explored. Committing to this style of staff training helps teachers develop a grasp of the scripted questions. Eventually they become second nature, like they were for Jess.

The next chapter moves us up the restorative practice continuum from small group conferencing to large group conferencing.

Chapter 17

The Large Group Conference

Large group conferencing works well for issues or incidents that involve a large number of students, usually from across cohorts or grade groups. Every now and then in schools, something goes wrong that sees many students involved. Examples of this may be an issue between groups of students from different grades, such as a scuffle over the use of a particular part of the schoolyard (turf wars or pitch battles). Had the soccer incident with the 14-year-olds from the previous chapter escalated to involve many students, a Large Group Conference could have been used to address the issue.

Case study: Four-square games out of control

By Tuesday, the behaviour book contained records of 11 Small Group Conferences and nine yard reflections that had been issued to students who had not conducted themselves restoratively. These conferences and yard reflections had all involved a group of students who played four square on the court near the toilets. When Sam, the principal, raised the issue in a staff meeting, there was a collective groan from staff who had all been in some way involved in the cacophony of *restoratives* to deal with various upsets, exclusions and even the odd fight on the four-square court near the toilet block. Some staff were shocked to hear that problems had re-emerged after what they believed had been a successful Small Group Conference.

Staff talked about the various restorative conference agreements that had been made between the students involved in the squabbles and quickly realised that there were many students using those courts who would come and go from the game, and disagreements and misunderstandings about the rules of the game had caused the conflicts. There were so many different interpretations of the rules and so many different players coming and going that conflict was inevitable. The socially powerful students were also bending the rules of the game to suit themselves. Things had reached a boiling point on Friday, when a fight erupted between five 11-year-old and 12-year-old students. Sam, the principal, had held a Community Conference (see Chapter 19) on Monday afternoon to address the previous Friday's incident. During this conference students and parents agreed that something had to be done about the confusion regarding the rules.

Conference preparation

The staff agreed that the four-square court near the toilet would be a no-play zone until a Large Group Conference could be held during lunch on Thursday. All interested students would be invited to discuss the problem, the harm that had resulted and to see what could be done to begin to repair the harm and make the four-square courts a peaceful and fair place again.

Kerry, the school's well-being coordinator, moved her release time around with Sam's help so she could be free the next day to plan and convene the conference that would begin at lunch time. She anticipated the conference would take about 1 hour.

The next morning, Kerry visited the classrooms of the students who used the courts and asked for students who were interested in being part of a conference to sort out the four square. Kerry explained that the outcome of the conference would be a written agreement by which everyone would be expected to abide. Despite the fact that the conference was planned for a lunch break, many students volunteered to be involved. Kerry capped the number at 25 students, knowing that more students would make the conference run too long.

On Thursday morning, with a list of 25 names from across four classes, Kerry set about writing the conference script and setting up a circle of seats in the drama room. She put out 27 seats (including two for the principal and herself). Kerry deliberately designed the conference script to get students talking about the harm that had been caused to others, not themselves personally. Many of the students had already discussed this during the myriad of Small Group Conferences that had led up to this point. Kerry included some activities students had learned in Classroom Circles such as mix-ups and pair-share, and feedback to make the conference run more effectively.

Knowing that there had been some parents involved in the Community Conference that Sam, the principal, had run previously, Kerry asked Sam if he could call these parents and ask them if they would tell him what they would like to say to the group about the effect that the bickering at the four-square courts was having on parents. The parents responded eagerly and gave Sam some statements to share with the students during the conference.

Kerry put the script questions into a PowerPoint presentation so they could be projected onto a whiteboard for the Circle to refer to during the conference.

Large Group Conference script

Kerry began the script for the Large Group Conference as follows:

> Welcome. Thank you all for agreeing to be here in your own lunch time so we can deal with the problems on the four-square courts. Your being here will help us all understand what's been happening, how people have been affected and what we can do to make four-square games fairer and more peaceful.
>
> Let's play a mix-up game. It's important that we hear the ideas of different people, not just our friends, so please change places if:
>
> - you are wearing anything black
>
> - your name has the letter 'a' in it
>
> - you have stripes on any of your clothes
>
> - you think it is important that we all play fairly at four square.
>
> Great – well done on changing seats so well.

Conference introduction

Kerry continued:

> Over the past few weeks there have been many problems and upsets on the four-square courts. Many of you here have been part of smaller conferences to fix arguments and fights over rules and unfair behaviour. Some here have been in yard time-out over these problems. The teachers discussed the problems in the last staff meeting and realised that things had become so bad at the courts that we all needed to work together to come up with an agreement to make four square safer and fairer.
>
> Today we will talk about the problems, not the people. In other words, we will talk about what's been happening, instead of naming and blaming. There will be a chance to say if you think *you* have behaved unfairly, but we won't be blaming one another for the problems. Have I explained that well enough?

If you need to leave the conference for a toilet break, just raise your hand and let me know.

Setting the ground rules

Kerry continued:

Remember, we are here to discuss problems, not people. We all know that there are people in the Circle who have said and done things that have caused harm. Some here have been only bystanders to harassment or unfairness. I'd like to thank those people for being here to try to fix the problems these behaviours have caused. So we can all have a fair say today, there are some rules we must follow:

- We speak respectfully at all times.

- We take our turn to speak – no interruptions, and you will need to be holding the talking stick to talk.

- You can pass if you wish.

- If you can't follow these rules, you will be asked to leave the conference, and decisions will be made without you.

Stand up and sit down if you think those are fair rules for our conference. Great, I think that was everyone. Let's get started.

Exploring the harm

Kerry continued:

Mr Bartlett [aka Sam], you have spoken to a few of the parents who have been involved in the problems regarding four square. Because these parents couldn't be here with us today but wanted a say, would you please read to the Circle what they wrote?

Sam reads what the parents wrote.

Put your hands up if you are surprised to hear how this has affected parents.

Kerry then moved around the Circle and paired students up for the next questions.

In your pairs, discuss and decide on two main things that have been going wrong at the courts. Be ready to share this with the Circle.

Now with your partner, decide on who you both think has been affected by these things and how. Be ready to share this with the Circle.

Once the pairs had shared, Kerry responded:

Put your hand up if you're surprised or shocked to hear that so many people have been affected by the problems on the four-square courts.

Exploring the issues and repairing the harm

Kerry continued:

Can you thank the partner with whom you just worked? Can the tallest person in your pair stand up and move clockwise, sitting down in the second empty seat they find?

Great – it was a bit messy, but we did it! I'll now move around the Circle and put you into your new pairs.

In your pairs, decide on two reasons for the problems we've had with four square. Remember to name behaviours, not names. Be ready to share these with the Circle.

This next part will take some courage. I will pass the talking stick around the Circle twice. If you feel that you have to take responsibility for any of the behaviours that have caused harm, this is your chance.

When the talking stick gets to you, you *can* tell us the names of anyone you believe you harmed and you can talk directly to that person if they are in the Circle. You might say something like, 'I pushed John the other day when he got me out and that was unfair. John, I want to apologise, I handled that badly.' John doesn't have to accept that apology, but I do want him to say that he heard it by saying something like, 'Thank you for your apology, Kerry.'

Remember, you can pass.

Agreement phase

Kerry continued:

> As the pairs shared what they believed had caused the problems, I recorded what was said. I'll now read these out.

Kerry read the reasons.

> Now I want to hear from each pair what *one* action will stop these problems from happening.

Kerry heard the ideas.

> Thank you for these ideas. I have recorded them and will now read them back. These actions will become our agreement for how four square will be played. Now, let me ask you:
>
> - Who would be interested in working with me later to finalise the agreement and help to get it signed, copied and shared with all of us and the teachers?
>
> - How should we respond if people break these rules?
>
> - When shall we meet again to review the agreement?
>
> - Who should be part of this review?

Closing the conference

Kerry closed the conference as follows:

> Thank you for being here today to work on the problems regarding four square. Our agreement will go a long way towards making it fairer and more peaceful. Once our agreement is typed up, we will bring it to your classrooms for everyone to sign. We will then copy the original and give everybody here and the teachers a copy.

> Before we finish, is there anything anyone wants to say?

Keystones for the Large Group Conference are shown in Figure 17.1.

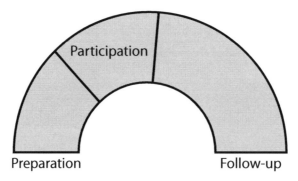

Figure 17.1 Keystones for the Large Group Conference
(Adapted from Jansen and Matla 2011)

Large Group Conference follow-up

The higher we move up the restorative practice continuum, the more important post-conference follow-up is. The long-term effectiveness of the Large Group Conference described will be reliant on the steps below being executed in a planned and prepared way. Trying to do conference follow-up on the fly, or after something goes wrong with the agreement (e.g. the students break the agreement), is a disastrous practice that sends a message to students and the community that restorative practice is a one-hit wonder with no follow through. In other words, HIGH on support but LOW on accountability. This is not the impression we wish to make.

Completion of the agreement

In the case of the four-square Large Group Conference, the agreement could be finalised with a smaller group of students who had volunteered. Agreeing on the wording of the agreement would be too difficult with 25 students, so convening a smaller executive group to do this would be more manageable. This group would meet to complete the agreement. The next step would be to either call the entire conference group back to present the agreement to them for feedback (and adjustments) or simply to have all students sign the original agreement.

Communication of the agreement

Once the four-square agreement was signed by all present in the conference, copies would need to be made and given to all stakeholders. Besides those who had attended the conference, all classroom teachers of the students involved and all staff who would be on duty at break times near the four-square courts would need to be aware of the agreement. Copies of the agreement could also be laminated (or as a teacher in one of my trainings once called it, 'law-minated') and placed in classrooms and clearly displayed near the four-square courts.

Agreement review meetings

As with most restorative processes from this point upward on the restorative practice continuum, scheduled review meetings where students come together to discuss how things are going are critical to changing attitudes and behaviours. In the case of the four-square agreement, the first review meeting would be best scheduled for 1 week after the conference, then 2 weeks after that, and then, if things were going well, less regularly. This seems like a lot of work, but when we consider that we're helping many students to change habits as well as altering their dynamics as a group, an investment of a few 20-minute review meetings is a small sacrifice. The alternative would be sending a large group of young people back into the schoolyard with an agreement and hoping that the group would be able to regulate itself without support. This would be setting them up for failure. (More about reviewing restorative conference agreements is covered in Part 4.)

Large group conferencing is a highly effective approach that always brings sensible solutions to large-scale problems. Simply imposing an arbitrary set of rules to be policed by teachers, or imposing a school-wide ban on a game or activity, always sets up a new layer of unrest and resentment among students. It also doesn't teach them a thing. The process of engaging students from all corners of a problem draws out the rational voice of young people as long as they sense that the problem is genuinely being solved 'WITH' them.

The next chapter looks at another form of large group conferencing: the Classroom Conference.

Chapter 18

The Classroom Conference

Occasionally an issue or conflict arises that affects an entire class group. This could be a fight between students in the classroom that has left other students and staff shaken, or a theft (or series of thefts) where a class has become fearful for their personal belongings. At other times an issue is more chronic and has caused harm over time. This could be a group of students behaving disruptively and affecting the functioning of the class, or a situation where a culture of poor treatment and harassment has become so widespread in a class that learning has ground to a halt and the good order of the classroom has been seriously affected.

When the harm is widespread across a class group, the process to address it will need to involve the entire affected group. This is where classroom conferencing can be suitable. Classroom conferencing can involve a student or a group of students being held accountable for their actions by the rest of the class (a confronting process that requires meticulous preparation), or a conference where, instead of identifying particular wrongdoers, the problems are the focus of the conversation (no naming or blaming of particular students) and people are given the choice and opportunity to take responsibility and make amends if they are able to do so. This chapter will look at this type of classroom conferencing, known as the No-Blame Classroom Conference (Thorsborne and Vinegrad 2004). This is an extremely powerful process that, when carefully prepared and meticulously followed up, can significantly improve the climate of a classroom.

Case study: No-Blame Classroom Conference

Jim's new appointment was to a middle school of about 500 students. The area was on the fringe of a rural city of about 90,000 people. John's previous school had been in his home town, 30 miles away – a small rural town with a school with enrolments of 250 students.

Jim was a traditional disciplinarian. Standing over 6 feet tall, he was a respected sportsman in his home town. He towered over his students and had a booming voice which he'd learned to employ to bring instant reform from any student who displeased him. Jim's student management approach occupied the 'TO' quadrant of the social control window. For 25 years, Jim's primary means of behaviour correction involved shouting, belittling and humiliating, and when a student was really having a bad day, Jim would keep them in during break times. In Jim's last school he'd had little need to send students to the principal's office because he carried enough authority in his own right and also knew most of his students' parents socially. In Jim's home town it was understood that, if he liked a young person, they would have a good year in his class, but if Jim believed a young person was a troublemaker, they were in for a bad year. Some parents had taken exception to Jim's methods and tried unsuccessfully to approach the issue with Jim and the school principal, but Jim was too set in his ways, and the principal, who at times wanted to challenge Jim on some of his methods, found Jim unmovable. Jim's respected position in the community also made it a very bad idea for the principal, who was a relative newcomer to the town, to put Jim off side.

As Jim got to know his new class in his new school, he concluded that difficult students made up the critical mass in his class. Of Jim's 31 students, 12 had some form of learning difficulty, four had attention deficit hyperactivity disorder and four others were downright quirky, with friendship problems. Their explosive dispositions meant that they were often arguing or fighting. These quirky kids were also being targeted and harassed by other students who enjoyed watching their explosive reactions to being baited as much as they liked watching Jim yell at them when they would set them up to get into trouble.

Assignments were rarely completed. Eight students in the class never completed work. Test results were terrible, with only a handful of students working at the standard required. The difficult students' parents were little help. They would make excuses for their children's behaviour, saying that they were being picked on and set off by other kids, and that Jim wasn't doing anything about it. Jim concluded that these parents had such little control over their kids that they would be of little assistance to him. Jim was on his own when it came to the difficult kids and was beginning to feel isolated.

Jim was struggling to manage very disruptive classroom behaviours from a group of girls. From the moment they walked into the classroom in the morning, their bickering and vindictiveness would start. The epicentre of this problem were Kyla and Olivia, who had been locked in bitter rivalry since preschool. Both girls were strong-willed, streetwise and smart-mouthed. For years they had competed for the loyalty of the other girls and were now starting to compete for the affection of the boys as well. Within five minutes of the school-day beginning, a look, a glare, an unkind remark or an accusation would result in sulking, tears, bad language, walkouts and arguments over allegiances (which were ever-changing). Their conflicts were endless and creative. Their drama occupied their minds, leaving little room for anything else, especially schoolwork.

Jim had never sent so many students administrative reprimands for disrespect, bad language, being mean, backtalking, harassment or fighting. He was finding that his revolving door of discipline was a very blunt instrument in his war against these behaviours. Jim may have been an authoritarian, but he wasn't stupid. He knew something needed to change, and he wasn't the only one noticing that things were getting worse. The high number of students Jim sent from the room was causing concern among the leadership.

Jim was almost at his breaking point when the principal, Susan, suggested he take a different approach to his unsettled class. In a meeting with Jim, Susan told him that, despite the complex learning needs of the kids, there was a deeper social issue at play. She believed the class had disconnected and segmented into factions who were at war with one another. There were many old conflicts and old hurts between students. Mistrust and broken relationships were everywhere and the students were in social-survival mode.

Susan empathised with Jim as he talked about how challenging the class was. Jim spun around the Compass of Shame between blaming the students and their parents, criticising Susan for not suspending the girls more often, talking about retiring early and blaming himself for having spent too long teaching in the countryside and becoming stale. Jim's main concerns were for the good kids in his class who were affected by the disruptive behaviour of the others because of time lost addressing the constant stream of inappropriate behaviours, particularly the bickering girls. Susan praised Jim for his diligence in addressing behavioural issues. Jim's approach was high on expectations and standards, and he communicated these effectively to the students. The problem was that there was not enough *support* offered by Jim to compliment the challenge he had rightfully posed to students about their behaviour. The students knew that this behaviour wasn't suitable but needed guidance (support) in how to change. Susan knew the pressure Jim was under and knew that, if she condemned his behaviour management, she'd have his resignation on her desk the next day.

However, Susan did say to Jim that she believed his approaches to classroom management were traditional and authoritarian, and that although this was highly effective in his last school, this leadership style was no match for this class. She paused before concluding, 'Jim, your current approaches, although diligent and well meaning, are damaging your relationships with the students and damaging their relationships with one another. I'd like to teach you how to work with a class like this.'

Susan explained the four quadrants of the social control window ('TO', 'FOR', 'NOT' and 'WITH'; see Chapter 3) to Jim. She explained that their task was to push Jim's practice more towards the 'WITH' quadrant. (Jim had already quickly identified that he was a 'TO' teacher.) Susan then proposed a restorative Classroom Conference as a starting point for addressing the ongoing issues. The form of Classroom Conference that Susan proposed was the No-Blame Classroom Conference (Thorsborne and Vinegrad 2004). Jim was sceptical but listened as Susan shared some before-and-after behaviour data and surveys from students from other classes where they had used the No-Blame Classroom Conference. Susan stressed to Jim that the success or failure of the process depended on the follow-up, which hinged on an agreement that the class and teacher would develop during the conference. This follow-up would involve the class meeting in a Circle, at least weekly, to talk about how the conference agreement was going, celebrating successes and dealing with any breaches of the agreement. The first thing that entered Jim's mind was the learning time that all of these review meetings would take up. He then thought that he was already losing learning time because of the current situation, and that this was worth a try.

Jim left Susan's office with a copy of the No-Blame Conference process, including the conference script that Susan would use when she facilitated the conference with his class. Susan had asked Jim to read through the script and make any changes to suit his class. He and Susan had arranged to meet in 2 days to plan the conference.

No-Blame Classroom Conference script

The following is the basis of the script that Susan and Jim would develop for his class.[1]

---

[1]   This script has been adapted from Thorsborne and Vinegrad (2004, pp.56–58).

Preparing the students

Susan prepared the students as follows:

> Thank you for agreeing to participate in a Classroom Conference, which will happen shortly [or tomorrow]. Before we have our conference, we need to understand what harm has been done to people in our class. I would like everybody to take five minutes and write down on the paper provided these things:
>
> - Write down what has been done to you – the verbal or physical harassment, the name-calling, putdowns and so forth.
>
> - Write down what has been done to others in this class – the words or actions that have been used to hurt people – what you've seen and heard happen.
>
> We need to hear about the bitchiness, the pushing, the fighting, the teasing and rumours, and the threats [whatever is appropriate]. Please do not put any names on this paper, not even yours. It is confidential, and what you write will not leave this room. If you need to write something offensive that has been said, please do so. You will not get into trouble; we need to know exactly what has been happening.

Introduction to conference

Early the next day (or immediately after preparing the students, depending on whether or not Jim and Susan wanted to leave time between introducing and running the conference), Susan facilitated the conference in Jim's class.

The following conference script is an example of the No-Blame Classroom Conference script that Susan and Jim would have modified for use with Jim's class. The full script, with all of the alternative wordings is included to give you a template to adapt for your own use.

> Thank you for participating in this conference. This Classroom Conference will take about 1 hour. This conference has been called because [please choose an appropriate statement or develop one of your own]:
>
> > Your teachers can no longer successfully teach this class, and many students in this class can no longer learn, and people are being harmed by this behaviour; or

Teachers and students have said that there are problems with people fighting and verbal harassment, which means that our class is not going well; or

People have said that there is a lot of trouble and conflict in our class which is causing harm to people; or

People are not being responsible for their behaviour, and people's right to learn and feel safe are not being respected.

We are here to talk about the harm that has been done by the behaviour of this class. We want to try to understand who has been affected by your behaviour and in what ways. You will be given a chance to talk about what things need to happen to make things better. People in this class who have been harmed by the behaviour will be given the chance to talk about how they have been affected. This is a No-Blame Classroom Conference. No one will get into trouble or be punished for what they say.

Conference rules

Susan continued:

We need to follow some rules so that everybody can be heard and make a contribution:

- What is said here today stays in this room.

- One person speaks at a time. To speak you must be holding our talking stick.

- You may pass if you wish.

- Tell us how you *feel* about what has happened, not what you think.

- If you can't follow these rules, you will be asked to sit outside the Circle, which means you will not be able to contribute or have a vote.

- You may leave the conference any time you wish, but you need to know that the school will manage your behaviour and what you may have done in a different way.

Do we need any other rules?

To all participants: I will now read some of the statements that you have all made. No names will be mentioned. After reading, I will roll up all of these statements to make our talking stick. What should we call this stick?

To all teachers present: I would like to ask the teachers present to tell us how they feel about what has been happening in this class.

- How do you feel about the behaviour of this class?

- What's it like to work with this class?

- What are the main issues for you?

To the class: We will now move around the Circle and ask how people feel about what has been done to them and others in this class. Do not mention any names.

Choose some of the following questions to help students elaborate on their responses:

- What has been happening to you?

- How has this affected you?

- What has changed for you?

- What is the hardest thing?

- How do you feel about what has been done to others?

- How has the class changed?

- What are the issues for you?

After the Circle has been completed once:

- Raise your hand if the talking stick should go around the Circle again.

- Raise your hand if you feel that this is harassment of people in our class and these problems need to stop.

Thanks, hands down.

To the class: We now want to explore who has been affected by the behaviour of the class. We will move around the Circle and ask you to tell us who has been affected and in what ways:

- Who else? Think of the people not here today.

- Can anybody tell us how [a particular person] has been affected?

- Raise your hand if you are surprised that so many people have been affected.

Thanks, hands down.

To the class and teachers: Now it is time for some courage and honesty. We need you to take responsibility for what you have done. Remember that what is said will stay in this room. No one will be punished. Tell us what you have done and what you need to do to fix things. You do not need to mention people's names. You may want to say, 'I have put people down by name-calling and to those people I apologise', or you may want to say, 'I have pushed and punched people at the lockers and I apologise – I will not do this again.' Raise your hands if the talking stick should go around this way, or should it go that way? The talking stick will pass in this direction. Let us begin:

- What do some teachers and students need to hear from this class?

- For what things are you apologising?

- Do people need to hear anything from you?

After the talking stick has circled once ask:

- Does the talking stick need to go around our Circle again?

- What else needs to be done to make things better?

- Have you heard the apologies that have been given?

- What else would you like to see happen?

We now want to talk about what other people could have done to prevent the harm:

- Who can tell us what other people could have done differently?

- Who stood there and watched and listened and knew that it was wrong?

- Who would do something about it next time?

- How can the class take some responsibility for what has happened?

Making the agreement:

- What needs to be done to make sure that this does not happen again?

- Do we need to make a formal, written agreement?

- What should the agreement say?

- Who should be responsible for monitoring the agreement?

- What should we do if this happens again?

- How can the class respond?

- Who should decide what happens when people do the wrong thing?

It is now time to close. Is there anything that anybody wants to say before we finish? Thank you for helping us with the conference today. Remember that what has been said here must stay in this room. What needs to happen to this talking stick? Where should all of the harm and hurt contained in this stick be placed? Does anybody have any suggestions?

Please help us to fix up the classroom before we leave.

Analysis of the No-Blame Classroom Conference process

Keystones for the Classroom Conference are shown in Figure 18.1.

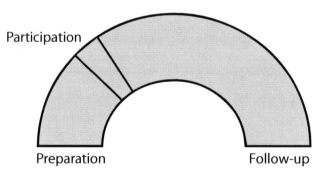

Figure 18.1 Keystones for the Classroom Conference
(Adapted from Jansen and Matla 2011)

Preparation

Thorsborne and Vinegrad (2004, p.61) provide a useful checklist for preparing a No-Blame Classroom Conference. This leads the facilitator through a series of checks such as arranging release time for teachers to attend, arranging a seating plan that will maximise student engagement and following through with the completion of all necessary paperwork and record-keeping after the conference.

Preparing the students

In the conference script above, you can see the script used to prepare the class for the upcoming conference. In this part of the process students confidentially write what has been done to them as well as what they have seen done to others (see Appendix 1). Students will want to know whether they can write bad language (the actual words) they have heard. In my experience, it is okay to allow this as it's important that everyone be clear about the extent of the harm.

Take time to answer questions before and after students record their experiences. You will be answering the same questions again and again. Saying 'Haven't you been listening?' is unhelpful. Be patient and repeat things, because nervousness about the approaching conference will cause students to listen intermittently and miss important information. Students will have questions about confidentiality and will need to hear several times that nobody will get in trouble for what is said during the conference.

Ask students to make sure that no one else can see what they write and to turn the paper face down once completed. Ask the class what harm might result if people put others under pressure to reveal what they wrote. Listen to responses and then ask for a hands-up vote of who agrees that nobody should ask others what they wrote.

The intention of preparing the students is not to make them fearful of the conference, it is quite the opposite. Young people need to be reassured that the conference will be fair and safe (with clear guidelines) and that it will be a chance to start to heal the harm caused so that the class can start to work better. Mention that some young people sometimes consider staying home on the day of the conference because they are worried. Say that students who have done this in the past have regretted this, because they have missed out on a very important turning point in the class.

Preparing the teachers

The No-Blame Classroom Conference is often a confronting experience for the teacher(s) who work closely with the class. They bring to the conference varying degrees of shame and distress about what this conference says about their management of the class. Because the teacher(s) will be taking part in the conference alongside students, as people affected by the behaviours of the class, they will need to be well prepared for the process. This process will mark the beginning of a new style of classroom management for the teacher(s) involved, so careful preparation is critical.

Below are some points to cover in preparing teachers for a No-Blame Classroom Conference:

- Be prepared to hear about incidents or ongoing issues about which you've not heard. This happens in all conferences of this nature.

- During the conference you will be asked to talk about how the behaviour of the class has affected you as a person as well as professionally. Students listen best when their teachers speak as a person. Heart talk gets students listening; head talk quickly switches them off. Decide how much you want to disclose when talking about what it has been like teaching the class. Plan what you want students to know beforehand. You might want to share how difficult it's been to deal with upset students and parents, and how this has affected you. You will be modelling the level of honesty we want from the students.

- Expect that some students will not talk during the conference, particularly students you will want to see take some responsibility. Understand that their silence will be withdrawal or avoidance responses from the Compass of Shame (see Chapter 11). Even though some students may not grasp the opportunity to take responsibility and/or apologise, they will still hear how their classmates and teachers feel about their behaviours. The behaviours that have caused upset and disruption to the class will be openly rejected for the first time by a unified group. This always hits home.

- Even though there may be times during the conference when you feel distressed or angry, give students the respect that you would like yourself. Using correct names, waiting your turn to speak and allowing the facilitator to direct the questions are important.

- If you have made some mistakes yourself, be open about them. This can be an opportunity for students to see the strength of honesty and humility. A teacher opening up and acknowledging that they could have handled things differently encourages students to do the same.

- It can feel strange to open up in front of students, but it is an important part of the restorative process. An agreement made about confidentiality at the beginning of the conference allays some of these fears.

- Your account of events should be addressed to the class, not specific students or the facilitator. It is important that the students hear what harm they have caused, but it can be detrimental to the process to have teachers demanding explanations or apologies. In the conference there is a chance for students to offer explanations and make apologies.

Preparing the parents

In some situations the school may decide it is not necessary to inform parents about a Classroom Conference ahead of time. In my experience, parents already know when a class has become unsettled and can be powerful supporters if they are kept in the loop.

Informing parents about the approaching conference and its aims is an important way of managing the messages and combating misinformation. Appendix 2 contains an example letter that can go home prior to the conference. Be prepared to take phone calls from parents in the time between sending the letter home and the Classroom Conference. For some classes it may be wise to post the letter rather than hoping it will get to parents in school bags.

Follow-up

The long-term effectiveness of the No-Blame Classroom Conference hinges on the commitment of the teacher(s) working with the class to create opportunities for the class to meet in a Circle regularly to review the conference agreement and follow through with agreed processes related to the agreement. The class teacher's ability to do this will depend on the level of support they receive from the school leadership.

The No-Blame Classroom Conference has the potential to be catalytic – to change the culture of a class group from one where students only look after themselves to a group where 'the kind of class we want to be' and 'how we treat one another' become the topics of ongoing dialogue. A shared concern for the welfare of fellow students can flourish with the right guidance from the class or care group teacher. Rogers (2006, p.86) talks of the importance of the establishment phase at the beginning of the school year when students are psychologically ready to discuss and decide on the classroom rules and core routines. For classes where relationships and behaviour are getting out of hand, a No-Blame Classroom Conference process creates a second establishment phase. The No-Blame Classroom Conference process clearly illustrates to the students that the current behaviour agreement has not worked effectively. Class groups are normally highly motivated to make constructive changes directly after No-Blame Classroom Conferences. If the teacher and leadership seize on this emotional inertia and invest time and effort into the conference agreement with students, a fresh start for the class is possible. (I have seen this happen many times.)

Following the No-Blame Classroom Conference

Ask two students to type up a 'draft agreement' from the handwritten agreement notes taken by the facilitator during the conference. It's a good idea to choose students most likely to break the agreement to do this. Two students who have a history of conflict might work together on publishing the agreement.

Once these students have completed the draft agreement, they present it to the class and get suggestions from the other students as to the wording. This might result in a few different versions of parts of the agreement. Use a 'dot democracy' process or a class vote to get an agreement on the best wording. For the dot democracy, lay different versions of the agreements on the floor, and each student gets a sticky dot to place on their preferred one. The ones with the most dots go in; others are omitted.

Students next sign the final agreement to confirm that they were present at the conference and were part of the decision-making process. If a student refuses to sign the agreement, never bring this to the attention of the rest of the class. Remain relaxed and say it will be discussed later in private. When talking with a student who refuses to sign the agreement, respectfully enquire about their concerns. They will have their reasons that will need careful unpacking and respectful listening. Gently point out that not signing the agreement may send a message to the rest of the class that they do not value what was agreed and could alienate them from the class. Point out that they will be expected to abide by the agreement regardless, as it reflects the school's values. Never force their signature – just gently make it clear that the agreement stands with or without their signature on it. It is advisable to have this conversation in the presence of a senior member of staff and/or with the student's parent present.

Copy the master agreement and send a copy home to each student with a parent letter similar to the suggested parent letter presented in Appendix 2 (Thorsborne and Vinegrad 2004, p.62).

Display the agreement in the classroom and decide what will become of the talking stick that was used during the conference. Many classes I have worked with have instructed me to take the rolled-up talking stick home and burn it, with the ashes being placed in a glass jar and kept in the classroom as a reminder of how things used to be in the class.

Ask students to complete a post-conference survey. (Appendix 3 is an example of this survey.) The results of this survey can be easily entered into a spreadsheet and presented to the class as a series of graphs to show comparisons of how the class felt after the conference at different times. It is a good idea to give this survey to students in the days immediately following the No-Blame Classroom Conference and then about a month later. Present the results to the class. What classes often see is a natural waning of enthusiasm about the impact of the class agreement. The class can be asked to share what they think this is telling them about the agreement. This is a reminder to everybody that maintaining a positive class culture takes hard work.

Keeping the agreement alive: The Agreement Review Circle

The following is a suggested format and script for running an Agreement Review Circle with a class following the completion of the class agreement. Each class will need practice to perfect their own process. The art is to keep the process moving, helping students to discuss the agreement honestly and frankly, but not allowing the process to descend into a witch-hunt for students who have broken the agreement.

Students bring their seats to a circle. Begin the Circle with a mix-up activity to break up friendship groups. Go through the rules for Circles:

- One person speaks at a time, and you must be holding the talking stick to speak.

- You may pass.

- Speak respectfully.

Teacher's opening remarks

The teacher can begin the agreement review by saying the following:

> We are now going to check in with how our class agreement is going. Putting your thumbs up says: 'I think we are doing a good job of sticking to the agreement.' Thumbs to the side says: 'We are doing okay – but we could be doing better.' Thumbs down says: 'We need to work harder – things are no better.'

Let the students indicate and briefly comment on what you see. If it's a disappointing result, just acknowledge it and move the meeting forward. Try not to personalise this – it won't help.

The process
Go around 1
The first time around the Circle proceeds as follows:

> We agree that honesty and the courage to repair harm is important. If you think you have upset somebody during the week, this is the time to deal with it.
>
> You may want to make an apology to somebody now, or just say to a person that you want to speak to them in private after this meeting to sort something out.

Go around 2
The second time around the Circle goes like this:

> Without using names, please mention if you've seen something this week that has concerned you and you want to bring it up in the Circle.

Students and/or the teacher can use this script: 'I was concerned by seeing someone…[describe behaviour]. It concerned me because…[describe concerns]. I hope those people have been able to sort the problem out.'

The teacher can then ask questions like:

- If you think you were involved in this, is there anything you'd like us to know about it?

- What happened?

- What were people thinking at the time?

- What are people thinking about that now?

- Who was affected and how?

- How does this affect our class agreement?

- How can this be fixed?

At this stage of the Review Circle, the teacher may believe that certain behaviours have broken the agreement. A well-written class agreement will specify what actions are to be taken in these situations, and the teacher will take care of ensuring that the agreement is followed. If sanctions are part of the agreed response, the teacher must not let deciding on these sanctions dominate the rest of the review process; rather, they can make a note of which students they will be talking with following the Review Circle. They can then move the process forward.

GO AROUND 3

The third go around involves the following:

> If you have seen somebody handle themselves, or handle a problem, really well this week, please share that with us, but begin by checking with the person who it is about by saying something like:

>> Ben, I saw you deal with a problem really well on [day] and I wanted to acknowledge it. Do you know what I'm talking about? Can I share with the group what I saw you do, or would you prefer I don't?

> If that person is happy for it to be shared, go ahead with *not* using the names of any others involved. This could sound like:

>> Ben, on Tuesday, you were upset by a name that somebody called somebody else. I could see you were upset and you checked straight away with that person if they wanted any help or advice. You didn't own the problem.

> If the other student is not happy for it to be shared, do not share details – just say, 'You handled it really well and supported our agreement.'

Conclude the Circle with a game.

Expect that there will be some very positive agreement reviews where interest and enjoyment prevail, and some reviews that will feel awful. This shows that the class is beginning to work better within Tomkins' Central Blueprint for healthy communities (see Chapter 8). Remember, all is not lost after an agreement review that unearths many issues. Before the No-Blame Classroom Conference, many of these issues would have resulted in more conflict and harm. One of the side effects of restorative practice is a phenomenon known in criminal justice as net widening. This means people report more problems than they previously did because they trust the processes to make things better more than previously.

About the case study: A dialogue between the conference script developers

Straight after the No-Blame Classroom Conference was concluded and chairs had been packed away, Jim and Susan de-briefed over a cup of tea in Jim's classroom. Jim commented on how honest the students were during the conference. He was surprised by how restoratively his class had behaved. The students had been very forgiving of one another. Most importantly for Jim, the students who he had never heard from, the silent majority, had been given a voice to say how the bickering and disruptive behaviour had affected them. The students at the centre of the disruption and bickering now knew that they were not the only ones affected by what was going on. The quiet students had taken a stand and talked about the kind of classroom they wanted.

Susan: And what epiphanies has this conference held for you, Jim?

Jim (after a moment of silence): I've been making the issues worse with my lock-step approach to poor behaviour. I haven't been putting the kids together to work things out. All I've been doing is talking about my class and my rules, and the kids have just fallen further into conflict with one another. In *my* mind, I had never worked with a group of kids who were so non-resilient.

Susan: These kids are hugely resilient. Many of them care for younger siblings or for their own parents and somehow manage to get themselves to school as well.

Jim: Yes, I understand that now – I guess what I mean is that before today the kids only had a limited set of ways to deal with conflict. Many of them said during the conference that payback was their only way to deal with being hurt or upset. Today, we gave these kids some different tools and they happily took them and used them.

Early Years No-Blame Classroom Conference script

The following script was created by Jane Langley in 2008 (unpublished). It is suitable for use with groups of children 3.5–8 years of age. This script may also suit older groups of students with special needs. A great resource for working restoratively with children who have special needs is *Restorative Practice and Special Needs* (Burnett and Thorsborne 2015).

Introduction to the conference

The conference can be introduced in the following manner:

Thank you for bringing your chairs and putting them in a circle so we can talk about:

- what happened today at the…[playground, sandpit, library, excursion and so forth]; or

- what's happening in our classroom that is making it hard for us to… [learn, treat each other kindly, complete our maths and so forth].

Conference rules

The conference rules can be communicated as follows:

Remember that when we sit in a Circle, it is so we can sort the problem out, so we can help make our classroom and playground the happy, safe and productive places we all want them to be. To do this we have two rules:

- One person speaks at a time, and to speak you must be holding our talking stick.

- You may pass if you wish.

The facilitator says to the class:

I am now going to pass the talking stick around the Circle, and I would like you to share the things that people are doing or saying [or what things people did say or do] that:

- have made it hard for you to learn; and/or

- have made you feel sad, annoyed, frustrated, mad or upset.

Optionally, after the Circle has been completed once, the facilitator may like to invite further responses if they feel insufficient information has been given by saying:

> Thank you for your honesty. It is important that we understand the sorts of things that have been:
>
> - happening in the classroom
>
> - happening in the playground, sandpit or wherever.
>
> Raise your hand if the talking stick should go around again because people have more things that need to be shared; or this time, when the talking stick goes around, I want you to give an 'I' statement such as 'I felt sad when he hit me' or 'I get annoyed when people keep talking and I can't get my work done'.

The facilitator should say to the class:

> Now is the time when you have the opportunity to fix things up:
>
> - To whom in the Circle do you need to apologise?
>
> - For what things do you need to apologise?

Optionally, after the Circle has been completed once, the facilitator may like to invite further responses if they feel that not enough students took responsibility for their behaviour by saying:

> Thank you to the people who accepted the opportunity to fix things up. If you missed fixing things up the first time the stick went around, or you have thought of someone else you need to fix things up with, put your hand up so the talking stick can go around again.
>
> Is there anyone who is not here that things need to be fixed up with? [For example, yard-duty teacher, specialist teacher, principal and so forth.]
>
> - How will we fix things up with that person?
>
> - Is there anything else that needs fixing up?

Accepting apologies

The facilitator can say the following regarding accepting apologies:

- Put your hand up if you accept the apologies that people have given.

- By putting your hand up you are forgiving people for the things that they did or said that upset you.

Thank you. It is great that all of you [or most of you] have forgiven each other for what has happened.

Moving forward

The facilitator can then say:

We now need to think about what choices you can make:

- tomorrow when you go back out to the playground

- when you go back to your tables

- the next time we go to the art gallery.

What choices can you make, or keep making, that will help our classroom [playground, excursion and so forth]:

- be fun, safe

- a good place to learn?

Closing the conference

The conference can be closed in the following way:

Thank you for being part of the Circle and working together to sort this problem out. I really liked the way that:

- people took responsibility for their behaviour

- accepted other people's apologies

- talked about what was happening and how they felt.

Now it's time to finish, so we need to put our chairs back and clean up the room.

This chapter has offered one effective form of classroom conferencing. As teachers and schools become more familiar with thinking and working restoratively, they will be able to devise variations of processes like the one in this chapter to suit particular classes and specific issues.

The next chapter looks at the most formal of restorative processes in schools: the Community Conference.

Chapter 19

The Community Conference

At the far end of the continuum, we find the Community Conference. This is a formal process, similar to restorative conferencing models used in criminal justice systems around the world. Community Conferences are typically reserved for issues where significant harm has been caused to people and relationships and there have been severe breaches of the school's behaviour code. Community Conferences are coordinated by staff who have trained in formal restorative conference facilitation. Community Conferences involve affected students, their parents or caregivers, other affected school community members and, sometimes, local authorities such as police.

Community Conferences end with an agreement being reached between all involved about what will happen to repair the harm, and new expectations of behaviour. This agreement is formalised as a document that is signed by the conference participants. It is then reviewed regularly in scheduled review meetings with the help of a facilitator. The Community Conference is the start of a larger process of relationship management (a term coined by Margaret Thorsborne), where students are brought back together to check in with one another and with the terms of the agreement. The agreement becomes the centrepiece of conversation. The simple act of bringing students face to face to review the agreement is a protective factor against further conflict.

Part 4 provides a series of chapters to help schools create the necessary systems required to systematise formal conferencing and relationship management processes.

This chapter is not a training manual. Community Conference facilitation is best undertaken by staff who have trained in the process with a recognised and experienced trainer.

Case study: Trashed on Facebook

On Sunday evening Louise, the head of well-being in a large private girls' school, saw on her calendar that there was an emergency 8 a.m. meeting the next morning with Georgia, a 15-year-old student, her parents, Steve and Kathy, and Mary, the school principal. *This can't be good* thought Louise as she read an email from Mary informing her that the meeting was to do with cyberbullying. Georgia's parents had threatened to involve the police and their lawyers (yes, plural).

Conference preparation

Georgia and her parents

The meeting commenced on time. Georgia was clearly distressed and her parents, Steve and Kathy, were visibly angry. Steve was ranting. 'We pay good money to ensure that our daughter is safe from this type of defamation, but here we are – Georgia's reputation in tatters and my wife being branded a common whore on social media in a post that has been seen by hundreds of kids. What type of a school are you running here? Don't you teach your students about the risks of social media?'

Mary, the principal, bristled at his words, and Louise knew it. 'Steve, we do everything possible to ensure the safety –'

Steve cut Mary off. 'So I'd expect then that the young lady who accused Georgia of sleeping with multiple boys and saying that she learned this from her mother will be immediately expelled by the conclusion of our meeting and a written apology will be made to our family. Good then, I think we're finished.'

Steve stood up. Kathy took Steve's hand and urged him to sit again. Georgia was quietly sobbing. Louise turned towards her and said, 'Georgia, this must be awful for you. Tell us what's happened.'

Georgia looked up. Steve reluctantly sat down. Georgia told of how she had learned yesterday of a post that had been written by Erin, on Facebook, accusing her of sleeping with three boys – all boyfriends of girls at the college. She sobbed as she said she knew the boys from a group at the mall, but their girlfriends had been there too, and besides that, she'd never slept with anyone, especially other people's boyfriends.

Steve was on his feet again. Louise knew he was anguished and angry, almost enraged. Steve was a successful businessman and wasn't used to feeling powerless. His little girl was in a situation that no amount of money or influence could save her from, and he didn't have the first idea about what he could do to stop her pain.

'Steve, I can't imagine what this is like for you at the moment, or you, Kathy,' said Louise. Steve took a deep breath and Kathy reached into her bag for a packet of tissues. She had tears in her eyes and her arm around Georgia. Her other hand was holding Steve's. She was doing her best to keep everyone steady. Louise understood affect and knew she had to sympathise with a family that was deeply distressed and fearful.

'Yes, I *am* angry, and Georgia and Kathy are hurt,' said Steve slowly and with less volume than before.

Louise knew that it was important that Steve had used the word 'hurt' because it was a start towards uncovering the distress and shame at the heart of his anger. 'What about you, Kathy?' said Louise.

Kathy thought for a moment, looked at Georgia, and then said in a very controlled voice, 'I'm not so worried about what was said about *me* – I can handle that. What concerns me is the effect this will have on Georgia and her friendships.' Her voice broke, and she paused to gather her composure as she looked towards the ceiling and blinked to hold her tears at bay. 'I guess I…' – she quickly corrected herself – '…*we* want some answers from Erin.'

'That sounds perfectly reasonable,' said Louise.

They all sat in silence for a moment to allow Kathy to add anything she wanted.

Louise then turned to Georgia. 'Georgia, what did you think when you first saw these posts?' Louise was now in the early stages of preparing Georgia and her parents for a potential restorative conference. Even if a conference was not possible, these were still the right questions to be asking Georgia to help her start to come to terms with what had happened.

Georgia replied, 'I went cold all over. I thought, *How could she accuse me of doing such an awful thing?* I've never done anything or said anything about Erin to deserve this. I'm so embarrassed. It's as though I've actually done what she said I've done, and I feel guilty about it, but I haven't done *anything*. It's so unfair and now everyone will think that I'm a slut, and that my mother is a slut. The looks and comments I'll get! It's over for me here, and I love this school and my friends. It's all done now.' She was sobbing deeply.

'For God's sake, Steve!' Kathy said. 'Go and hug your daughter! She needs a hug from her father!'

Steve sat next to Georgia and put his arm awkwardly around her.

Louise felt tears welling in her eyes and looked at Mary, who seemed shell-shocked. Louise knew that Georgia's distress had infected everyone in the room. Louise didn't know whether it would be a good thing for Steve and Kathy to see that she was distressed. Her next thought was, *I don't care if they see me upset – we're all human before we are anything else!* Louise reached for a tissue.

Steve saw this. His entire body slumped and he again let out a long breath and said, 'What are we going to do about this?' This time, it was a question, not a demand.

Louise composed herself and looked at Mary. Mary nodded as if to say, 'You've got this.' Louise addressed Georgia directly. 'Your dad has asked a good question, Georgia. I guess from the school's side, there are many things we could do about this. We're not the type of school that has a one-size-fits-all approach for these types of situations.' Louise paused for a moment. 'Georgia, I'm going to ask you to think about what might make this better for you. It's a tough question because, right now, we'd all understand if you think nothing will fix this.'

Georgia sat up from leaning into her dad and thought for a minute. 'I want to know why, I want to know what I did for Erin to say these things.'

'And we want the post deleted from Erin's Facebook account,' said Steve.

Mary, who had recovered, said to Steve, 'Our next meeting is with Erin and her parents, and that's the first thing I will address.'

Louise explained to Georgia, Kathy and Steve that there was a process called a restorative conference, where if Erin was remorseful for what she had done, there could be a meeting of the girls and their parents to discuss the matter and the harm that had resulted. The group would decide on a way forward together.

'What if Erin isn't sorry and isn't interested in doing anything about this?' asked Steve.

'Well,' said Louise, 'then we'll investigate the matter and make a decision about an appropriate course of action. Unfortunately, that won't teach Erin much. In my experience, a restorative meeting is the best way to get answers for the types of questions that you have.' She looked at Georgia. 'Georgia, what do you think of the idea of sitting in a room with your mother and father, and Erin and her parents, to talk about what's happened?'

'It would be better than Erin just getting some punishment and then just blaming me for telling on her, or doing the same thing to someone else.'

'So, if Erin and her parents are open to the idea of a meeting, you would be prepared to give it a try?'

'Yes.'

As the meeting concluded, it was agreed that Louise would be in touch with Steve immediately after her meeting with Erin and her parents about whether a conference with the girls and their parents would be going ahead. It was also agreed that if Georgia, Steve and Kathy were not satisfied with the outcome of any such conference, they would be free to pursue the matter in any way they saw fit, and the school would act within the guidelines of its own policies to make decisions at that point as well.

Louise explained to Georgia that the conference would probably be tomorrow. She asked Georgia about how she felt about being at school while these rumours were circulating.

'I was going to keep her at home today,' said Kathy.

'That just makes it look like I'm guilty,' responded Georgia.

'It's entirely your call as a family,' said Mary. 'We understand either way. If you decide you want to stay at school, Georgia, we could set you up to work in one of the private study rooms in the library, if you'd prefer.'

'I'd like to do that,' said Georgia. 'I want to go to pastoral care and see my friends before lessons begin.'

Louise felt a wave of uncertainty. 'What will you say if you are questioned by your friends about the post on Facebook?'

'I'll just tell them that we are in the middle of sorting it out.'

'And if they probe?' asked Mary.

'I'll just say that it's confidential.'

'I think that's the fairest thing you can say at the moment, especially seeing that we haven't spoken with Erin yet,' said Louise.

Mary added, 'In fact, Georgia, I'd insist that you say just that. None of us needs this mess getting any worse for you and Erin. A pile of rumours floating around about what's going to happen would make this worse. What do you think, Kathy and Steve?'

Kathy nodded. 'Yes, confidentiality is important for both families'.

'That's ironic,' Steve scoffed. 'Erin wasn't very confidential in her defaming of Georgia – and you.'

'There's no point causing any more harm,' said Kathy.

Steve nodded in resignation.

Mary summarised that Georgia would work in the library for the day, and that if she needed to talk to either her or Louise, she could come and find them. Mary also told Georgia that she would be the first to know when the meeting with Erin and her parents was finished. The meeting concluded at 8.50 a.m.

Erin and her parents

At 10.15 a.m. a sheepish-looking Erin and her parents, Elizabeth and Paul, entered Mary's office. Erin had not been in classes that morning. Louise had informed Erin's pastoral care teacher of the issue and asked that he discreetly direct Erin to reception as soon as she arrived. Mary had called Elizabeth as soon as the meeting with Georgia and her parents had concluded and informed her of the issue.

Louise thanked Erin and her parents for coming and then cut straight to the chase. 'Erin, we've been made aware of a troubling post on your Facebook about Georgia and her mother.' Louise waited.

Erin finally muttered, 'Yes.'

Louise paused and gave Erin plenty of time to continue.

Paul broke in, saying, 'What's Erin being accused of here?'

Louise gently said, 'Erin, what do you need us to know about what may or may not be on your Facebook about Georgia Banks and her mother, Kathy?'

'I said something about Erin sleeping with a few boys,' said Erin after a few moments of contemplation.

Paul inhaled loudly and sat back in his seat.

'Will you show us the post please, Erin?' asked Mary.

'I've deleted it from my account.'

'Thank goodness for that,' said Louise.

'The damage has been done, I suppose,' said Elizabeth, glaring at Erin.

Erin had gone even paler.

'When did you delete it?' asked Elizabeth.

'I deleted it as soon as I was asked to come to the office this morning.'

'On your phone?' asked Paul.

'Yes.'

'Open your Facebook, Erin, and take me to the place that post was and show me that it's gone,' said Elizabeth.

Erin showed Elizabeth that the post had been deleted.

'Do you mind if I have a look too?' asked Louise.

Erin showed both adults. There was no sign of the post.

'Georgia and her parents must be furious,' said Paul.

'Yes, they are very concerned and have some questions for Erin, but I think they are mostly interested in this mess being sorted out,' said Louise.

'What questions?' asked Erin.

'What types of questions would *you* have if you were Georgia?' asked Mary.

Erin paused for a moment, looking at her feet. 'I'd want to know…why.'

'You've got it, Erin,' said Mary. 'That's exactly what Georgia wanted to know when we met with her and her parents this morning. Her mother was mostly concerned for *her*, but she might also wonder what she did to be talked about in the way she was in your post.'

Elizabeth cut in, saying, 'Oh God, Erin, what did you write?'

Tears began streaming down Erin's face.

Louise stood up and moved next to Erin with a box of tissues. 'Erin, those awful feelings you have now are what will help you to fix this. Start by telling us exactly what the post said.'

Erin sobbed.

'Take a moment, Erin. Would you like a glass of water? My mouth goes pretty dry when I feel bad about something *I've* done,' said Louise.

Mary was already there with a glass of water when Erin looked up. Erin had a sip and then put the glass down on the table. 'I said that Georgia had slept with Ali and Emma's boyfriends, and that she had probably learned that kind of boyfriend stealing from her mother.'

'Why on earth would you say that kind of thing – on Facebook or anywhere else, for that matter?' asked Paul. 'We've talked about this over and over. That's it! That phone and all of your screens are off limits for a very long time.'

Louise asked gently, 'Erin, what were you thinking when you posted that?'

'I don't know... I was annoyed that she was flirty with the boys when we were at the mall last week.'

'Oh my God...boys again,' said Elizabeth, sighing.

'I don't know if she slept with any of them,' Erin said. 'I just said it.'

'What do you think about that now?' asked Louise.

'I shouldn't have – it was a mean and stupid thing to do. I don't know why I did it. I wish I could take it all back.'

Louise paused. 'Who has been affected by this post?'

Erin looked at Louise like it was obvious.

Louise nodded. 'Who else besides Georgia has been affected?'

'Her mother...probably her whole family.'

'And what about people here, in this room, not counting myself or Mrs White?'

'It's affected my mother and father.'

'I think your actions have affected *you* too,' added Louise.

Everyone sat silent for a few moments.

Paul broke the silence. 'Mrs White, do we need to call a lawyer?'

Mary answered, 'The fact that Erin is taking responsibility for her actions makes that less likely. Georgia and her parents were waiting to see if Erin is in fact sorry for this and whether she would be prepared to meet with them to discuss the matter in a restorative conference. You would both be present to support Erin, of course. The purpose of the conference would be to talk about what happened, who has been harmed and how, and then to see what we can do to minimise the damage.'

Louise looked at Erin. 'Erin, the type of meeting Mrs White is talking about is a bigger version of the small restorative chats we use when things go wrong.'

'Yes, I knew that as soon as you asked me what I was thinking.'

'Then I've got another question: How do you think this has been for Georgia?'

'It's probably awful. She's probably feeling like everyone thinks she's a slut.'

'That's what she pretty much said this morning,' added Mary.

'Are you prepared to meet with Georgia and her parents as soon as we can arrange it?' asked Louise.

'Yes.'

'It will be a tough meeting for you.'

'It needs to be tough,' said Elizabeth.

Louise was relieved that Erin's parents hadn't jumped to her rescue. The fact that the school's intention was to get Erin to take responsibility for her actions and not to punish her was a part of the reason that Steve and Kathy were supporting the school's course of action. There were other schools where Erin would have been immediately suspended, pending investigation. The police would have been called and Erin's time at the school would likely have been at an end. Louise had lived that type of scenario too often in other schools and had seen the devastating impact it had had on all involved. Louise had already asked Erin the questions that she would be asking her in the conference in front of Georgia and her parents. She explained this to Erin, who was prepared for the conference. Louise went through how the conference would run as well as the questions that she would ask Paul and Elizabeth during the conference. Louise made it clear that once the conference was completed and an agreement had been made as to what would happen to repair some of the harm caused, the matter would be over in the school's eyes, except for follow-up meetings regarding the conference agreement.

Mary explained that the decision regarding whether or not to take the matter further – that is, outside of the school – would be a decision for Georgia and her parents.

Erin was asked about the types of questions she thought she might face from the other girls about the Facebook comments, her lateness back to class and why Georgia was studying in the college library. After some discussion, it was agreed that Erin would study at home until the conference so that she would not have to face these questions.

Conference proceedings

The Community Conference was scheduled for the next morning at 9 a.m. Louise created the seating plan for the Circle (Figure 19.1), which had Georgia on one side of the Circle, flanked by her parents Steve and Kathy. Erin would sit directly across from Georgia, flanked by Paul and Elizabeth. Louise sat between the families.

Louise created name tags for the girls and their parents and created the conference script (below) that would guide her through the conference. She also ran off a blank conference agreement template that she could quickly take notes on during the agreement phase of the conference. This would later be published, signed by the girls and their parents, and copied.

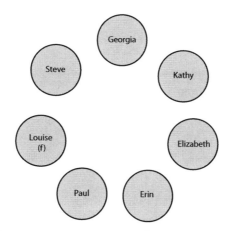

Figure 19.1 Community Conference seating plan

Community Conference script

The script went as follows:

Welcome. As you know, my name is Louise, and I will be running this conference. I'd like to thank you all for making the effort to attend. This is a difficult and sensitive matter, and your participation will help us deal with it. The conference will deal with the incident where Erin posted comments on Facebook referring to Georgia as a slut, accusing her of sleeping with the boyfriends of students and suggesting she had learned to behave this way from her mother, Kathy. These comments were posted last Friday evening. College policy states that this is a college matter and can be addressed by the college.

We will focus on what Erin did and how her behaviour has affected Georgia and her family. We are not here to decide whether Erin is a good or bad person. We want to explore how people have been affected and see whether we can begin to repair the harm that has been done.

I met with you all prior to this conference, but you've not yet met one another. Before we begin, I'd like to introduce everybody here and briefly indicate their reasons for being here.

Of course, there are some ground rules for our meeting today:

- As difficult as this matter is, we must all remain respectful in the way we speak to one another.

- We will take turns to speak – no interruptions.

- If you need to leave the conference for a moment, please tell me.

- If at any point I feel that we are making matters worse, I will call an end to this meeting and we will explore alternative ways of addressing the matter.

How do those rules sound to everybody?

Everyone will be given a chance to be heard. This means we will be here for about 1 hour.

Comments to Erin

Louise said the following to Erin:

Erin, you have admitted your involvement in the incident. You are free to leave this conference at any stage, but if you do, this matter will be dealt with differently. This matter will be finished when this conference is over and you have completed what people ask you to do to repair the harm. Is that clear?

TELLING THE STORY

Louise continued addressing Erin:

Erin, to help us understand what harm has been done and who has been affected by this incident, could you begin by telling us what happened?

- What were you thinking when you referred to Georgia as a slut?

- What were you thinking when you accused her of sleeping with the boyfriends of other students?

- What were you thinking when you made comments mentioning Georgia's mother?

- What were you hoping would happen?

- What have you thought about since you posted the comments?

- Who do you think has been affected by your actions, and in what way?

Exploring the harm

Louise then addressed Georgia regarding the harm that had been caused:

- What did you think when you first heard of the comments on Facebook?

- What about since then?

- How has this affected you?

- How did your family and friends react when they heard about this?

- What has been the worst of it?

Next, Louise turned to Georgia's parents (Kathy and Steve):

- What did you think when you heard of the comments on Facebook?

- What's happened since?

- What changes have you seen in Georgia?

- What are the main issues for you?

- What has been the worst of it?

Finally, Louise addressed Erin's parents (Paul and Elizabeth):

- How difficult is this to hear?

- What did you think when you heard?

- What's happened since?

- How has this affected you?

- What's been the worst of it?

Acknowledgement and apology

After everyone had answered, Louise addressed Erin again:

> Now that you've heard from everyone about how they've been affected by what you have done, is there anything you want to say to Georgia and her parents, or anyone else here? Is there something that people need to hear from *you* right now?

Agreement

In terms of an agreement, Louise said the following to Georgia, Kathy and Steve:

> What would you like to see happen as a result of our meeting here today that might start to repair the harm caused?

She then turned to Erin, Paul and Elizabeth:

> Does that seem fair? Is there something you'd like to see happen that might help?

Finally, she said to all:

> • Who will be responsible for supervising the terms of this agreement?
>
> • When should the girls and I meet to check on how the agreement is going?
>
> • How would you all like to be kept in the loop?

Closing the conference

In closing the conference, Louise said the following:

> I will now record the agreement that has been reached here. This will formally close the matter, subject to completion of the agreement. You will each be asked to sign it and you will be given a copy before you leave.
>
> Is there anything else anyone wants to say?
>
> You have all worked hard to resolve this incident, and the agreement you have reached should go a long way towards repairing the harm done. While I write the agreement, which I'll ask you to sign before you leave, please enjoy the refreshments we have provided for you.

FORMAL RESTORATIVE CONFERENCE AGREEMENT
BETWEEN GEORGIA BANKS AND ERIN STARK

Conference date: 22/11/16

Conference participants:

Georgia Banks, Steve Banks, Kathy Banks, Erin Stark, Elizabeth Stark, Paul Stark, Louise Laylaw (facilitator)

What's been happening (the problem that brought us to conference)?

On 18/11/16 Erin posted on Facebook that Georgia had slept with several boys and that she had learned this behaviour from her mother (Kathy). This is not true and was posted with malicious intent. The post was taken down by Erin on 21/11/16.

We agree that:

- Erin will post a retraction of her comments on her Facebook page and an apology to Georgia and her family. This will be posted by 8 p.m. this evening.

- Louise will arrange a meeting of the girls that Erin and Georgia agree would have seen or heard about the post, and Erin and Georgia will share the facts of the matter with them.

- Erin will not post defamatory material about any other student of this school on social media again.

- Erin and Georgia have agreed to arrange for a cyber safety expert to speak to the middle school about the legal implications of posting defamatory material on social media.

This agreement will be monitored by:

Erin, Georgia and Louise. The first agreement review is scheduled for 29/11/16 at 9 a.m.

If this agreement is broken/how we will handle it if this happens again (or conditions are not met):

- If Erin breaches this agreement, she will be required to repair the harm caused.

- Erin may face suspension and loss of all school Internet access.

Signed:

The agreement was signed by all present in the conference, including the conference facilitator.

Analysis of the Community Conference process

What made this Community Conference possible?

This conference went ahead because of a few important reasons. First, Georgia was interested enough in Erin's reasons for doing what she did to be able to overcome the negative affects and agree to be part of a conference. Second, Erin was able to deal with her shame well enough to take responsibility for her actions and the harm caused. This made her capable of being part of the business of reparation. Only through meeting with both girls and their families prior to the conference was Louise able to explore the incident, and the feelings involved, so she could assess the suitability of a conference. Had Georgia been too fearful (or disgusted) to consider the thought of meeting with Erin, Louise would have explored other avenues of restoration and accountability to help Georgia move forward. Had Erin not shown any remorse or understanding of the harm caused by her actions, a conference would have been unsuitable. In the event that Erin showed no contrition, Louise would have had to have chosen a non-restorative sanction for Erin. This would have done little to meet the needs of either girl, or their families, but at least there would have been accountability.

Keystones for the Community Conference are shown in Figure 19.2.

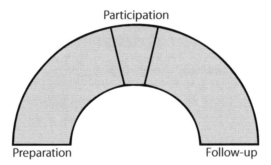

Figure 19.2 Keystones for the Community Conference
(Adapted from Jansen and Matla 2011)

Preparation and follow-up

The success or failure of the Community Conference lies in meticulous planning and methodical follow-up. The steps Louise took towards preparing this conference are summarised by O'Connell *et al.* (1999, p.52).

Facilitator's preparation checklist

The facilitator's preparation checklist should comprise the following (adapted from O'Connell *et al.* 1999):

- Have you a clear understanding of the incident?

- Is a conference needed?

- Has the wrongdoer(s) admitted responsibility?

- Have you invited all necessary participants?

- Have you spoken or met with all participants and secured their attendance?

- Do all participants understand the conference process and its purpose?

- Do all participants know how to contact you?

- Have you reserved a suitable room?

- Do participants know the time, date, location and how to get to the conference?

- Have you developed a seating plan?

- Have you developed a script for the conference?

- Have you thought about how the conference may unfold?

- Do you have plans for what to do if the conference does not reach an agreement or the wrongdoer fails to satisfy the conference agreement?

- Do you have the following ready for the conference?

  - the script and a clipboard

  - paper or template for the agreement

  - the seating plan

  - name tags or labels for participants

  - a box of tissues

  - refreshments for afterward.

Conference follow-up would involve the finalising of the conference agreement and having it signed by all involved. It would then be copied and given to both girls and their parents. Louise would schedule an agreement review meeting with the girls. Agreement reviews would follow until the girls and Louise were satisfied that the agreement no longer needed to be reviewed.

As you have seen, this type of restorative process is highly rigorous and highly emotional. Its success depends on meticulous preparation that involves a great deal of careful listening by a trained facilitator. Everyone involved tells their story twice: once while being prepared for the conference and again during the conference. By the time the affected parties come together, the facilitator has heard everyone's story and understands their wishes for an outcome. You will find out how the agreement between Georgia and Erin panned out in Part 4.

The next chapter covers a process called the Leaving Well Conference. This conference does not involve a happy ending for a young person and therefore is placed separately, at the far right of the restorative practice continuum. It is, however, a process that makes the best of a bad situation and honours the dignity of a young person who has reached the end of the road in a school.

Chapter 20

The Leaving Well Conference

Sadly, there are times when a school is limited in its capacity to address the challenging behaviours from a young person, and the school chooses to expel a student. Expulsion sits at odds with restorative principles because it is not reparative and often deepens the cycle of alienation and exclusion that fuelled the misbehaviour in the first place. This book does not advocate the use of expulsion. It does, however, acknowledge that there are times when a school finds itself under-skilled and under-resourced to meet the high needs of some students. There are also times when the collective disgust about a young person's behaviour becomes so severe and widespread among a school community that expelling a young person becomes a politically motivated decision.

Despite the fact that expelling young people is the most un-restorative thing a school can do, it does not have to take on a cold and inhumane feel. The Leaving Well Conference[1] is a ceremony of departure that acknowledges the connections a young person has formed with people in a school and honours their good qualities. For young people like Adam in the case study that follows, the Leaving Well Conference is an important reminder of their intrinsic worth in the saddest of circumstances.

Case study: Adam

The problem

Adam, a 12-year-old, had made sexual suggestions to a number of the girls such as, 'Would you like to increase the world's population?' He was at times quite physical with them and pinched some of the girls' nipples in an inappropriate move called 'nipple cripplers'. Stroking their hair and commenting about the fragrances of their shampoo and how attractive he found them was not

---

[1]   The Leaving Well Conference was developed and documented by the late Geoff Blair, along with his colleagues from Victoria, Australia. At the time of Geoff's death he was working as a well-respected and sought-after independent restorative practice consultant.

uncommon behaviour for Adam. When challenged on this behaviour, Adam would jokingly claim that he was doing a survey of the most popular shampoo and would put his nose in the girls' hair. On other occasions he asked the girls highly inappropriate questions about pubic hair. Adam had gone to primary school with these girls and it appeared that he had formed quite good relationships with them.

Unknown to teachers, Adam had told the girls about his upbringing and the trauma associated with it. When he was three years old he had been kept in a cage with the pet dog. He had communicated through barking. Adam was removed from home and began moving from one foster family to another. He had been in 30 different homes. Despite his trauma, Adam's cognitive functioning hadn't suffered. His intelligence was commented on by students and teachers.

The girls became so distressed about the physical attention from Adam that they approached the assistant principal, reporting that they were uncomfortable with Adam's behaviour towards them but insisted that they didn't want to get Adam in trouble. The assistant principal approached the school's attendance officer about what some of the options were for the school and the girls. The attendance officer discussed this with the well-being manager, and Geoff, a restorative practice facilitator, was approached to run a restorative conference.

Through his work with other traumatised students, Geoff had come to the conclusion that one of the best ways of minimising the impact of this type of issue in a school setting was to take a restorative approach. Geoff made arrangements to visit the school to commence the preparation interviews of all those affected by Adam's behaviour.

The assistant principal and her pastoral care teacher acknowledged that Adam was challenging but that they had not given up on him. Geoff spoke with a teacher assistant who commented on Adam's academic abilities. She said she enjoyed working with him when he was focused.

Geoff interviewed the girls, who talked about what Adam had been doing and how this made them feel. Geoff asked the girls what they wanted to see happen, and they replied that they just wanted it to stop.

Geoff interviewed Adam after he had spoken to everyone else. Because of his past, Adam was slow to give clear answers to the restorative questions. When he finally understood that the interview was not to punish him, but to help him to be accountable for the behaviour that had upset the girls, he stopped trying to distract Geoff and openly admitted what he'd said and done to the girls. Geoff made arrangements with the assistant principal for a restorative conference to be held a few days later.

The first Conference

On the day of the conference, the assistant principal had organised a room. Chairs were in a circle. In attendance were Adam, the assistant principal, Adam's teacher, the teacher assistant and the six girls who had asked for help. There was also an observer from the regional office.

Geoff used the Community Conference script. The first questions were for Adam. Adam knew what was coming because Geoff had prepared him. Not being certain of how it was really going to work or how the conference would feel, Adam initially resorted to trying to change the subject and asked questions that were irrelevant to the conference. Geoff knew, from the Compass of Shame (see Chapter 11), that this was an avoidance tactic. These strategies were a very vulnerable boy's only defences against the awful thoughts and feelings with which he was dealing. Geoff stayed on script, gently asking Adam questions and helping him remember what he had said in the preparation interview before the conference: 'You'll remember, Adam, that when we spoke the other day, you talked to me about how you had… [names the behaviour]. Tell us about that.' Even though this was difficult for Adam, Geoff didn't allow him to duck or weave. With some help, Adam soon acknowledged that what he had done had had a negative impact on everyone in the room.

The girls spoke about how they felt when Adam had done the things that had made the conference necessary. They commented about how they enjoyed Adam's company, how he made them laugh and how smart he was. They also spoke candidly with Adam about how they did not enjoy the touching and sexual innuendoes.

The teacher and the aide commented about Adam's talents and how they enjoyed his company – most of the time. They told about how they felt distressed when Adam made others feel uncomfortable. They offered strategies for ways he could improve his behaviour and what the girls should do if this happened again.

The assistant principal spoke about how this situation had affected her. She spoke about her distress when dealing with the parents of the girls. She talked about how it had been hard work to get angry parents to agree to allow the girls to be part of the conference. She said that Adam's behaviour had to change quickly. The assistant principal was supportive of Adam but stated quite clearly that she had a responsibility for the well-being of all students.

Adam made genuine apologies to all in the room and guaranteed that his behaviour would change. Agreements were documented and the conference was concluded. Things had been fixed up. The teachers conferred, and we were confident that what was brought up in the conference had been dealt with fairly and Adam had accepted responsibility for his actions.

A week after the conference, Adam phoned to tell Geoff how things were going. (This had been one of the agreements reached in the conference.) He told Geoff that he had stuck to the commitments he had made in the conference and that school was fun. The assistant principal confirmed this and commented on the effectiveness of restorative practice. A couple of weeks later, the attendance officer informed Geoff that things were still going well. The young people were happy. The invasive and sexualised behaviour had not returned.

Expelling Adam

A few months later, the attendance officer informed Geoff that Adam had got himself in trouble at school and that his enrolment was to be terminated at the end of the year. Adam was to be put on the Second Chance Protocol, which is a way of giving students a fresh start at another school. Adam had been isolated from the other kids in the school because his behaviour had deteriorated.

There had been no repeat of the behaviour that had been addressed in the conference. Other students were unhappy with some rough physical treatment from Adam, and the teachers didn't seem to have the stamina to work through the issues. Geoff was torn because he had been responsible for working with students like Adam in his previous work as a teacher. There were times when kids were in such a bad space, so deep in shame and self-disgust, that they would shut down in their shame (withdraw) and not be open to acknowledging or repairing the harm they were causing. Geoff did not want to rescue Adam, but he was becoming aware of his responsibilities as an employee of the region and to the kids whose well-being he and his colleagues needed to look after.

In an attempt to get an understanding of how things had gone wrong for Adam, the school's well-being team had a chat. A few issues came to light: Adam's foster caregiver had gone on holiday. Adam's learning aide had gone on long service and, due to an extensive construction project, Adam's favourite place in the schoolyard (the downball courts) had been destroyed. Routines and familiar relationships had shifted significantly, and Adam's world had tilted on its axis. Adam wasn't taking it well and had acted out. The school had run out of ideas and had fallen back to punitive sanctions to address Adam's reactions to the changes in his world. The results of this were, of course, not good.

The regional well-being team respected the decision of the school to expel Adam and decided to make efforts to bring a sense of optimism to Adam's inevitable departure from the school. The team wanted to make sure that Adam was not getting another cross of failure next to his name. They wanted Adam to leave well.

Leaving Well Conference preparation

Geoff arranged a meeting for the second last week of school. The usual preparation for a conference would not happen this time. The assistant principal arranged for students to attend.

In attendance were Geoff, a colleague from the regional office, Adam, the assistant principal, Adam's pastoral care teacher, Adam's carer and five students from the previous conference. Geoff met with the students before the conference and let them know that they would be asked:

- to share one thing about Adam at school that they really enjoyed

- to give Adam one piece of advice about what he could be or do so that he would have success at his new school.

Geoff let the assistant principal know that he would ask her what the school had gained or learned from having Adam as a student.

It was important that Adam hear this from the people with whom he had relationships that had broken down. There were some concerns that Adam would not show up to the meeting. It had been made clear to Adam that the decision about his leaving would not change. Geoff could understand how Adam might see no benefit from attending the meeting.

Leaving Well Conference

It wasn't long after everyone arrived that Adam and his carer appeared. Everyone was relieved to see Adam. Geoff began with the usual 'thank you for attending this meeting'. Geoff then made it clear that the decision had already been made about Adam changing schools.

The assistant principal spoke first. She restated the school's decision but also spoke directly to Adam and said that he was a wonderful young person who hadn't been able to find his place at that particular school. She said it was a tough decision to make, and the choice to discontinue his enrolment had not been taken lightly.

Geoff asked the students their questions and they all spoke about Adam's sense of humour, how clever he was and how they would remember lots of good times. The advice they offered was positive and supportive: 'You make us laugh' and 'You stand up for your friends'. They advised Adam to 'make friends with people who would treat you well, have fun and think before you act'.

All of the suggestions and comments were written down by Geoff's colleague and placed in a small bag that Adam could take away with him. Adam would have a tangible reminder of his friends and their warm thoughts for him. A chocolate Santa Claus was given with the paper and placed in Adam's bag. (In the planning meeting it had been mentioned that Adam liked chocolate, so this tiny gift was a fitting gesture.) When Adam saw the chocolate he said, 'I eat chocolate when I feel sad.' Adam then said, 'What about the others?' Then he said, 'That's okay, there's plenty here for them.'

Geoff then asked the assistant principal a question about the school. She said that she had learned that they needed to sort out issues a bit more quickly than they had in Adam's case. She mentioned that teachers needed to pick up signals that things weren't going well (a mild attack-other response to her shame).

Geoff asked Adam to commit to two of the suggestions the other students had made. Adam chose the 'making of good friends' and 'having fun'. The students had organised a farewell Christmas card for Adam. The assistant principal asked Adam to read aloud a couple of things that were said. He read them all. Adam's carer asked if she could take a picture of Adam and the five other students. The students were keen and they went to a courtyard just outside.

The Leaving Well Conference took 20 minutes. Before everyone left the school, Geoff spoke with the assistant principal and asked her what the meeting had been like for her. She said that they spend so much time giving farewells to graduating students at formal ceremonies but not much happens for kids like Adam when their time is up. Geoff and the assistant principal made a commitment to make sure that from then on, when young people had to go, their leaving would be done well.

Conference preparation

The following steps are taken to prepare the Leaving Well Conference, which were used in this case study:

- Ask for volunteer students who have had positive experiences with the student who is leaving and prepare them with the questions they will be asked during the conference.

- Prepare a significant teacher (who has a relationship with the student) and a member of leadership with their questions.

- It may be appropriate to invite a member of staff from the student's new school to attend (with appropriate permissions from the leaving student and caregivers) so they can get some insight into the student who will soon be in their care.

- Prepare slips of coloured paper for positive comments and advice for the future.

- Provide a small bag for the student to hold the slips of paper.

- Provide refreshments for the end of the meeting.

- Provide a box of tissues.

Conference introduction

The Leaving Well Conference was introduced in the following manner:

Thank you for attending this meeting. We are here to say farewell to Adam and wish him all the best in his new school.

As you all know, the very difficult decision about Adam leaving our school has already been made and will not be changed. This meeting will give everyone here a chance to talk about the good times they shared with Adam and share some words of hope and advice to help Adam be successful in his next school.

- To begin, I will go around the Circle and ask everyone here to tell us their name and how they know Adam.

Once completed:

- Thank you all for that information. Now I will ask each of the students to share one thing about Adam that they really enjoyed at school. I will record these comments on pieces of paper that Adam can take away.

Once completed:

- Thank you, everyone, for sharing that. Each of the young people here have thought of one piece of advice for Adam about what he could be or do so that he will have success at his new school. I'll now ask each of you to share this with Adam. I will again record these comments on pieces of paper that Adam can take away.

Once completed:

- I now want to ask the assistant principal what she thinks the school has gained or learned from having Adam as a student. Can you share that with us?

Thank you for that.

- Adam, I will ask the assistant principal to read back to you the pieces of advice that people have shared with you about having success in your next school.

- When you have heard them, choose two that you think you will commit to in your next school that you think will make a difference.

Thank you, Adam.

- Before we finish and have some refreshments, is there anything anybody would like to say?

Thank you, everyone, for coming to this meeting today so we could give our friend, Adam, the send-off he deserves.

Components of the Leaving Well Conference

The Leaving Well Conference only has two phases: preparation and participation. Keystones for the Leaving Well Conference are shown in Figure 20.1.

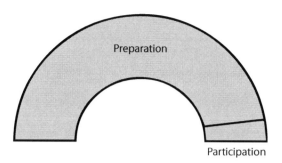

Figure 20.1 Keystones for the Leaving Well Conference
(Adapted from Jansen and Matla 2011)

Preparation runs along similar lines for preparing a Community Conference. The checklist below may be helpful in preparing a Leaving Well Conference:

- Have all necessary participants been invited?

- If the student has already started (or enrolled) in their new school, have arrangements been made to have a member of staff from the new school attend?

- Have all participants had the purpose of the conference explained to them?

- Do all participants understand the questions they will be asked during the conference?

- Does the leaving student clearly understand that the decision about their expulsion will not be reversed?

- Do all participants know how to contact you?

- Has a suitable room been reserved?

- Do all participants know the time, date, location and how to get to the conference?

- Has a seating plan been developed?

- Do you have the following ready for the conference?

  - the script and a clipboard

  - slips of paper, a bag and a small parting gift

  - the seating plan

- name tags or labels for participants

- a box of tissues

- refreshments for afterward.

This concludes our journey of case studies along the restorative practice continuum. You have read a wide range of situations involving younger and older students with many variations of the restorative script being used. What has tied all of these approaches together has been a wish for the schools to work 'WITH' young people to keep them connected to each other, their teachers and their schools. This has, however, never been at the expense of accountability. In each case study, the young people involved have been asked to take responsibility for the effect of their actions on others. It has been made clear to young people in all instances that, if they could not do this, the school would ensure accountability for them in another form.

In the next chapter, Margaret Thorsborne and I give you a *head start* towards the level of understanding and mastery that the teachers in the case studies demonstrated. We will re-introduce the conference script (restorative questions) and go through each of these questions, one by one, explaining their intentions. We offer different ways to *word* these questions to help young people to *do* the quality of thinking that restorative practice is designed to promote. We will also delve into the complex and necessary business of what to do when things don't go as we planned (as they often don't).

   We aim to help you avoid the drudgery of mindlessly ploughing through the scripted restorative questions in a way that gets little to no engagement from young people. We want you to have understanding and options so you can help young people over the line when it comes to the business of dealing restoratively with tricky situations and tricky feelings.

Chapter 21

The Path to Better Restorative Conversations

More often than not, young people have the solutions to their own problems; they just need to be asked the right questions.

— Hansberry (2009, p.50)

Restorative questions

By now you've seen many different forms of the restorative questions or conference scripts in the case studies and read some of the theory of restorative practice that explains why questioning is so critical to the restorative approach. Chapter 4 introduced a form of the restorative questions that helped Jason and Tristan consider the effect of their bickering on themselves, their mothers, their classmates and their teachers. In Chapter 5, we looked at Howard Zehr's comparison of the questions asked in traditional discipline systems compared with questions that restorative discipline systems ask when things go wrong. Chapter 8 introduced you to Silvan Tomkins' Central Blueprint and how the restorative questions facilitate this process, and Chapters 15 through 20 covered the points of the restorative practice continuum, introducing a variety of different restorative scripts.

Table 21.1 presents a shortened version of the foundation conference script with the questions that are asked to students involved in an incident or conflict that has caused harm. Scripts just like this have been reproduced in many forms as wallet-sized cards that are used in schools, centres and workplaces.

Table 21.1 Foundation restorative questions for
both the mistake-maker and the harmed

Restorative questions for the mistake-maker	Restorative questions for the harmed
1. What happened?	5. What did you think when this happened?
2. What were you thinking at the time?	6. How has this affected you and others?
3. What do you think now?	7. What's been the worst of it?
4. Who has been affected by what you did, and how?	8. What needs to happen to fix this?

After hearing the harmed person's idea:	
9. What do you think of the harmed person's idea?	
10. Is there anything else that you might need to do to fix this?	

The restorative questions as you have seen them in this book have their origins in the restorative conference script that was developed in the early 1990s by a team of police, government officials and academics who were trialling the restorative conferencing process as a means of diverting young offenders away from the court system. These scripted questions worked so well in encounters between offenders and victims that subsequent extensive research was undertaken to find out what made processes where restorative questions were asked to participants so consistently successful. A range of theories and approaches emerged to explain the effectiveness of the scripted questions within the process. Some of these were a Socratic questioning style, reintegrative shaming theory (Braithwaite 1989), fair process (Kim and Mauborgne 2003) and Silvan Tomkins' affect script psychology (covered in Part 2). Others have shown that the conference script can be successfully adapted as a preventative intervention as well. (For comprehensive examples of such proactive adaptations of restorative questions, see Thorsborne and Vinegrad 2004.)

Restorative questions provide us with a script and format to follow when working through incidents of harm, conflict or wrongdoing with young people. The scripted nature of the questions keeps our conversations with young people on track. The questions support a focus on reflection, understanding, responsibility-taking and repair on the part of those involved. This can help teachers assist students to move through dialogue around incidents of harm or conflict without completely taking over, that is, doing things 'WITH' students, instead of doing things 'TO' them, 'FOR' them or 'NOT' doing anything at all!

More often than not, young people have the solutions to their own problems; they just need to be asked the right questions. And we need to learn how to listen! Regardless of the context, good teachers know how to ask good questions to promote learning. When teachers move their practice away from asking questions to just telling, lecturing or scolding, young people lose the opportunity to work with others to find constructive ways forward. The opportunity for learning and resilience-building is lost.

Using restorative questions effectively

Using the restorative questions begins to feel more natural as teachers gain experience and fluency with them, and develop a better understanding of the emotions (affects) that motivate young people to do what they do.

Restorative questions are most effective in the right hands. Teachers who have a genuine interest in young people and their sense of agency always find that restorative language is a natural fit with their values and existing practices. The questions work well for them. These are the 'WITH' or authoritative teachers (described in Chapter 3) who have developed high emotional intelligence and value humanity and dignity in their interactions with young people. These teachers believe that young people are innately good, regardless of how challenging their behaviour might be at the time.

Alternatively, teachers with a punitive ('TO') view of the world find the restorative questions ineffective because their attitude is all wrong. Young people quickly smell a rat and begin to defend themselves by withdrawing their cooperation and switching into self-protection mode by employing Compass of Shame defences (see Chapter 11).

What follows has been compiled in consultation with Margaret Thorsborne. Our intention in writing this chapter is to help teachers to better understand the purpose and intent behind the restorative questions so they can use them more effectively to help young people in a range of situations.

Memorising the foundation script

If you are new to speaking restoratively, the first thing to do is to have the questions committed to memory (or at least keep a card with the questions handy). The questions are the skeleton of restorative dialogue, and it is the task of the person asking them to put 'muscle and flesh' on the questions to make them meaningful and relevant to all young people involved in the dialogue. In the case studies earlier in this part you saw several adaptations of the foundation conference script asked in many different ways to suit the situation, the age of the students and the individual style of the teacher.

WARM conversations

To help with memorising restorative questions, Jansen and Matla (2011) have developed a popular mnemonic they call the 'WARM' conversation (Figure 21.1). It's a useful way of recalling the essence of a restorative conversation when we don't have the script on hand. It encapsulates the key ingredients: warm in manner, calm in tone and keeping to the essence of a conversation.

Key thought: Warm in manner, warm in words, warm in approach	
W	*What:* happened? (Tell the story.)
A	*Affect:* Who was affected/how does that line up with our school/class expectations? (Explore the harm.)
R	*Repair:* What needs to happen to repair them? (Repair the harm.)
M	*Move forward:* What do you need to do so this doesn't happen again? (Move forward.)

Figure 21.1 WARM conversations
(Adapted from Jansen and Matla 2011)

Engagement: Changing brains

Good restorative work is an exercise in engagement. I'm often asked by teachers what to do about the student who seems to be just going through the motions in restorative processes and giving formulaic responses. In my experience, this is a young person's response to a teacher who is just going through the motions themselves, asking formulaic questions and not watching carefully for emotion and not working to engage the young people involved. This is why we wrote this chapter: to give teachers alternative ways to ask restorative questions to engage young people. It's no surprise that the young people we will be asking restorative questions to most of the time are our least engaged and the least invested in our school rules and norms. These are the young people who need our best work and our deep interest in their answers.

The order in which we ask young people the questions stays relatively unchanged, but there are infinite ways in which these questions can be worded to either enhance understanding for participants or to probe further into young people's minds to explore intent, thinking, feelings and so forth. Just rattling off the questions will be met with limited success. We want to get young people thinking in new ways about themselves and others, about their emotions, cognitions, motivations and conduct. We need to get young people thinking outside of themselves. This is not easy work because it involves stimulating new neural pathways and diverting activity away from well-worn existing pathways, which only result in old habits. Novelty is the best way to do this, so the way we pose restorative questions needs to be dynamic. This is no different to how effective teachers think hard about the questions they ask in class or in assessment tasks.

Being gently relentless

In small or large group conferencing, it is essential that the teacher facilitating the dialogue between parties remain as impartial as possible. We are the first to admit that this can be extremely difficult, especially if you find yourself dealing with the same student(s) a few times over a short period or when what they've done has particularly offended you. Impartiality, however, does not mean that we are easy on students. In exploring incidents of harm, the teacher is gently relentless in getting meaningful and understandable responses to the script questions. It is the teacher's role to do their best to make sure that everyone in the conference hears and understands the different stories, feelings, thoughts and intentions of the others who are present. The facilitator uses a style of polite, curious enquiry that 'picks up every rock and lets some air in underneath'. The following sections unpack the basic restorative questions and give some examples of other ways of asking these questions.

In writing this, we have tried to avoid the terms 'victim' and 'offender' and have replaced them with terms like 'the wrongdoer/student who caused the harm' and 'those affected/harmed'. The terms 'victim' and 'offender' belong in a criminal justice context, and we believe that they are not helpful labels for school-aged children.

Questions for the person or people responsible

'What happened?'

'What happened?' is an easily understood question and doesn't require too much adapting. However, in the context of restoration, it is a crucial question because it invites everybody to tell their story. Getting a chance to tell others what happened to us is a critical part of the healing process, whether we were the ones who caused the harm or were the ones on the receiving end. When we share our experiences with others and are listened to, the awful feelings we have about the problem are reduced in intensity. Nathanson (2004) tells us that creating a context where negative emotions are shared and people can empathise with each other works to reduce negative feelings and helps people get to a place where they can start to deal with the present and look for ways to begin to repair harm (the future). This affective exchange (sharing of feelings) is also healthy for building and maintaining relationships and a sense of community (see Tomkins' Central Blueprint in Chapter 8).

When not to ask 'What happened?'

There are many times when it is not necessary or, in fact, might be unhelpful to ask, 'What happened?' In the case study in Chapter 15, where six-year-old Steph disposed of her rubbish in an air conditioner cage and not the bin, Peter didn't ask her what had happened because he saw what had happened. Asking her what had happened may have given Steph unnecessary wriggle room and perhaps an opportunity to bend the truth. All teachers have been in a situation where something has taken place in front of their eyes and a young person has then re-storied what happened when asked, 'What happened?' This creates an unnecessary opportunity for some young people with a propensity to bend the truth. A good rule of thumb is that, if you saw it, skip asking 'What happened?' for low-level incidents.

Other ways to ask 'What happened?'

One can ask 'What happened?' in numerous ways, such as:

- 'What's happening?'

- 'Tell us what happened' or 'What were you thinking when you...?'

- 'Can you share with us what happened from your side?'

- 'So, tell us what was happening the way you saw it.'

- 'What was happening when you became involved?'

- 'What's happened and what was your part in the problem?'

- 'Can you tell us some more about that? And what happened next?'

'What were you thinking at the time?'

This question works in a couple of ways. First, it works to establish the wrongdoer's intent at the time(s) that hurtful actions occurred. Second, it gives the facilitator and the rest of the group (or other party) an idea of the moral and social development of the student being questioned. It is also a glimpse into some of the private logic that students involved use (their private and unconscious ideas about the world). It gives us clues about where this person is with their understanding of the needs and feelings of others and their own moral code and set of values.

Even though this question appears once in the script, in actual fact, it may need to be asked many times. This is simply because it is highly likely that the incident being explored will have many parts to it (more than one taunt, put-down, push, punch). The wrongdoer's intentions need to be explored for every key moment – every time they did something different – working with the timeline as events unfolded. This 'unpacking' of the wrongdoer's thinking and intent for each choice they made is critical to the outcome for both parties as they come to understand the reasons and intent behind someone's actions. Being able to make sense of what happened (even if only through the wrongdoer's possibly distorted perspective) is important for those affected by harmful behaviour. It also means the wrongdoer can reflect on their own behaviour and draw some conclusions that may not have been apparent at the time of the incident.

There is another benefit from asking a young person, 'What were you thinking when you...?' It is very likely that the young person will also describe what they are feeling. Sometimes if we ask that feeling question directly, it can send the young person's brain into a state of stuckness. Asking the thinking question can allow a kind of back-door entry into that vital piece of information about that young person, without asking directly.

When not to ask 'What were you thinking at the time?'

The question 'What were you thinking at the time?' is not included in the Early Years scripts in Chapters 16 and 18. It is deliberately omitted because it is a difficult question for young children to answer. 'What were you thinking?' has a meta-cognitive aspect in that it requires that we recall, or make a guess about, what our internal dialogue may have been at a particular moment in the past – a theory of mind, in fact. This requires good recall, an awareness of our own thoughts and the skills to articulate this to somebody else. Many young children (normally under seven years of age) aren't developmentally able to do this. This is also the case for young people with deficits and delays in intellectual functioning.

Other ways to ask 'What were you thinking at the time?'

Other ways of asking 'What were you thinking at the time?' include:

- 'When you did…, can you tell us what was going through your mind?'
- 'What made you decide to do/say that?'
- 'What was happening for you at the time that you did…?'
- 'What did you hope would happen when you…?'
- 'What were you expecting would happen?'
- 'How did you come to think that doing…was okay?'
- 'What was going on in your head at that time?'
- 'What was going on for you at that time?'
- 'If we replayed the video file to the point where you…, tell us what you were thinking.'
- 'What was the purpose of doing it that way?'
- 'If you did know what you were thinking, what would it be?'
- 'What were you saying to yourself at that moment?'
- 'What were you wanting to happen?'

If a student is reluctant to share what they were thinking about, or is simply having trouble verbalising an answer because they are in a state of 'freeze', a good strategy in a more formal conference is to ask their parent (or support person) either of two things:

- '[Parent's name] you know your child [use their name] better than we do. What do you think they might have been thinking?'

- 'When we talked yesterday about this, you said… Did I get that right?'

Often the young person will say that the parent or support person has answered incorrectly and will correct them.

'What do you think now?'

This is a critical part of the process because it is where those who have been harmed may see for the first time that the wrongdoer acknowledges that what they did was wrong. This question gives the wrongdoer(s) the opportunity to take responsibility for their behaviour. This is the point where you may see those who are angry and upset visibly relax as they think to themselves, 'At least they know they did the wrong thing.'

This question again gives clues about the wrongdoer's stage of social and moral development. It asks the student to share whether they have re-evaluated their actions since the incident and, if so, what types of judgements they have made about their own conduct. In the heat of the moment, we all have the potential to say and do things that we re-evaluate in light of the fallout from our actions (with the benefit of hindsight). This question can let us (and more importantly those harmed) know how the wrongdoer appraises their own behaviour now that they have had time to reflect.

People are so often judged on the choices they made in difficult or tense situations. If the incident is the first time the harmed student came into close contact with the wrongdoer, it is understandable that they might judge the wrongdoer's entire character based on their behaviour during the incident. All participants in the conference, especially those harmed, will be interested to see whether what the wrongdoer did during the incident was normal behaviour for them or simply them having a bad day. The wrongdoer gets an opportunity to show that they have appraised their own behaviour and now regrets their actions. It might even be useful to reserve this question until after the wrongdoer has heard from the person harmed.

Other ways to ask 'What do you think now?'

'What do you think now?' can be asked in the following ways:

- 'In the time since you did..., about what have you thought?'

- 'What do you think about that decision now?'

- 'What do you think about your choice at that time now that we're having a chat about it?'

- 'What do you think about the way you behaved?'

- 'What have you thought about what you did since it happened?'

- 'Looking back on when you did that, what do you think now?'

- 'Have you thought about it since? What do you think about what you did?'

- 'If you had your time again, what would you do differently?'

- 'Now that you've heard from…what do you think now about what you did?'

If they don't take responsibility

Sometimes, when asked 'What have you thought about since?' (or a variation of that question), students will respond 'Nothing' in a snotty tone, or may try to defend or justify their behaviour in some way. This often comes as a nasty surprise to the facilitator because they initially believed that the wrongdoers would take responsibility for their actions. This is more often than not a Compass of Shame defence (see Chapter 11) and signals that the young person is feeling particularly wobbly. If the young person has been well prepared before the meeting (like in the case of a more formal conference), the teacher can help them by saying something like, 'When we spoke before about this, you told me that you thought that… What has changed for you?' This works more often than not to help a young person back onto the right track so the conference can continue.

If a young person remains stuck and cannot acknowledge their behaviour as harmful, the teacher makes the decision to continue to conference, or to abandon it on the grounds that the wrongdoer(s) is not taking responsibility for their behaviour. It is important to understand that the wrongdoer hasn't yet heard the stories of the students and others who have been harmed. This is a judgement call, and in making this decision, the teacher needs to put the needs of the harmed student(s) first, and ask himself or herself the question, 'Is this making things worse or better for the harmed student(s)?'

All may not be lost, however. The facilitator may choose to stay with the process and close off their questioning style with the wrongdoer(s) by asking questions like:

- 'Was what you did fair or unfair? Tell us how it was unfair/fair.'

- 'Was that the helpful or the unhelpful thing to do? What was helpful/ unhelpful about what you did?'

- 'Was your choice to do that a good one or a poor one?'

- 'Did that choice make things better or worse?'

- 'Was that behaviour kind or unkind?'

This is a very powerful tactic that takes the question from being open – 'What do you think now?' – to a closed question where the young person is given the chance to appraise their behaviour in a series of contrasting options. The teacher will gently and calmly ask these closed questions, one after another, with long and deliberate pauses between them, until a young person is able to respond appropriately. This is not mere trickery; it is calling a young person to their values and giving them more than one chance to process the question and then put their best foot forward. Sometimes the facilitator needs to do this because the student simply hasn't understood the question before and needs a very basic closed question. Other times, the student is having difficulty with the shame of the moment and needs support from the teacher.

It's humbling but important to remember that most people (including adults, of course) have significant trouble admitting when they have done the wrong thing. This is the shame–humiliation affect at work. People have to feel very safe in a process before they can admit that they did something harmful. It is no small task!

'Who has been affected by what you did, and how?'

This two-part question aims to see if the wrongdoer(s) understand who has been affected by their actions. Asking them 'How?' goes a step further and asks the wrongdoer to share their understanding of how those harmed may have been affected.

This is an opportunity for the young person(s) who has caused harm to show others in the meeting that they understand at least some of the ways in which their conduct has affected others. Those affected by the wrongdoing will often need to have their upset acknowledged by those responsible for it. This is another very important step in making young people accountable – to have them take responsibility for the harm their behaviour caused. Here, they begin in a way to own the harm. These questions require wrongdoers to show a degree of empathy and reflect upon how those affected by their deeds may have experienced what they did, and how this may be affecting them.

Other ways to ask 'Who has been affected by what you did, and how?'
Ways to ask 'Who has been affected by what you did, and how?' include:

- 'Who has your behaviour affected?'

- 'How do you think…has been hurt or upset by what you did?'

- 'When you…how do you think it was for…?'

- 'What do you think it was like for…when you…?'

- 'You said that you… How do you think that was for…?'

- 'When you did…, how do you think it was for…?'

Questions for those affected or harmed

We now turn our attention to the questions in the script that are asked of the students who have been harmed.

'What did you think when this happened?'

This is the important time where those who've been harmed tell their story. They have listened to the wrongdoer(s) speak and now have their opportunity to share their version of events.

Other ways to ask 'What did you think when this happened?'
One can also ask 'What did you think when this happened?' as follows:

- 'Tell us your story.'

- 'Tell us your version of events and what you thought when this happened.'

- 'When this happened to you, what were you thinking?'

- 'When you first realised what…did, what did you think?'

- 'What was going through your mind when this was happening?'

- 'What have you thought about [how have you felt] since?' (Optional)

This last question is not included in the foundation questions (see Table 21.1) but can be an important question to ask in higher-level conferences. It allows the affected student(s) to share the way the incident has affected them in the time since the incident. It is very important for them to share their concerns and fears. This builds a picture for the wrongdoers of how the incident has stayed with them in the time since the occurrence. This is an empathy-building experience for wrongdoers as they are given an insight into how it has been for the students affected by their actions:

- 'What has it been like for you since that moment?'

- 'What has [school, recess time, lunch time and/or being in this class] been like for you since it happened?'

- 'How have you felt about things since it happened?'

- 'What has it been like to be around [wrongdoer's name] since it happened?'

- 'Since this happened, what sort of things have been going through your mind?'

- 'Can you share with us some of the things that you have thought/how you have felt about this since it happened?'

'How has this affected you and others?'

This question is the clincher and is an opportunity for the harmed student(s) to share the impact of the incident. In asking the harmed student(s) these questions, the facilitator needs to prompt them to talk from their heart about the effect of the incident. If the harmed person happens to be a teacher, this is especially important because students don't often think about how their inappropriate behaviour may be affecting teachers on a human level.

Sometimes those harmed will rely on head talk and skirt around the edges of their experience in answering this question. This is usually due to a fear of being seen as weak by those who have wronged them. In this case, the facilitator can re-question carefully to encourage them to dig deeper in their responses.

Hounding is not recommended for either the harmed or the wrongdoers. The affected person's response to this question can be developed in the chat with them before the conference (conference preparation) to the point that they feel that they are confident to share the full impact with others and not leave anything out.

Other ways to ask 'How has this affected you and others?'

Other ways of asking 'How has this affected you and others?' are:

- 'How have you been affected by what happened?'

- 'What impact has this had on you?'

- 'Since this happened, how have things been different for you?'

- 'Since this happened, how have things changed for you?'

- 'Since this happened, what's been different about coming to [school and/or class]?'

'What's been the worst of it?'

This very important question aims to uncover the deeper hurts that the incident has caused for those harmed. It is an important question to ask in higher-level conferences (i.e. Large Group, Classroom and Community Conferences), because it helps to crystallise the suffering and can help both the harmed student(s) and others realise the extent of the harm done. Often young people have difficulty answering this question because it requires them to cognitively rank the different effects of the incident on them and choose what has been the hardest thing about what happened. In Community Conferences attended by parents, this question is very important for them to answer in front of their children so that they get to hear about their suffering. Alternative wordings of this question can be:

- 'What's been the hardest thing for you?'

- 'Out of all of this, what's been the most difficult thing to cope with?'

- 'What's been the worst thing out of all of this for you?'

- 'What's been the hardest to handle out of this?'

- 'What's been the hardest of it all for you?'

- 'As the mother/father of [the person harmed], what's been the worst of it?'

- 'Out of all of this, what's been toughest to deal with?'

'What needs to happen to fix this?' (To help those harmed first, as a priority)

It is important to acknowledge that not all harm can be simply fixed. Sometimes, it is better to talk about making things better. This acknowledges that we may be able to improve a situation but may not be able to make things completely right again. This question is asked of those harmed before it is asked of wrongdoers. As the needs of those harmed are paramount when working restoratively, it becomes obvious that they be asked first what they need.

You may wish to ask the question in one of these ways:

- 'What do you think needs to happen to put things right again?'

- 'What do you need to have things fixed [as much as they *can* be]?'

- 'What things do you think need to happen to put right some of the harm?'

- 'What needs to happen to clean up this mess [metaphor]?'

- 'What would make things better for you right now?'

- 'What would make it alright/safe for you to come back to [school and/ or class] now?'

Asking the harmed student first gives the wrongdoer the opportunity to take cues from the harmed student and gives them a better chance of answering the same questions helpfully.

'What do you think of [the harmed person's] idea?'

- 'What needs to happen to fix this?' (Now directed to the wrongdoer)

The wrongdoer gets an opportunity here to take the lead from those they have harmed in suggesting ideas about reparation. They also get the opportunity to say what else they believe needs to happen over and above the affected student's suggestions, allowing them to show goodwill and their possible desire to go the extra mile to make things better.

Other ways to ask

'What's been the worst of it?' can also be asked in the following ways:

- 'What do you think needs to happen to put things right again?'

- 'What do you think needs to happen to have things fixed [as much as they *can* be]?'

- 'What things do you think need to happen to put right some of the harm?'

- 'What do you think you need to do to repair some of the damage?'

- 'What do you need to do to clean this up?'

- 'What do you think would make things better for [student's name] right now?'

- 'Is there anything else you can think of that might help?

Supporting follow through

Wrongdoers need to be supported in doing what they have agreed to do to make amends. Because of our anger with the wrongdoer's actions, it is normal for us to sometimes feel that they should make amends all on their own without any help, but this can lead to problems. Restorative work is about adults offering students high levels of support as well as high expectations and behavioural boundaries.

As restorative practitioners, it is our obligation to support both those harmed and those responsible to work through incidents of harm. We need to help wrongdoers to get over the line in this respect because, as we all know, there is a difference between agreeing to a plan and actually being able to follow through on it. If a wrongdoer begins to renege on their agreed obligations, it is often because they feel unable to deliver to the satisfaction of those they harmed (fear) and would rather not try at all than risk falling short of expectations. It may be that there are some simple things that are preventing wrongdoers meeting their obligations that can be easily problem-solved.

To ensure that there is an acceptable outcome for those harmed and wrongdoers, we need to assist them in almost any way possible to follow through. The result of not doing so can cause more pain for both parties – with the harmed student(s) losing trust (again) in our restorative systems and the wrongdoer being effectively thrown on the scrap heap or written off as a bad person. This failure around follow-up is one of the reasons why some parents and staff think that restorative problem-solving is too soft. We need to teach young people the importance of keeping promises, trust and integrity.

Have you noticed the missing question?

In all scripted restorative questioning we never ask, 'Why?' It is a very deliberate omission because many of the young people we work with have had the 'why' question used on them with such rancour and accusation that it immediately triggers defensiveness. Asking 'what', 'how' and 'who' questions delivers far better results.

When agreements are broken

Regardless of how well a restorative process goes, there is always the possibility that one or more of the students will not do what they agreed to do to repair the harm, or will perhaps repeat the behaviours that they agreed not to repeat. This is called 'breaking the conference agreement'. This presents schools with a tricky situation. (See Chapter 26 for tips on dealing with this situation.)

Apologies

This is a very big area and there is a large body of literature dedicated to exploring the notion of apology and how remorse is conveyed in socially and culturally appropriate ways. Sometimes apologies occur spontaneously and sometimes restoration will be achieved without 'sorry' being uttered once. In my experience, people look for the word 'sorry' more often when other indicators of remorse are not being shown by a person who caused the harm. There have been many occasions when I have been prompting a young person to make an apology during a conference and another student (the harmed) has said to me, 'It's okay, Mr H, I know they are sorry.' On other occasions, I've had the parents of harmed students say that to me during Community Conferences. So why was I so hung up on wanting to hear 'sorry' or 'I apologise' when the way that the young person had responded to the script questions and their body language was clearly communicating remorse? Perhaps I was investing too much in apology.

Experience has shown me that pushing hard for an apology during a conference is fraught. I have seen this derail conferences. A teacher hounding a young person to make an apology makes everyone in the room awfully uncomfortable (triggers more shame in everyone). There are other ways if a young person cannot say 'sorry'. We can't assume that the wrongdoer understands how to make an apology or has the ability to follow through with a sincere, socially acceptable apology. A conference may not be the best place to teach them in front of others, seeing they already have enough shame to deal with. Some of us have been socialised to understand what a sincere apology needs to look, feel and sound like. We have had it modelled to us and may have had some real-life apology practice ourselves.

There are also young people who have very limited experience with apologising – and may not have heard it happen in their family of origin or indeed a previous school or community.

Sometimes a young person's facial expression or body language won't look apologetic as they apologise. It is helpful to consider that this may be a result of nerves, a shame response or, again, a lack of understanding of what a socially acceptable apology should look like.

When an apology seems insincere or is not forthcoming

These questions, asked respectfully, can be helpful:

- 'For what exactly are you apologising?'

- 'You have agreed that an apology is needed for what you did. Is there any way I can help you to do this?'

- 'I'm confused. When you and I spoke before this conference [or chat], you took responsibility and told me that you thought an apology might be one way to sort the problem out. Now you're having trouble with this. Can you help us understand what's happening?'

- 'Would you like to make this apology here in this conference or later in private?' (Check that this is okay with those harmed.)

- 'I'm noticing that you are not looking very sorry. I might be wrong, though. Can you please explain to us what is happening for you at the moment?'

- 'Is there something about which we still need to talk?'

- 'We've heard you say "sorry". How will "sorry" look tomorrow, next week or next month?'

A teacher can ask some questions that may lead a young person to conveying their regret or to help him or her be aware that their body language is not matching what they are saying:

- 'If we could go back in time and this happened again, would you do the same thing?'

- 'What do you think [student's name] needs to hear from you right now?'

- 'What do you think people here need to hear from you right now?'

- 'Was it your intention to make [student's name] so afraid/miserable?'

- 'How do you think [student's name] was affected by what you did?' (Re-visiting this question can help re-establish the wrongdoer's understanding of the harm they caused and can sometimes be acceptable to a harmed student.)

- 'How do you want to be remembered, as someone who was kind or unkind? So what could you say about that now?'

When apologies aren't accepted by those harmed, it can create a very sticky situation. It shows that they may not have been satisfied by the outcome of the conference. In this case, these questions can be asked:

- 'What can…do to show you they really *are* sorry?'

- 'Is there anything else that needs to happen for you to believe that they are sorry?'

- 'What else could…do to show they are sorry?'

- 'Is there something else happening here that we don't understand yet that you could share with us?'

It's really a matter of assisting the negotiations and keeping in mind the multiple purposes of the restorative process, whether formal or informal, to repair harm done and make things right so that the dignity of all parties can be preserved and/or recovered, and a level of harmony restored.

This whole chapter emphasises the need for educators to be more effective at helping young people work through their difficulties with each other, their learning, their classmates and their teachers. We need to learn to listen more carefully so that young people know we are truly interested in them, that we care about them, whether they have done harm or been harmed. This means being curious, respectful, polite, gentle and relentless – that is, less of us and more of them!

The next chapter will look at using Circles in classrooms to build relationships, cohesiveness and emotional literacy. Circles, known also as Circle Solutions, originate from Circle Time. Despite misconceptions, Circles don't have a place on the restorative continuum as an approach for addressing particular incidents of conflict, harm or disruption. Rather, Circles work as an underpinning pedagogy that oils the wheels for restorative practices, teaching young people a range of important skills that equips them to work restoratively.

Chapter 22

Circles for Building Community and Teaching Restorative Thinking

If the purpose of restorative practice is to restore relationships in the wake of wrongdoing or conflict, then the role of Circles and Circle Solutions, variations of which are known as Circle Time, Learning Circles, Tribes or Circle Work Time, is to help build the relationships children consider worth restoring. Circles are a practical way to skill young, developing human beings to listen with understanding, tune into feelings, share opinions and begin to see the world from another's viewpoint. These are the very skills children need to function successfully in any social setting.

– Hansberry and Langley (2013)

Circles and restorative practice have different purposes but at the same time are highly complementary pedagogies. They both build safer and more connected school communities and improve learning outcomes. They also share a theory of psychology (i.e. affect script psychology) that explains why they work so effectively to build and maintain safe and peaceful schools.

Circles provide a fun and interactive time where students join together and engage in a range of activities, many of which are playful. The goals are to build group cohesion and a sense of community by building familiarity between young people as they playfully and respectfully interact through the positive affects of interest and enjoyment. Circle sessions also provide a great forum to teach young people the skills to think and behave restoratively.

Circle activities are designed to mix up student groups and get them interacting outside of normal social groupings. Activities promote the sharing of ideas, values, thoughts and information between students and adults in pairs, threes, fours or as a whole Circle. A talking piece is often used to indicate whose turn it is to speak. When holding the talking piece, students can have a say on a particular topic or can choose to pass.

Circle Solutions gives young people a safe space to consider the diverse social
and emotional issues that impact on their lives. Structured activities enable
children to think through the fundamentals of relationships together with
their peers and begin to see that there are ways to be in the world that make
them feel better about themselves and others. (Roffey 2014, p.4)

Affect script theory: Why Circles build community and restorative practice repairs community

Circles maximise positive affect in groups. Interest and enjoyment are maximised
(in line with the first imperative of Tomkins' Central Blueprint; see Chapter
8) through fun and connecting activities with others that are interesting and
enjoyable. In a Circle everyone can see everyone else's faces (the primary site
of affect), so affects become incredibly contagious. Through this mutualising
of positive affect, classes are brought closer into community through a shared
interest in enjoying themselves. Good feelings about one another develop.

Shared positive affect is critical to building connected communities. When
there is a sense of genuine interest in one another as well as a genuine interest
in how interested others are in us, things go better and we recover faster from
inevitable relational hiccups. Contrast this with a classroom where individuals
have become self-interested and care little for the interests of those around
them. In those settings, small conflicts quickly escalate because young people
don't know if others are interested in their needs. Negative affects (shame, fear,
anger, distress, disgust and dissmell) dominate and drive negative defensive
behaviours that lead to even more negative affects. In those classrooms, social
capital is low and young people and teachers can become unwell in all sorts
of ways.

Restorative practice serves us well when the social connections that bind us
(our interest in others and their interest in us) are compromised by conflict or
wrongdoing. This is, of course, inevitable from time to time. When someone
acts in a way that triggers negative affects in others, these affects need to be
expressed (in line with the third Central Blueprint imperative) so they can
be mutualised and, through this mutualisation, be minimised (the second
imperative). Harm and conflict throw our Central Blueprint out of balance, and
we can no longer maximise positive affect (the first imperative) and minimise
negative affect (the second imperative). In this situation we tend to become *out
of balance* and preoccupied with trying to avoid (minimise) negative affect (the

second imperative) and may withdraw from our community or self-protect by acting in ways that are out of character. This is not good for life.

Restorative practice helps humans work together to appropriately express the negative affect related to a harmful event (in line with the third Central Blueprint imperative), so everyone becomes interested in repairing the harm caused (relieve negative affect – the second imperative) and return to positive affect (the first imperative). This is a social process that is based on our earliest attachment scripts that tell us that other people are our best relief from negative affect.

The ASPIRE Principles of Circles

Six principles – agency, safety and choice, positivity, inclusion, respect and equality (ASPIRE) – underpin all interactions in Circles and become the basis of the Circle guidelines which are stated at the beginning of every session and sometimes during sessions to remind or re-focus students. The descriptions below are adapted from Roffey (2014, p.5), one of the best resources available for schools wishing to embed Circles. These principles become the basis of a very simple set of Circle guidelines for Circles that work well from early years through to adulthood:

- One person speaks at a time.

- You can pass.

- No put-downs are permitted.

Agency

It is everybody's job to create a safe and positive atmosphere. Students work together to build solutions to class issues (the 'WITH' quadrant) rather than being told what to do by adults ('TO'). Giving young people agency helps change from an external locus of control, where everything is done 'TO' you or 'FOR' them, to an internal locus of control where young people learn that they can effect change.

Safety and choice

Nobody is pressured to speak, and participants may 'pass' as often as they like. Teachers must not challenge this. By being in the Circle they are still watching, listening and learning. Young people usually begin to contribute once they build up the confidence from watching others. Allowing the right to pass is often a challenging notion for teachers, but with experience in Circles they soon see that the vast majority of young people eventually take up the invitation to speak when it is their turn.

Positivity

Circle activities deliberately trigger positive emotions (the affects of interest and enjoyment). When people feel better about themselves and others, they have more emotional resources to cope with challenges (Fredrickson 2009). An increased sense of belonging raises resilience. When there is a need to discuss an issue that is creating negative emotions within the group, the group becomes focused on seeking a solution. The focus of the group becomes: 'What will help us build a friendly, inclusive, fair and happy classroom/group for everyone?'

Inclusion

Everyone in the group is welcomed to the Circle and are expected to work with all of their classmates. Mixing up groups of young people so that they break out of their cliques and get to know one another better is a key feature of Circles, and young people accept this readily when an adult takes the time to explain this to them. I often ask groups of students, 'Why would someone like me ask you to play silly games that get you away from your normal friends and sitting with someone you might not know?' Even five-year-olds more often than not understand that this makes for safer schools!

Respect

We respect what everyone has to say, and the way we listen to each other matters. Issues may be discussed but not incidents (incidents are discussed in restorative conferences). There is no blaming, shaming or naming. Young people who experience respectful treatment are more likely to act respectfully towards others.

Equality

There are equal opportunities to contribute. No one group or person is allowed to dominate. Knowing that everyone has their turn promotes cooperation.

What does a Circle look like?

Circles are an elegantly simple pedagogy with each Circle session following the same formula and operating by the same set of principles. You will know that you are running successful Circles if you and the students are by and large enjoying yourselves. The descriptions below have been adapted from Hansberry and Langley (2013).

How do people sit?

Everyone, including the adult leading the session, sits in a chair in the Circle. Teachers often ask if students can sit on the floor instead of chairs. In my experience, young people are able to maintain attention for longer when seated in chairs. Having everyone in chairs also keeps the shape of the Circle, especially in mix-up games where people move to different seats to work with a new partner or grouping. In classes where students often sit on the floor, using chairs signifies the importance of coming together as a group in a Circle. All classrooms can build a routine for moving furniture to set up a Circle with some patience and practice.

How long should a Circle session run?

Circle sessions work best when they are short. The idea is to leave young people wanting more! If students groan in disappointment when told that the session is complete, it's an indicator that you've timed the session well. A period of 10–20 minutes is ample for young children and no longer than 25 or 30 minutes is suggested for older students. When a Circle begins to feel as though it is dragging, it has gone on too long. Keeping sessions short maximises success.

Circle format

Some Circle books suggest an identical format each session. I have found that starting and finishing a Circle session the same way each time is enough. I find that Circles with students from around eight years of age and above run well with the following format:

- welcome by teacher and reminder of the guidelines for the Circle

- a quick energising activity

- a lively mix-up activity to get young people out of their typical social groups

- the introduction of a topic or question (session theme) for the group by the teacher

- paired or small group discussion on the topic or question, and feedback to the Circle by the pairs or groups

- a whole-group game

- a calm closing activity, guided meditation or visualisation.

Although activities in the middle of the session can be omitted or changed, a reminder of the rules and a mix-up activity at the beginning, and a calming concluding game at the end of the session, are critical. Teachers of students younger than eight years of age may leave out the energiser and/or shorten the time students spend in pairs or groups discussing the question or topic. They may also use the whole-group game as the closing activity to keep the session under 20 minutes. When I train schools in Circles, people are always surprised at how tricky it can be to keep sessions to the suggested time limits.

What does a commitment to regular Circles achieve?

Those who commit to working regularly in Circles with young people report that relationships and cohesiveness naturally build and student behaviour improves as class groups come closer into community with each other, sharing and aligning values. Social and emotional learning and certain parts of the academic curriculum can be delivered in Circles because of the high levels of engagement and interaction. The following list has been adapted from Armstrong and Vinegrad (2013, p.17) and reflects what I have witnessed to be the social and emotional learning outcomes of a commitment to regular Circles:

- *Stronger relationships*: Students get to know one another and become skilled in friendships and repair of relationships. Familiarity in schools is one of the most powerful protective factors against violence and bullying. As students get to know each other better, prejudices (based on the affect dissmell) break down and students take on a more flexible and tolerant approach to one another.

- *Enhanced engagement and participation*: Students become involved in decisions ('WITH') that affect them and learn to trust that what they say will be listened to by the rest of the Circle. The normally shy and quiet students (the silent majority) slowly find their voice in Circles and begin to participate and enjoy the interactions with peers.

- *Improved attendance*: Students look forward to Circles because of the added sense of belonging, respect and friendship. Students have reported that Circle Time is the one time in the school week they don't have to worry about schoolwork and can just relax in the company of classmates.

- *Reduction in conflict and violence*: Issues and tensions are eased as students become more familiar with one another and more skilled in perspective-taking and problem-solving and talk about how they want to be treated and what this means for their own behaviour.

- *Cooperation and community*: Moving away from compliance and control ('TO'), students become increasingly thoughtful and caring because adults share this responsibility of creating safe and friendly classrooms ('WITH'). Circles provide the ideal forum for social and moral values to be understood and modelled.

- *Resilience*: Having fun and laughing together (interest and enjoyment) promotes a sense of connection and raises levels of oxytocin, one of the feel-good neurotransmitters. Positive emotions foster creativity and problem-solving; they enhance people's ability to think. They also help undo the effects of negative emotion, as people bounce back more quickly from adversity (Fredrickson 2009). Circles offer the perfect forum for teaching restorative thinking and behaviour, and with this comes the resilience needed to recover from injustices, mistakes and wrongdoing.

- *Reduction in referrals*: Schools which have collected data on the impact of regular Circles have seen reductions in behaviour referrals to senior staff and increases in teacher morale as more connected and resilient classes have resulted in lower levels of disruption and harm. McCarthy (2009) reported improvements in student behaviour, with students being more courteous, paying more attention to teachers, showing more care towards classmates and involved in less incidents of bullying.

- *Enhanced health and well-being*: This becomes an obvious outcome of Circles when considering how the above factors impact uniquely on student well-being. Students' care and concern for each other increases and students learn problem-solving and communication skills.

- *Social capital*: Social capital is a term for explaining what happens in the myriad of interactions that occur every day in schools and classrooms that facilitate participation, engender relational trust and promote reciprocal support. To build social capital, young people and adults need ongoing opportunities (not just one-offs at the start of the year) to talk together about:

  - how people talk about (and to) each other in our class and whether this is helping or hindering our class

  - how people are acknowledged, valued and supported in our class

  - helpful ways to deal with conflict in our class

  - whether or not people are treated equitably in our class and what it means to be equitable.

- *Positive attitudes*: Circles raise levels of optimism and hope. Positive regard for the class, school and broader community strengthens the learning environment and students feel better (more interest and enjoyment) about their classes and their school.

Circles versus restorative conferencing: What's the difference?

Sometimes, groups may use their time in a Circle to share and discuss issues that are negatively affecting the group, but with the strict understanding that there is no naming, blaming or shaming. Circles should not be a forum for asking wrongdoers to take responsibility and make amends. This is the realm of restorative conferencing. However, tricky issues that affect the class might be aired during Circles, without naming any names, to clarify the issues, get people's thoughts and feelings, and help the group identify the prevailing thoughts or values in relation to an issue (e.g. teasing) that may have become a problem for the class. An experienced teacher will cleverly facilitate Circles to ensure that they don't turn into a restorative conference. If it is clear that an issue raised in Circle Time needs a restorative process, a restorative conference can be planned for an appropriate time, involving those affected by the problem.

A commitment to regular Circles, at least once per week, takes class groups to a point where restorative practice will work much more effectively because:

- an ethos of caring and understanding has developed among students and staff

- students have become accustomed to working in a Circle and have developed Circle skills like listening to each other, withholding judgement, taking turns to speak, responding succinctly and using a talking piece

- students will have built relationships with one another that they will consider worth repairing when conflict damages those relationships.

Will Circles 'work' straight away?

Running Circles may not be smooth sailing right from the outset. I remember one particular class of eight-year-olds where our first attempts lasted only about five minutes before the tricky behaviours of a few highly anxious students caused the Circle session to end before all hell broke loose!

When the Circle pedagogy is first introduced to a class or group, things can be a little wobbly for a while as trust and familiarity builds. Classes which are accustomed to teachers who normally lead from the 'TO' quadrant of the social control window can become quite disoriented when they are suddenly encouraged to talk with one another, listen, be playful and share their thinking. This approach will be a completely new way of interacting for some groups. It's best to start with a focus on games (such as sentence completions) and slowly introduce activities that get young people speaking to the entire Circle. In time, partner and small group work can be introduced. Young people will first need to learn that Circles are fun and a safe place. In time, they will develop the skills and trust one another to handle topics and issues that involve levels of personal disclosure.

Hansberry and Langley (2013) offer helpful advice to teachers introducing Circles and also explain the main reasons that young people misbehave. They also include strategic ways for teachers to respond to tricky behaviours that stay true to the guiding principles.

Savvy responses to misbehaviour always begin with a 'least intrusive' response (Rogers 2006, p.30). Simply making eye contact and using a hand signal or a pre-arranged private cue to remind children of what they should be doing are 'least intrusive' and draw as little attention to the offending children as possible. Good behaviour management strategies preserve dignity and keep relationships intact. This is crucial within the context of Circle Time, because building relationships is our purpose.

Building community: Not left to chance

In schools, interactions take place between people all day long in varying contexts. As schools buckle under the weight of increasing political demands – curricular, assessment, child protection, industrial matters, risk management and so forth – opportunities for teaching young people to connect in meaningful ways are reduced or forgotten completely. I often refer to this as 'taking our eye off the relationships ball'. Student behaviour soon deteriorates spectacularly and community breaks down.

Young people, like all humans, are hardwired for social attachment. This means that young people will connect with each other regardless of what is happening in their educational surroundings. Sometimes, in some cohorts, these connections form spontaneously in healthy ways (respectful, kind, non-dominant), without adult intervention. We can all remember 'that amazing class' that just got along with one another most of the time, where everyone seemed happy and levels of inclusion and acceptance were high. In that class, young people took care of one another and mostly acted in one another's interests. When conflict occurred, the high baseline of familiarity and a willingness to listen to one another saw that resolution and restoration were never too far away. When those classes had a visiting teacher, even a bad one, they came through unscathed. Those classes had high social capital.

Alternatively, we can all recall those classes that were incredibly hard work, where social capital was low and negative affect dominated. Upset and conflict constantly simmered and the class was segmented into those kids who were in and those who were out. In some of those classes, cruel was cool and students became completely preoccupied with minimising negative affect by either being the first to attack others through teasing and put-downs, or keeping very quiet. Learning came a distant second to social survival. Conflict in those groups quickly descended into harmful words and acts, or was carefully played out in a covert form of relational violence, where the damage was done in the form of looks, quiet put-downs, posts on social media and strategic social isolation. In those classes the vulnerable students were often preyed upon and a socially powerful group dominated. When a visiting teacher took that class, unless they were highly skilled in classroom management and building rapport fast with students, the class would descend into chaos and the fallout would last for days.

Sadly, without interventions that build cohesiveness and community in class groups, the second type of class above is more often the case. This is not because young people are amoral or innately bad; it is because young people today are bombarded by messages from popular media that show people behaving at their worst. The producers of reality TV programmes know that the best ratings come from conflict and questionable behaviour. News and current affairs programmes saturate us all with images of conflict playing out in neighbourhoods, cities and countries, often on a deadly scale. This is what makes it newsworthy. A high-level tennis player abusing the chair umpire and smashing a racquet will be the opening story on the sports segment. Video footage of a schoolyard fight is far more likely to go viral than the story of a bullied young man who turned his life around in a new school by holding doors open for other students. Pornography, now so easily accessible, sends all the wrong messages to young minds about intimacy and relationships. Good news stories of kindness, human connection and compassion only occasionally break through the fog of the rude, angry and self-interested.

Young people are extremely vulnerable to this poor modelling, and in schools we often see its impact on the developing identities of young people and the group cultures of classes, pastoral care groups and even entire grades of students. We see how these influences play out on how young people form and maintain relationships and how they deal with conflict. To create safe and peaceful places of learning, educators have to engage in the moral and emotional labour of creating opportunities within teaching and learning time where we can offer guidance to students in this connecting process. We might deliver the most current curriculum content supported by high-quality pedagogy, but students, especially in adolescence, will be largely preoccupied with their innate need to connect with each other.

Circle is a proven pedagogy that guides young people to form healthier connections and provides a fertile seedbed for restorative practice in schools.

Where can I be trained in Circle pedagogy?

The following organisations all offer high-quality training for schools in the implementation and ongoing use of Circles:

- Hansberry Educational Consulting (www.hansberryec.com.au)

- Circle Solutions Network (www.circlesolutionsnetwork.com)

- Inyahead Press (www.inyahead.com.au).

For more information in relation to the UK, contact Sue Roffey via email at Sue@sueroffey.com. Details of courses being offered internationally are given at www.sueroffey.com/news-upcoming-events.

Now we have explored the full length of the restorative practice continuum as well as Circles to build community and restorative skills, we will now move our focus to an aspect of restorative practice that will determine whether it succeeds or fails in your school. This is the all-important follow-up, accountability and relationship management.

PART 4

Following Through Restoratively

Managing a Restorative Programme through Follow-Up, Accountability and Relationship Management

Chapter 23

'What Have We Agreed to Here?'
Holding Young People Accountable

In some schools restorative practice has unfairly gained a reputation for being soft and low on accountability. In my experience, a key factor in this state of affairs has been a lack of rigour in conference follow-up. Inevitably, students have lost faith in conferencing to deliver lasting change, and schools have either abandoned restorative practice or become caught in a state of limbo between restorative and punitive approaches. In this limbo, schools have begun to slip back towards old, punitive approaches.

In Chapter 14 the restorative keystones model (developed by Jansen and Matla 2011) was introduced to illustrate how good restorative work involves three stages: preparation, the actual restorative conversation or conference (participation) and then follow-up to help young people remain accountable to their commitments made in the participation stage and to manage relationships (Figure 23.1).

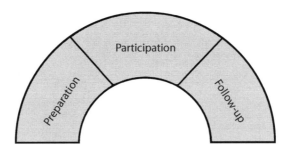

Figure 23.1 Restorative keystones

Jansen and Matla (2011) assert that, without attention being given to all three of these keystones, cracks will appear in the restorative process and the benefits of the process will be lost as the situation returns to how it was (or worse than it was) prior to the restorative intervention. Part 4 is dedicated to the last of the keystones: the follow-up phase. This part contains information and resources for developing a school-wide restorative conferencing programme.

Formal conference agreements

The centrepiece of conference follow-up for higher-level conferences (Large Group, Classroom and Community Conferences) is a formal record of what was agreed in the conference. This is called the conference agreement. Conference agreements outline:

- what has been done, or still needs to be done, to repair the harm

- how behaviours will change following the conference

- agreed actions if the previous two points are not adhered to

- the people who will monitor the agreement

- when agreement review meetings will take place and who will be involved in review meetings.

In the case studies in Part 3, formal conference agreements are mentioned several times. In the Large Group Conference involving the students playing four square, a conference agreement was created with the students that laid out the new rules of the game. Following the conference, a small committee of students would draft the conference agreement and present it to all who were involved in the conference. The agreement would then be monitored and reviewed regularly.

The No-Blame Classroom Conference with Jim's class saw the creation of a formal conference agreement that detailed the new agreed expectations for classroom behaviour as well as a weekly process for review, where the class would meet weekly in a Circle to review their new agreement, celebrate successes and address any problems.

The Community Conference to address the defamation of Georgia and her mother by Erin on Facebook concluded in a formal conference agreement between the girls and their parents as to how Erin would repair the harm by retracting her comments and apologising publicly. The agreement also documented a commitment by Erin to work with Georgia to organise a cyber-safety seminar for the middle school. Erin also committed to change her online behaviours, and this was clearly documented in the agreement.

In the Small Group Conference to address the situation between the soccer-playing boys, Jess, the teacher, asked the boys whether their agreement to politely return soccer balls to their game of origin should be formally recorded. In this situation the boys agreed to keep their agreement verbal. The boys weren't left completely unaccountable to their verbal commitments, however. Jess made a note in the staff bulletin about the conference and the agreed actions, so other teachers could support the boys to keep things peaceful.

Matching process to agreement type

Figure 23.2 illustrates the different types of agreements that can come from different processes on the restorative practice continuum that you read about in Part 3. As we move along the continuum from left to right, the restorative process used increases in formality to match the seriousness of the issue or incident being addressed.

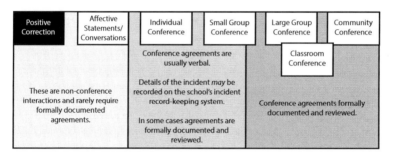

Figure 23.2 Matching process to agreement type

Keeping in line with this increasing level of formality, the way conference outcomes are documented must also increase in detail and formality. More importance also needs to be placed on processes to monitor and support students so that they remain accountable to the agreed conference outcomes. In other words, the more serious the problem, the more formal the restorative process used and the more work put into documenting and following up on the agreements made during the conference.

It is important to understand that there are no hard-and-fast rules about which type of restorative process will require which type of agreement. Figure 23.2 shows how there can be an overlap between process type and agreement type. There will be times when a lower-level process, such as an Individual Conference or a Small Group Conference, might require a formally documented and reviewed agreement. These times might be the following:

- When students (or staff) request that their agreement be formally documented and reviewed. At the conclusion of a lower-level conference, it's a good idea for a teacher to ask, 'Is our agreement a verbal agreement, or do we need to make it formal and write it down and review it later?'

- When parents of students request a formal written agreement.

- If teachers suspect that bullying behaviour may be behind the issues addressed in a lower-level process, and want to monitor the dynamics more closely.

- A student(s) involved in the issue has a history of repeated behaviours of the same nature and needs extra support to remain accountable.

- A student(s) involved in the issue has had difficulty honouring verbal agreements from previous low-level conferences and needs extra support to remain accountable.

When we ask young people to work together to resolve conflicts and incidents of wrongdoing, it is our responsibility to provide support and clear accountability processes to give them the best chance of honouring commitments and undertakings. Failing to create and maintain systems of post-conference follow-up results in young people (and their parents) losing faith in restorative practice.

Developing a school-wide conferencing programme

What is hopefully emerging is a clearer picture of how restorative processes need to be supported by a greater system of follow-up. As you read further, you will discover that good conference follow-up is a no-stone-left-unturned process that involves lots of time and coaching of young people as well as meticulous information-sharing with stakeholders. There are no 'silver bullets' in the process of teaching young people to manage upset and conflict. This is the stuff of peace-building. It is laborious as well as up close and personal.

The remainder of this book comprises six chapters related to conference agreements, plus a chapter with my closing thoughts.

Chapter 24

Creating Conference Agreements

This chapter provides a template for a restorative conference agreement. Schools develop their own forms to suit the needs of their own conferencing programmes, but a template like this can be a good place to begin. The person who facilitated the conference ideally produces the final draft of the conference agreement from their own notes taken during the conference. The wording of the conference agreement is very important and needs to express the tone of the conference. The conference facilitator has the best chance of correctly capturing the intent and tone of the conference in the formal agreement. Delegating this to somebody who was not in the conference can result in some of the important details being lost.

Once the agreement draft is finalised, I like to get the students (and adults) who attended the conference to run their eyes over it to see if there has been anything missed before asking them to sign it.

FORMAL RESTORATIVE CONFERENCE AGREEMENT BETWEEN [STUDENT(S) NAME(S)]

Conference date:

Conference participants:

What's been happening (the problem that brought us to conference)?

A detailed account of the incident(s) that caused the need for the conference goes here. This helps parents and teachers understand the event that necessitated a conference (if they weren't present in the conference) as well as making it easy for all to remember and reflect upon the incident when this agreement is reviewed in scheduled review meetings.

We agree that:

This is what is agreed upon by all involved to repair harm and make sure we don't have a repeat of this incident. Include the behaviours that all have agreed will not occur again. Use concise bullet points here about the 'when' as well as the 'what', as well as 'with whom' and 'by when', of the agreed undertakings. Clarity of expectation is extremely important here.

This agreement will be monitored by:

Write the names of the people who will be responsible for making sure that:

- agreements are lived up to/undertakings are honoured
- plans for repair are followed through (if required)
- agreed conditions are met if the agreement is broken.

Include the names of the students involved here to show that we have a shared responsibility in taking care of the agreement and each other.

If this agreement is broken/how we will handle it if this happens again:

It is critical during the conference to agree on what will be a fair way to deal with it if the students fail to honour the undertakings laid out above, or engage in further harmful behaviour that they agreed to cease. These agreements are added below. I have facilitated many conferences where participants have felt that this is not necessary, and I have had to ask them to humour me so we could come to some agreement! When a conference is going well and students have taken responsibility for their behaviour, it is normal for people to believe that this part isn't required. Avoid this pitfall – this part *is* necessary! Options may be that:

- Another conference meeting is called so the person who broke the agreement can explain their reasons for breaking the agreement to everybody (possibly with parents this time if they weren't included in the original conference).
- A previously agreed-upon formal consequence may be imposed.

Signed:

The agreement is signed by all present in the conference including teachers of students (if applicable), parents of students (if required) and the conference facilitator.

Chapter 25

Recording and Managing New Conference Agreements

When schools begin to use restorative conferencing as a way to involve young people more in finding solutions to conflict and ways forward after wrongdoing has caused harm, they soon find that they need a process (and policy) for managing conference agreements. Once a conference agreement has been published, printed and signed by all those who attended the conference, it becomes the conference agreement original or agreement master copy. From this point it needs to be:

- photocopied and distributed to all conference participants

- centrally filed and the location of the electronic file recorded for ease of access to the electronic version

- communicated (as appropriate) to school staff who may come into contact with students affected by the agreement

- reviewed regularly with all involved students.

Although conference agreements may have a level of confidentiality, it is important to ensure that staff who come into contact with the involved students are aware of the existence of an agreement. Relevant staff being aware of the general nature of the agreement is critical in helping the affected students to stay accountable to the agreement.

The suggested process below may be used by the school to manage new conference agreements along with existing conference agreements:

1. The original conference agreements are created from the school's agreement template (see Chapter 24).

2. For ease of access, conference agreements are electronically saved to a folder titled 'active conference agreements' on a shared drive that is

accessible to relevant staff (any teachers who may come into contact with any of the students named in the agreement). It is wise to add a common file-path footer to all conference agreements so the electronic file can be located from any hard copy; for example:

Agreement Between Georgia Banks and Erin Stark/Restorative Agreements and Documentation/Restorative Agreements/Agreements.

Staff who have access to conference agreements might be:

- classroom or pastoral care teachers of involved students

- grade coordinators and/or heads of house

- school counsellors

- school psychologists

- school leadership.

A hard-copy original of the conference agreement is printed and signed by those present at the conference. I write 'original' or 'master' with highlighter pen on the original hard copy (so as not to show up on photocopies).

If the agreement cannot be completed and printed immediately after the conference, participants can be called back to sign the agreement at a later time. Alternatively, the original agreement can be sent home to all families involved, one at a time, for signing. This obviously takes longer and runs the risk of having the original signed agreement lost in transit. With follow-up phone calls and prompting, this can work successfully and be sent to all families in an envelope with the following on the front:

This envelope contains the original Restorative Conference Agreement Between Georgia Banks and Erin Stark. Please read the agreement carefully, sign and return the next day.

☐ Georgia, Steve and Kathy Banks (sent home 14/11/16)

☐ Erin, Elizabeth and Paul Stark (sent home 15/11/16)

(Managing staff member to tick box when returned to school.)

When this original is returned, signed copies will be sent to all involved. This original will be kept at school and used for regular agreement reviews. Thanks for your assistance.

3. Once the original conference agreement is signed by all who participated in the conference, a copy should be produced for:

    a. students who participated in the conference

    b. adults who participated in the conference (staff and parents)

    c. class teachers of conference participants and all other staff who work with the young people involved

    d. the school records and/or discipline files of students involved.

4. The signed original should be placed and kept in a central location (perhaps a folder that stays in the school's administration area).

5. For students who have specified actions to undertake to honour the terms of the agreement, it is a good idea to complete and attach an accompanying parent letter for conference agreements (see Chapter 29). For ease of access, a template for this letter should be kept on the school's network in a location that is accessible to all conference facilitators. Classroom teachers, pastoral care teachers and heads of house who facilitate restorative conferences with their students can also access the template.

6. *Restorative conference agreement termly review procedure*: It is absolutely critical to review active conference agreements with students at scheduled meetings following the conference and in the first week (if possible) of each new school term. This is a vital process as it keeps the terms of the agreement fresh in the minds of students and can be used to deal with any relationship hiccups from the school holidays before they begin to cause problems at school. This process also brings the students together and has the potential to improve relations between them. (It is often a relationship breakdown that brought students to a restorative conference in the first place.) Chapter 27 offers clear guidance on reviewing restorative conference agreements with students.

7. *Updating the 'agreement summary' with the details of the agreement*: In Chapter 28 you will learn a process to ensure that appropriate staff members are aware of conference agreements that affect particular students. The centrepiece of this process is a document that contains summaries of current (active) conference agreements. This 'agreement summary' needs to be kept updated with the details of active conference agreements and

distributed to all teaching staff who will have contact with affected students in the classroom or schoolyard.

This is necessary to make staff aware of the agreements that exist between students and how these agreements may affect future disciplinary decisions for students named in an agreement. Teachers, of course, are not expected to memorise all of the agreements that exist between students, but they do need a document to refer to so they can quickly determine and take into account whether students are affected by a conference agreement or refer the issue to a grade coordinator or someone else with authority.

8. *Updating the student behaviour database to show that a conference agreement is linked to that incident*: Different schools use different types of databases to keep records of disciplinary issues. Regardless of the system used, any record of a behavioural incident will normally contain details of the incident as well as the consequence chosen by the school to address that incident. When a restorative conference has been held, the database record must indicate this and refer the reader to relevant documentation associated with that conference (usually the conference agreement).

Access to restorative conference agreements

All staff working in any way with the students named in the agreement should have access to the agreement on the school's network. Information contained in agreements may be important in deciding on an appropriate course of action for disputes or incidents involving students with existing conference agreements. (Note: It is advisable to inform conference participants that certain school staff may have access to the conference agreement before they sign the agreement at the conclusion of the conference.)

Chapter 26

After the Conference
Relationship Management and Accountability

Agreement review meeting

Any conflict or incident between students that leads to a restorative conference can be deep-seated with a long and turbulent history. Restorative conferences begin to address the harm caused in the past, but it is the conference follow-up that is critical to helping young people manage their relationship in the future. For students with a history of conflict, the days and weeks following the conference are very important in determining whether things between them will become more trusting or whether they will spiral into further conflict and harm. The written agreement from the conference becomes the centrepiece of this dialogue.

Bringing students together to review a conference agreement is a powerful, proactive measure that goes a long way to minimise the risk of further conflict. The more positive exposure students have to each other after the conference, the less likely they will be to break the agreement.

Chapter 7 introduced Silvan Tomkins' affect script psychology and the nine innate affects. An aim of the restorative conference process is to bring out the negative affects that students have built up about one another, by allowing appropriate expression of these bad feelings, which allows healing. As the conference process draws to a close, the negative affects are reduced and the positive affects begin emerging between students.

It is crucial to bring the students together regularly after the conference to build on the interest and enjoyment that was generated during the conference. This typically occurs in the context of a conference agreement review meeting, where students are brought together in a formal meeting to check in with one another about how they are going in adhering to the conditions of the conference agreement. This meeting works best when it is coordinated by the adult who facilitated the original conference, or an adult who was present at the conference.

When agreements are broken

Regardless of how well a restorative conference goes, there will be times when one or more of the students will not do what they agreed to repair the harm, or will repeat the behaviours that they agreed not to repeat. This is called 'breaking the conference agreement'. The following sections give some advice on how to deal with this scenario as well as how to deal with our own feelings of disappointment (as teachers) when students break conference agreements.

Expectation clarity

During the final stage of a restorative conference, it must be decided (and recorded in the agreement) what will happen if the agreement is broken. A common response for breaking a conference agreement involves the convening of another conference where those who broke the agreement are asked to explain (i.e. justify) their reasons for breaking the agreement. This approach does mean more work for the school, but under some circumstances it is a very powerful and illuminating strategy. Other sanctions for breaking agreements can involve the use of traditional school consequences.

If a condition of the agreement is broken, it is natural to feel despondent and think that the conference was a waste of time. In this situation, staff and other adults who were involved in the conference process can feel extremely disappointed. In these situations, it is important to focus on the positives from the conference and ask ourselves, 'What would have happened if we had not conferenced this issue? Would the students have taken responsibility for their actions? Would there have been any restoration?' This has always helped me when conference agreements have been broken. What is easily forgotten is that the young people who find themselves in restorative processes are often those with the most inconsistent behavioural and social functioning. A few bumps along the road are to be expected. We are dealing with young people who often fall victim to a lack of experience and poor impulse control. It is also important to recognise that the students themselves will also feel disappointed if and when one of them breaks a conference agreement. Be ready for some young people to show this disappointment through being angry – for example, blaming each other or blaming a teacher (attack-other Compass of Shame responses). They will need help with these feelings, and getting the students together quickly to deal with the matter is important.

Dealing with broken agreements

There are many reasons a young person will not or cannot do what they committed to do during the conference. A student's failure to comply with the agreement always needs some investigation to uncover the reason(s) they didn't follow through with that to which they committed, before all involved are brought back together to address the broken agreement. It can be the case that the problem is relatively simple and can be quickly and discreetly addressed. However, if the decision is made to bring students together to deal with a broken conference agreement, it is important to first of all remind yourself that you will be modelling to the students what it means to be restorative.

Bring the affected students back together, look at the agreement together and follow it to the letter. Remember to keep the focus on the important stuff – the restoration – but at the same time, follow through on any agreed formal sanctions for breaking the agreement. This communicates to young people that the school is serious about helping them to live up to the conditions of conference agreements. Even though discussions in the review meeting may turn to the 'how' and 'when' of the formal consequences for the student(s) who broke the agreement, be sure to communicate to the students that repairing the harm is the most important thing.

When it has been established how the agreement was broken, encourage the student(s) who broke the agreement to explain their reasons for breaking it to those present in the review meeting. Young people need to be helped to examine the reasons for the decisions they make. If the agreement came from a Community Conference, it may be appropriate to invite everyone back who was present (including parents) at the original conference and have students explain themselves to this group. This is indeed very tough and highly confrontational. The thought of being held to account for breaking the conference agreement in front of all who took part in the initial conference acts as a powerful deterrent.

Once young people have been held accountable for breaking the agreement, it is important to give them an opportunity to make it better again (e.g. to apologise to others), so the shaming process remains reintegrative and not a ceremony of stigmatisation. In some situations the original conference agreement may need to be amended. It is important to record on the original agreement that it was broken (how and by whom), as well as the resulting actions. This can be done by hand writing a record on the back of the original copy of the agreement with brief details of the incident, the actions taken and the date.

When discussing how the agreement was broken, it is helpful to use the restorative scripted questions to address what happened and work on repairing the harm all over again. Keep the focus on repair. Do your best to keep the formal consequence in the background. Sure, it needs to be followed through, but it is not the main point of the exercise – the young people feeling better is. Young people tend to follow our lead. Punitive school environments create punitive young people. If students pick up that we are more interested in 'who gets what' consequences, this will also become *their* focus. If students get the impression that we are more concerned that they mend the bridges and restore safety and relationships, they will be more likely to focus on that. When discussing the agreed sanctions in the agreement with students, I often say to them, 'Yes, we did agree that x, y and z would be the consequences if the agreement was broken; that is important and we will follow through on that. However, the really important stuff is the fixing. This is what will make it better for everybody and this is what we need to look at first.'

Students (and sometimes teachers), through their disappointment, say things like 'The agreement isn't working' (as if the agreement is this entity far removed from them that has power of its own!). I empathise with their frustration in this situation and then say something like the following: 'The agreement is nothing more than a piece of paper with some writing on it. It is your hard work and commitment to keeping your promises to each other that makes it work. The only way this agreement will make things better will be through your hard work.' I say this kind of thing often to young people to give them a message that it's their responsibility to change their behaviour and stick to the agreement. I make it clear that the power to make things better lies exclusively with them. And of course, this is in contrast to many messages that young people receive today about personal responsibility.

Young people always need support to adhere to conference agreements. With some young people who have never repaired anything properly in their lives and never been shown how to make good on their misdeeds, we will need to go to great lengths to help them meet expectations. Students living with attachment disorders are one example of young people who will need a great deal of support in repairing harm and adhering to conference agreements. Sometimes we make the mistake of walking out of a conference, hopeful and pumped up, thinking that the students will stick to the conference agreement. Then, we are reminded that they are, in fact, inexperienced in many areas of life. They often look to our wise guidance (well, hopefully wise!) and the occasional prod to follow through with their commitments.

The teacher's job

It is sometimes the case that teachers will agree to certain undertakings as part of the conference agreement. Because it is the role of teachers to model the restorative spirit to students, it is critical that teachers honour their commitments. Failure of teachers (or other adults in schools) to do so is often bitterly disappointing to students and sends all the wrong messages.

Chapter 27

How to Review Conference Agreements

Creating a process for reviewing conference agreements is an important part of a school's conferencing programme. Without a whole-school process to check in on agreements made in restorative conferences, repair of harm and long-term behaviour change is less likely for many of the most troubled students. Bringing students together to review conference agreements on a regular and ongoing basis is a critical component to a whole-school programme of restorative practice and signals to students that the school wants to support them to live by the school's code of conduct and to improve and manage their relationships.

Reviewing conference agreements also sends a clear message that the school is serious about holding students accountable to the commitments made during restorative processes. The review process helps to keep students accountable to one another and puts a relationship management process into action. The simple act of bringing students together to review an agreement can build on the positive feelings that were created in the repair stage of the initial conference and reduce the likelihood that students will harm one another in the future. Familiarity builds safety.

Social-skilling opportunities

For students who struggle with social skills, agreement review meetings create wonderful teachable moments where the students and the teacher can talk about the new behaviours that students may be trying out. As well as documenting what has been agreed that needs to happen to repair harm, a conference agreement will also contain information about behaviours that will need to cease immediately (e.g. hitting, teasing) and new, more positive behaviours to take their place. When we frame the conference agreement as a new set of skills to learn, we can help students view it in a more positive light and provide a wonderful springboard for a conversation about the new skills in the agreement.

The most powerful restorative moments I have experienced have been when students in agreement review meetings have spontaneously given one another advice for handling tough situations or conflicts. Keep in mind that these are students who were, at one point in time, in serious conflict with one another. This peer coaching between students strengthens social bonds and creates powerful learning opportunities. In these moments, clever teachers just sit back and allow the conversation to flow, occasionally asking questions like:

- 'How do you handle it when that happens?'

- 'How does that work for you?'

- 'What have you tried that's different when that happens? How did it go?'

- 'What do you think is the reason people might do/say that?'

- 'What is a smart/not so smart thing to say to yourself when that happens?'

- 'How have you seen others deal with that well/poorly?'

- 'Did you make that skill up or learn it from someone else?'

Gently questioning young people helps them to reflect on their own habits of reacting to different situations and hear from peers regarding how *they* deal with things. I find it really works to take on a 'dumb teacher' façade and listen as though I've never heard of the ideas the students are discussing. It is like they are teaching me, as well as one another, good strategies for managing friendships and handling tough situations. This involves letting go of the idea that I am the only one in the room with ideas about handling conflict, and it is an extremely powerful way to get students talking and sharing strategies when their normal shame defences are down. Young people really tune into one another in these moments.

It is often the case that students who find themselves in frequent conflicts are very inflexible in their thinking. These young people benefit greatly from conversations with other students where different points of view and ways of thinking are aired.

The three Es: Engagement, explanation and expectation clarity

Schools that conference issues but then neglect the need for ongoing review of written agreements can expect a short life for restorative practice. Conference agreements complete the three Es that are required for a fair process to exist: engagement, explanation and expectation clarity (Kim and Mauborgne 2003). Without all students being clear about the expectations of them to repair harm, as well as new expectations and standards for behaviour, the effects of the conference will likely be short-lived.

How an agreement review might run

Usually, 15 or 20 minutes per conference agreement review meeting is enough time to explore issues, to follow through with agreed actions in case of a breach of agreement, or to make changes to agreements if necessary.

Students enter the room, and seats are arranged in a circle. The original signed conference agreement should be accessible. (I like to have it at the ready.) A copy of the original agreement can be made for each student or, alternatively, they may be asked to bring their own copy of the agreement to the meeting. (I do both.)

The reviewing teacher might begin by saying:

Hello [students' names], thanks for coming to review your agreement. Make yourselves comfortable.

It is important to observe the students' body language towards each other as they enter. This gives important clues as to how things are between them and whether there will be issues raised.

We are meeting to check on the agreement you have together, but before we do, we need to remind ourselves of what happened to make us need this agreement. Who would like to read our agreement?

If none of the students volunteer, the teacher can read the agreement. The 'What happened?' section is of particular importance as it reminds everyone of the incident that necessitated the need for the original conference.

After the agreement has been read aloud, the teacher says:

So, tell me, how's our agreement going?'

Here students share whether they believe the agreement is going well, whether somebody believes the agreement has been broken or whether somebody has not followed through with agreed actions. If the agreement is going well, the teacher may respond:

> That's wonderful to hear. I can see you are all happy with things and it's fantastic to see that you are showing commitment to the promise(s) you made to each other. Can I please get you to sign the agreement so as to record that we met today to review this agreement and that all is going well?

The review date is handwritten on the back of the agreement and a couple of notes may be made about the review.

> Well [names], thanks for coming. It's great that things are going well. If I don't see you before, I'll see you at the next agreement review on [date].

If students report problems, this is where things get tricky, and you need to be willing to explore how they believe the agreement has been broken. Some helpful questions are:

- 'Exactly how do you think [student name] broke our agreement?'

- 'Which part of the agreement do you think has been broken?'

- 'What did we agree would happen if this agreement was broken?'

Even though the agreement will likely specify what will happen if the agreement is broken, this discussion needs to be backgrounded for the time being so that the conversation can remain restoratively focused and the behaviour that broke the agreement can be explored by using restorative questions. As mentioned earlier, this process becomes a restorative process in itself to explore the incident(s) in which the agreement was believed to be broken. This allows for some degree of reparation to take place between students.

Needless to say, a student who broke the agreement will be preoccupied with thoughts of the consequence for breaking the agreement, but in spite of this, it is advisable to work on restoration before turning attention to the practicalities of following through on the agreed sanctions for breaking the agreement.

Even though it can be tempting to go straight to sorting out the details of following through on the agreed sanctions, this doesn't allow for the student who broke the agreement to explain their reasons for doing so, or the circumstances that led up to their breaking the agreement. Often, it is the case that responsibility for doing the wrong thing needs to be shared between students and it isn't as simple as one person having broken the agreement. There's always a story!

After stories about the breaking of the agreement have been shared and all circumstances discussed, the black and white of imposing the agreed consequences must be followed through. After all, this was agreed to and detailed in the initial conference. To not follow through with these agreed actions devalues the conferencing process and also sends a message that the school is not serious about following through on conference agreements.

So, the message here is that when a conference agreement has been broken, do your best as the teacher to facilitate the repair of relationships between students before imposing any agreed sanction. This shows students that even though the school values following through on what has been decided in the conference, the repair of the relationship is the most important thing. It is a matter of being careful about where the main importance is placed – restoration first and sanctions second.

Students who have to face an agreed consequence for breaking an agreement will not be happy about receiving the consequence but will usually not protest as much as they otherwise would have. Don't be too bothered if students protest about the 'unfairness of it all'. They are still learning to live with the consequences of their actions and are some way off from being mature enough to say, 'Fair enough, we all agreed and I need to accept this consequence.' It is also important to remember that the protest may be about the student feeling disappointed with (ashamed of) themselves for breaking the agreement. If they become angry with you, it is likely an attack-other Compass of Shame defence (see Chapter 11) that they are using to deal with their shame and disappointment with themselves. If protest comes, it's best to say in a calm and friendly tone, 'I can see you're uptight about this at the moment, but I want you to remember that we all agreed. I know you're not happy with this, but it is what we all agreed would happen.'

After this, try not to defend your decision(s) by arguing with the young person. Stand firm but friendly on the matter. Often some soothing words like 'You're showing a lot of maturity by accepting this…' (even if they are not accepting it) can settle down agitated students. Something else you can say with students having difficulty accepting a consequence is:

> [Student's name], try not to stress out too much. Yes, you broke the agreement and we're dealing with it like we said we would. This doesn't make you a bad person – just someone who made a mistake. The important thing is that things are getting back on track, and when you have done [the consequence], we can go on with life. Just work really hard not to break the agreement again because it will be harder to win back people's trust if you do.

The key message here is: *You have done a bad thing by not sticking to the agreement, but this doesn't make you a bad person. Life will go on and it will be okay.*

Handing down sanctions and maintaining dignity

When following through on the agreed sanction, it is best to have this discussion with the wrongdoing student(s) after the other student(s) involved in the agreement have left the room. This way, the other students are part of a process where the breaking of the agreement is explored in a restorative fashion, but they don't have to feel awkward and ashamed as the sentence is handed down to the wrongdoing student(s).

Removing the other students from this process also makes it more likely that peace will remain between the students. The students who didn't break the agreement will be content to know that the agreement is being enforced without having to be in the room while this occurs. (In other words, it avoids a lot of weirdness between the students.)

Documentation

Documenting the breaking of the agreement in the review notes is crucial. It is also important to document details of how the agreement was broken and by whom, as well as the details of how and when the agreed sanctions were followed through. You may wish to staple a copy of any official consequence documentation regarding the sanction used (e.g. detention forms) to the agreement original. This makes accountability easy, and in future reviews, it can be seen that breaking of the agreement was dealt with in line with the agreement.

Making agreements inactive

If a period of time has passed where there have been no problems with the conference agreement – that is, all involved students have kept to their part of the deal by adhering to the agreement and relationships have improved – students may agree to making their conference agreement inactive. I have found that two review meetings over two school terms (approximately six months) is a good length of time for this. For me, the process of making an agreement inactive has involved a quirky little ritual whereby a corner of the original agreement has been torn off and shared around participants (including myself) to eat! (This can be likened to smoking the 'peace pipe'.) Students have certainly enjoyed watching me eat paper, though this isn't for everyone, of course.

If an agreement is made inactive, do not discard the original agreement. Keep it with other inactive agreements so it can be called upon for future reference or simply made active again if the same students have a similar issue which requires another conference in the future.

If an agreement is made inactive, a letter can be sent home to inform parents. (See Chapter 29 for an example of an information letter that can be sent home to parents when this happens.)

Summary

Reviewing restorative conference agreements can be an affirming and rewarding process, but it can also be challenging for the adults and young people involved. For a school committed to a restorative approach to discipline, it is a crucial part of the behaviour management process. As an adult facilitating the review, it is important to model restorative attitudes to students, as they will follow our lead. In the challenging situation where one or more students have failed to meet the agreed expectations for repair and future behaviour as outlined in the agreement, the focus needs to be primarily on what needs to happen to repair the harm this failure has caused. Imposing the agreed sanctions is important, but it is secondary to restoring people's rights and relationships.

Chapter 28

Keeping Colleagues in the Loop about Conference Agreements

A restorative conferencing programme will deteriorate without the support of all school staff. This support is only possible when staff have access to information about conference agreements. Nothing erodes colleagues' enthusiasm for any new initiative faster than being starved of relevant information about the initiative. I've seen leaders in schools neglecting to be considerate of the needs of those they expect to support restorative practice and then wonder why they are receiving so much resistance from staff. In my experience, the vast majority of staff will have a genuine interest in supporting young people to live by the conditions of conference agreements and, when given the right information, will do a very good job of this. Paranoid leaders who deliberately restrict the flow of this information to staff cripple the restorative process and demonstrate their lack of faith in colleagues to act professionally.

Below is an example of a summary of conference agreements that can be distributed to staff at the beginning of each school term (or four times during an academic year).

Summary of Restorative Conference Agreements: Term 3, 2016

Dear Colleagues,

As part of our behaviour development processes, we keep track of and review restorative conference agreements.

The process of bringing students together to go over their agreements is a preventative measure that keeps students accountable to one another and clear about their obligations to each other and our school community.

The original conference agreements are kept in the administration area, and all involved parties (students, parents and teachers) have copies of agreements.

This document is a summary of all of the current (active) agreements. You have been given a copy to inform you of existing conference agreements in case you happen to be working through an issue with students who have a pre-existing agreement with each other. These agreements often outline how future problems between certain students are to be handled. If you are helping students deal with a problem, you can ask, 'Do you have an agreement with each other or the school that I need to know about?' Students are normally forthcoming with this information.

If you wish to see a copy of the original agreements, please don't hesitate to see me or to get on the administrative network and follow the file path in the agreement summaries below.

Please have a look at the summary agreements to gain an awareness of who has agreements with whom.

Overview of current agreements at Justicetown School

1. Joe Dirt and Jim Dust

2. Janet Plant, John Mud and Class 6/7B

3. Georgia Banks and Erin Stark

4. Four-square players

Non-active agreements are agreements that students and I have decided no longer need reviewing. These are also kept in the office.

Restorative Conference Agreement
Between Joe Dirt and Jim Dust

Conference held: 3/2/16

Facilitated by: Bill Hansberry

Full conference agreement on file at: J:/COMMON/RPCoord/documentation/RJ/Agreements from conferences/Joe and Jim 030216.doc.

Agreement summary

- Joe will not be involved in any further teasing of Jim.

- There will be an immediate time-out for Joe for deliberate teasing. (Be wary – Jim can sometimes make up things to get attention.)

Review meeting notes

Review meeting 1

Reviewed 2/5/16: The boys reported that all is going well and signed the master agreement as a record of having reviewed the agreement.

Review meeting 2

Reviewed 31/7/16: The boys reported that all is going well except for Jim making an issue out of something that wasn't teasing. The misunderstanding was addressed in the review meeting. Both boys signed the master agreement as a record of having reviewed the agreement.

Restorative Conference Agreement Between Janet Plant, John Mud and Grade 6/7B Class

Conference held: 19/5/16

Facilitated by: Jane Langley

Full conference agreement on file at: J:/COMMON/RPCoord/ documentation/RJ/Agreements from conferences/Janet, John and class 190516.doc.

Agreement summary

- Janet will keep her hands and feet off people in the classroom – no more hugging, pulling on people's arms/legs or other touching.

- Violence is never okay at school – office time-out will be given immediately for violence in lesson time.

If agreement is broken

- Janet will get immediate office withdrawal.

- If John and Janet fight again, there will be serious school consequences and a conference involving parents and class.

Review meeting notes

Review meeting 1

Reviewed 26/5/16: All is okay so far – both students are keeping their agreement and enjoying the calm. Both students signed the master agreement as a record of having reviewed the agreement.

Review meeting 2

Reviewed 12/6/16: There was a problem last week when Janet thought that John had disrespected her. Mrs Harper helped Janet speak to John calmly and they sorted it out. There was no violence. Both students signed the master agreement as a record of having reviewed the agreement.

Restorative Conference Agreement Between Georgia Banks and Erin Stark

Conference held: 22/11/16

Facilitated by: Louise Laylaw

Full conference agreement on file at: J:/COMMON/RPCoord/ documentation/RJ/Agreements from conferences/GBanks and EStark 221116.doc.

Agreement summary

- An information-sharing Circle will be called to put the record straight on the rumour that Erin started.

- Erin will not post defamatory material on social media about any students at this school again.

- Georgia and Erin will plan a cyber-safety seminar.

Review meeting notes

Review meeting 1

Reviewed 29/11/16: The information-sharing Circle has been completed and went well. Erin really stepped up. Both girls signed the master agreement as a record of having reviewed the agreement.

Review meeting 2

Reviewed 6/12/16: All is well – Erin has made preliminary enquiries about the cyber-safety seminar for later in the school year. Both girls signed the master agreement as a record of having reviewed the agreement.

Review meeting 3

Reviewed 1/3/17: All is well – Erin and Georgia have a phone meeting arranged with CyberSmartKids to plan a workshop for the middle school. Both girls signed the master agreement as a record of having reviewed the agreement.

Review meeting 4

Reviewed 1/4/17: The cyber-safety seminar went very well. Both girls have agreed that all terms of the agreement have been met and the agreement can become inactive. A letter to this effect is being sent home by Mrs Laylaw to both sets of parents. Both students signed the master agreement as a record of having reviewed the agreement.

Restorative Conference Agreement Between Students Who Play Four Square

Conference held: 19/7/16

Facilitated by: Kerry Green

File held at: J:/COMMON/RPCoord/documentation/RJ/Agreements from conferences/4square/170716.doc.

Agreement summary

- The students have created an agreed set of rules for all games. An executive committee of players has taken on this job.

- These are the rules for all break-time four-square games: [rules].

- Not playing by the rules may result in losing the right to play and/or being called before the four-square committee.

Review meeting notes

Review meeting 1

Reviewed 25/7/16: The four-square executive group has formed and taken new game rules to all classes and posted them near the courts. There have been no fights so far. Executive members signed the master agreement as a record of having reviewed the agreement.

Review meeting 2

Reviewed 8/8/16: All is going well – play is safe and friendlier. Executive members signed the master agreement as a record of having reviewed the agreement.

Review meeting 3

Reviewed 29/8/16: There was a kicking incident on the court between two girls. The other players on the courts calmed the incident and the two girls had a Small Group Conference with two executive members to deal with the problem. No ban was given, but both girls are on notice. Executive members signed the master agreement as a record of having reviewed the agreement.

Review meeting 4

Reviewed 27/9/16: All is well with the rules. Teachers and students report that four square is much more peaceful these days. Executive members signed the master agreement as a record of having reviewed the agreement. Agreement review meetings will no longer be conducted unless required.

Chapter 29

Keeping Parents in the Loop about Conference Agreements

Parents and caregivers play a critical role in helping children do what needs to be done to recover from mistakes and indiscretions. Trust is everything when it comes to working with parents. In my experience, parental resistance to a school's approach to discipline often stems from:

- a distrust of school staff

- a lack of transparency in school discipline processes

- a lack of understanding of what the school is trying to achieve (especially if they see the school's approach is overly punitive)

- confusion about what the school requires of them as parents/caregivers to support their children.

Restorative discipline has a huge advantage over punitive responses to harm and wrongdoing because of its transparent and collaborative nature. Those involved in an issue or incident become active participants in deciding how a situation will be made better. In the case of more serious incidents, conference agreements help parents understand their role in helping their children do the agreed repair work.

On occasions when parents have not been able to attend the actual conference with their children, a later meeting has been planned when the young people can take their parents through the conference agreement and ask for their input. The case study in Chapter 4 involving the ongoing conflict between Jason and Tristan is an example of this.

In lower-level situations, where parent involvement is not usually required (e.g. Individual or Small Group Conferences) and agreements are not usually documented, schools need to be very deliberate about how they communicate restorative outcomes to parents. Many young people need help to communicate to their parents how things have been resolved. In my experience, nothing beats a phone call or, if possible, a face-to-face conversation with a parent, where a member of staff who facilitated the restorative process can run the parent(s) through what happened, how it was resolved, as well as some guidance as to how they can support their child.

Below is an example of a form that can be sent home to parents that accompanies the copy of the conference agreement. This form is primarily for parents or caregivers of students who attended the conference as the wrongdoers. Regardless of whether the parent attended the conference or was contacted by a member of staff about the conference, I like to attach this form to the agreement copy.

Accompanying Letter for Restorative Conference Agreements

Dear Parent/Caregiver,

Please find enclosed a copy of the restorative conference agreement that we made in our conference on [date].

All those affected by this agreement have signed the original, and this original is now kept at the school.

This agreement will be reviewed in a series of short meetings with the students involved until the agreement is made inactive.

Your part in helping your child adhere to this agreement:

It is very important that, as adults, we give the children support to meet the expectations laid out in this agreement. It is often the case that children don't know where to start when needing to make things better with others after a problem, or how to follow through with meeting the conditions of agreements that have been made in a conference.

Just leaving children to their own devices and expecting that they will stick to this agreement, without any help, can be a recipe for further problems and can lead to the agreement being broken.

You can help your child and support us at the school by:

- reading through the agreement carefully with your child to make sure you both understand what is expected

- checking that your child understands what will happen if they break the agreement or don't meet the expectations laid out in the agreement

- checking in with your child occasionally about the agreement by asking them how it is going – be careful *not* to ask too often because that may cause your child to think that they have to 'create' problems to tell you about

- keeping the agreement in a set place at home (perhaps stuck on the fridge) and going through it occasionally with your child to keep it fresh in their memory.

It is important to understand that this conference agreement is within the School's Behaviour Development Policy and will be taken into careful consideration in any future incidents involving the students named in the agreement.

If you have any questions, please do not hesitate to contact the conference facilitator (named on the attached copy of the conference agreement).

Thank you,

[Signature]

Making conference agreements inactive: Informing parents

A conference agreement reaches the end of its life when all agreed repair work has been carried out and the relationship between the involved students has stabilised to a point where further conflict is unlikely. In other words, as a general rule of thumb, two agreement review cycles (two school terms or six months) need to have passed during which no issues have arisen and neither party has broken the agreement. (If the relationship is still strained, however, one should continue to help the young people by scheduling further review meetings.)

If all has gone well, I ask the students what they think about making their agreement inactive. I explain that the agreement will still be kept by the school and that they are still expected to stick to the terms of the agreement, but they will no longer be required to attend review meetings unless there is another problem between them, in which case the agreement will be reactivated. If students agree that this is a good idea, the agreement becomes inactive. The fact that the involved students have repaired their relationship to this point is celebrated with words of praise, handshakes, high fives or even a previously negotiated incentive.

The letter below can be sent home to inform parents or caregivers of their child's success.

Restorative Conference Agreement Made Inactive

Dear Parent/Caregiver,

This letter is to inform you that the restorative conference agreement your child [name] had with [other name] has been so successful that in our recent review meeting on the [date], we decided to make their agreement inactive. This means that we will no longer need to meet to talk about how the agreement is going because:

- all conditions of the agreement have been met and things have been put right

- the relationship between the students is going well

- the students have made the agreement work by sticking to it.

The agreement will be kept in our records in case the students involved have another problem so that we can either make it active again or use it to help us with making a new agreement.

Please congratulate your child on sticking to their agreement. They should be very proud of themselves.

Regards,

[Signature]

Chapter 30

Concluding Thoughts

As I conclude this book, I feel as though I have thrown all I can at you in the way of logic, research and sound argument about the merits of working restoratively in your school, centre or system and the students and staff who are a part of this. However, you already know that logic, research and sound argument are never enough on their own to change hearts and minds.

Tell stories

Because humans are motivated by emotion, it will be the stories – the case studies – in this book that have determined whether or not you've decided that restorative practice is (or still is) a way forward for you and for your school, centre or system. Have I told these stories in a way that has captured your imagination? Have stories within the case studies helped you to imagine a school, centre or system in two or three years from now where young people and staff are able to do business in a more restorative way? Have I helped you imagine a calmer, gentler and kinder school? Has my experience and the experiences of the researchers, authors and practitioners referenced in this book got you to imagine? Have we lit, or rekindled, a fire in your belly for a more peaceful school and a more peaceful world? It is through listening to one another's stories that we are reminded of our shared humanity, which we all feel, and we are all programmed with the same nine innate affects; despite the fact that we all respond differently to events, we essentially feel in the same ways.

Restorative practice is about honouring people's stories and the emotions attached to those stories. Stories transmit culture, so as you embark on, or continue, your implementation of restorative practice, keep telling stories of your successes and failures in working with young people. Make it okay for young people to tell their stories to one another. Most importantly, when you are being told a story, listen with a burning intent to hear and see all. Watch for affect and emotion and try to pay attention to your own feelings as you listen. Working hard on this ability will make you more effective at helping people than you ever hoped.

Share your practice boldly

As others begin to show an interest in the way you work with young people (this interest may be disguised as criticism), invite colleagues to attend restorative conferences, especially if they have been affected themselves or if they can act as a support person for the young people involved. Invite colleagues to look on as you use lower-level restorative practices such as Individual and Small Group Conferences. Boldly offer to prepare and facilitate Classroom Conferences in their classes to address issues. Be as brave as we ask young people to be with one another. Plan and run Circle sessions in classes with your colleagues and then, at the end, make time to ask them what you might have done better. Try not to let the fear of making mistakes keep your practice behind closed doors. Instead of intimidating your colleagues with perfect practice, being open and honest with them about what you could have or should have done differently will inspire them to take risks and try to use restorative practice themselves.

Use restorative practice to its fullest potential and include parents

Have a cohort of your staff trained in Community Conference facilitation (covered in Chapter 19). These are conferences where parents attend with their children and become an important part of the process of repairing harm. Failing to use the restorative continuum to this extent will convince your staff, students and parents that restorative practice is just for the minor issues and the good kids. Schools who do not invest in training staff to conference at the Community Conference level tend to exclude parents from restorative processes that involve their children. Without being in on the process, parents are left to guess what goes on behind the closed doors of a restorative process. Believe me, under these circumstances, parents will often make all the wrong assumptions about restorative practice. I have seen this over and over again. So train staff to the full extent of the restorative continuum so that they are confident to involve parents in restorative processes.

Leading restorative cultural change

If you are a school leader, then understand that you will be leading from the front. There's simply no way around this. Restorative practice only changes the culture in schools where the principal has a well-articulated vision for restorative practice and a steadfast belief in working restoratively. These leaders also:

- behave restoratively with all members of the community, especially when things are not going well

- continue to develop their restorative leadership style

- articulate their vision for restorative practice publically and actively promote restorative practice as the way to do things

- actively learn more about restorative practice through professional reading, viewing and attending trainings

- openly coach others by modelling restorative practice to them – mistakes and all!

- admit their mistakes quickly and emphatically

- adequately resource the development of restorative practice in monetary terms.

These behaviours are the opposite of merely announcing that restorative practice will be implemented across the school and then delegating the implementation (as an add-on) to someone else's very full role description.

The change you will be asking some members of your community to make in their thinking about how we should address conflict and wrongdoing is enormous. Along the way you will find some of your own core beliefs about behaviour management exposed and challenged:

Moving from a punitive rule based discipline system to a system underpinned by relational values requires a change in the hearts and minds of practitioners, students, their parents and the wider community. Without understanding the enormity of this task a few good people in each school will be working very hard to make a difference, with limited impact. (Blood and Thorsborne 2006, p.1)

Manage staff restoratively

Blood and Thorsborne (2006) make the very important point that, in implementing restorative practice, school leaders sometimes fail to use the relational approaches with their own staff that they ask teachers to use with students and parents.

In their zeal to see restorative justice embedded, school leaders may use coercion and even bully-style tactics to push staff to change their practice to become more relational and restorative. A restorative mode of leadership requires leaders to work with staff in the same spirit that they want staff to work with students.

Restorative schools simply don't happen in the absence of restorative leadership.

The school's leadership, with the principal leading from the front, must embrace and model restorative approaches in their work with students and in their management of staff.

Lead from the front

Principals should be trained conference facilitators – out there planning and facilitating restorative conferences.

Your staff are watching your every movement to gauge your level of investment in restorative practice, so please take my word for it – you won't achieve a restorative school through delegation. Lickona (2004) talks about the hidden curriculum in every school and classroom which is all about how people treat one another, how teachers treat young people and how young people treat each other. Attend carefully to this culture and be deliberate about the type of culture you want to build.

Build the implementation team around yourself. Restorative values must be lived by those leading the implementation. I have seen many leaders completely delegate the implementation of restorative practice to others in the school and, you guessed it, the new practices haven't taken hold in any meaningful way. It is a tragedy when such a potentially powerful way of doing things is passed over because the leadership fail to go beyond paying it lip service.

Support, support, support – oh, and more support!

Marshall, Shaw and Freeman (2002) tell us that restorative practice requires teachers to redefine their role in behaviour management to relationship management and that teachers need time and support to grapple with questions about the impact of punishment and potential alternatives based on a restorative philosophy. They remind us that teachers require understanding and time to practise and refine new skills and to reflect upon their own style. This occurs best in an environment that is challenging yet supportive – in other words, high control/high support (see the social control window in Chapter 3).

> The onus is…on school systems to ensure that teachers have access to substantial professional development that allows for progressive skill development with the aim that teachers will be able to confidently apply and model effective relationship management skills. (Marshall *et al.* 2002, p.7)

Experience has taught me the importance of supporting colleagues, even when I didn't agree with what they wanted to do to a student. There were many occasions when an angry colleague wanted blood from a student and I believed a restorative conference would deliver far better outcomes. On these occasions I followed my colleague's preferred option (within reasonable limits), but I also negotiated for a restorative process to precede, or follow, the sanction that my colleague was asking for. If I had not supported my colleagues in these circumstances, their trust in me would have taken a blow and, with it, may have ruined any chance of them coming round to a more restorative approach in the longer run. I sometimes made the decision to lose a battle to win the war. Some of the colleagues I supported in this way ended up being the school's biggest advocates for restorative practice. People ultimately engage in something new (and frightening) through their relationships with those they trust who are already doing the new thing. If these relationships are damaged, the opportunity to influence others is crippled.

Commit to ongoing professional learning

As we near the end of this book, painfully aware that there is so much more I would like to share about implementing restorative practice in schools, I ask you to tap into the wealth of knowledge out there about restorative work in schools. I have lost count of the books, articles, videos, PowerPoint presentations on the web, VHS videos, DVDs, YouTube clips and documentaries I've devoured over the years. Tap into this powerful resource and benefit from those who've taken this journey before you.

Remember, just you alone doing restorative work well in your school is not enough. You must sell restorative practice to your community. To do this, you need to be one of the best-read experts in your school. If you have a passion for the possibilities of safer schools and more connected communities, let this passion stir you to embark upon your own learning journey into this joyous and hopeful field.

Finally

A commitment to restorative practice involves a deep commitment to the nitty-gritty work of building a more peaceful world. In a political climate where politicians gain votes through making humans fear one another, those who stand for reparation-based justice face a challenge. Are you up to it?

Appendix 1
Pre-No-Blame Classroom Conference Student Reporting Pro Forma

Write down what has been done to you: the verbal or physical harassment, the name calling or put-downs and so forth.

. . . .

. . . .

. . . .

. . . .

. . . .

. . . .

Write down what has been done to others in this class: the words or actions that have been used to hurt people – what you've seen and heard happen.

. . . .

. . . .

. . . .

. . . .

. . . .

. . . .

Appendix 2

Example No-Blame Classroom Conference Pre-Conference Letter to Parents

Dear Parent/Caregiver,

For some time now the teachers and students in class [class number] have had some concerns about the levels of disruption occurring. Students and teachers have been complaining about the loss of focus on learning because of the behaviour of many of the students.

As you know, [school name] works under the restorative practice framework that focuses on firm and fair approaches to discipline, with an emphasis on students taking responsibility for unacceptable behaviour and making commitments to put things right. In light of this, we will be holding a No-Blame Classroom Conference for all [class number] students on [date]. The purpose of the conference will be to give the students and staff a voice about what has been happening, and to come to an agreement about how to repair harm and ensure that the students treat each other respectfully and fairly.

In the conference each student will have the opportunity to speak their mind about issues related to the behaviour of the class as well as other issues of harassment, bullying or disruptive behaviour within the group. We will hear from those responsible for, and those affected by, the unacceptable behaviours.

This conference, as the name suggests, will not be a naming-and-blaming conference. There will be no punishments for any of the issues raised during the conference. It is a chance for students to talk freely about what has happened, who has been affected and what needs to happen to make it right again. Those responsible for the harm will be given the opportunity to take responsibility and make suggestions about what can be done to repair the harm caused.

The conference will conclude with the drafting of a formal written agreement. This agreement will formalise agreed expectations on how students will treat each other in the future. Our agreement will also clearly specify agreed responses for breaches of our agreement. [Facilitator's name] will be facilitating the conference so that the teachers are free to take part in the conference with the students.

It is important to make clear that this is a disciplinary-educative process and not a punitive one. As aforementioned, nobody will be punished for what comes out in the conference. The goal is for students to take responsibility for harm caused and repair the harm – something that rarely occurs under threat of punishment.

Our aim is to restore and strengthen relationships so that this group can better settle into their learning.

A copy of the agreement will be sent home after it is completed and signed by all involved.

You can do the following to help us in preparation for this conference:

- Do not interrogate your child about what's been happening, as this may undermine their willingness to speak openly during the conference.

- Encourage your child's attendance for the conference, as students who stay home can often feel out of the loop in regards to commitments and agreements made during the conference. These processes often bring groups of students closer together.

- Quietly ask your child how they feel about what's been happening and the upcoming conference, and how they believe the situation can be made better.

- Reassure your child that nobody will be punished for what's said during the conference.

Please contact [person's name] if you have any questions about the process, and be assured that we have your child's best interests at heart.

Regards,

[Signature]

Appendix 3

Example No-Blame Classroom Conference Post-Conference Survey

We are interested to see whether or not students in our class believe there have been any changes to the behaviour of people since the No-Blame Classroom Conference and the making of our class agreement. Please answer the questions below (circle one answer for each question) as honestly as you can.

1. What did you learn during the conference that you might not have known before? (Please comment.)

    ....

    ....

    ....

2. Has the class changed at all since the conference?

    Definitely yes   Yes   Unsure   No   Definitely not

3. How is the class agreement going?

    Very well   Okay   Unsure   Badly   Very badly

4. Since the conference, the way people treat each other in our class is:

    Much better   Better   No different   Worse   Much worse

5. Since the conference, the amount of harassment, bullying and put-downs in our class is:

    Much less   Less   No different   Better   Much better

6. Have you noticed people who were targeted or hassled before the conference being treated more fairly by people in our class?

    Definitely yes   Yes   Unsure   No   Definitely not

7. Since the conference, have you been making an effort to treat anyone in the class differently?

    Definitely yes   Yes   Unsure   No   Definitely not

8. Since the conference, I think more carefully before I do or say something to somebody.

    Strongly agree   Agree   Unsure   Disagree   Strongly disagree

9. I felt better/worse about being in this class after the conference.

    Better   Worse

Thanks for your time and care in filling out this survey.

References

Abramson, L. (2014) 'Being Emotional, Being Human: Creating Healthy Communities and Institutions by Honoring Our Biology.' In V. Kelly and M. Thorsborne (eds) *The Psychology of Emotion in Restorative Practice*. London: Jessica Kingsley Publishers.

Ahmed, E. and Braithwaite, V. (2004) '"What, me ashamed?" Shame management and school bullying.' *Journal of Research in Crime and Delinquency 41*, 3, 269–294.

Al-Ghani, K.I. (2009) *The Red Beast: Controlling Anger in Children with Asperger's Syndrome*. London: Jessica Kingsley Publishers.

Armstrong, M. and Vinegrad, D. (2013) *Working in Circles in Primary and Secondary Classrooms*. Queenscliff, Victoria: Inyahead Press.

Baumeister, R.F., Twenge, J.M. and Nuss, C. (2002) 'Effects of social exclusion on cognitive processes: anticipated aloneness reduces intelligent thought.' *Journal of Personality and Social Psychology 83*, 4, 817–827.

Blood, P. and Thorsborne, M. (2006) *Overcoming Resistance to Whole-School Uptake of Restorative Practices*. Paper presented at the International Institute of Restorative Practices, 'The Next Step: Developing Restorative Communities, Part 2' Conference, 18–20 October, Bethlehem, Pennsylvania.

Braithwaite, J. (1989) *Crime, Shame and Reintegration*. Cambridge: Cambridge University Press.

Burnett, N. and Thorsborne, M. (2015) *Restorative Practices and Special Needs*. London: Jessica Kingsley Publishers.

Deppe, S.L. (2008) *Affect and Script: Building Relationships and Communities*. Available at www.iirp.edu/pdf/ON08Papers/ON08_Deppe.pdf, accessed on 26 October 2011.

Fredrickson, B.L. (2009) *Positivity*. New York, NY: Three Rivers Press.

Garbarino, J. (1999) *Lost Boys: Why Our Sons Turn Violent and How We Can Save Them*. New York, NY: Anchor Books.

George, G. (2015) *Affect and Emotion in the Restorative School*. Available at www.rpforschools.net, accessed on 6 March 2016.

Gladwell, M. (2005) *Blink: The Power of Thinking Without Thinking*. Boston, MA: Little, Brown and Company.

Hansberry, B. (2009) *Working Restoratively in Schools: A Guidebook for Developing Safe and Connected Learning Communities*. Queenscliff, Victoria: Inyahead Press.

Hansberry, B. and Langley, J. (2013) *The Grab and Go Circle Time Kit for Teaching Restorative Behaviour: 13 Sessions for Junior Primary.* Queenscliff, Victoria: Inyahead Press.

Hendry, R. (2009) *Building and Restoring Respectful Relationships in Schools: A Guide to Using Restorative Practice.* Oxon: Routledge.

Hopkins, B. (2011) *Restorative Classroom Practice: Using Restorative Approaches to Foster Effective Learning.* London: Optimus Education.

Hopkins, B. (2014) 'Restorative Classroom Practice: Revised Edition August 2014.' In-house training resource (yet to be published). Transforming Conflict, The National Centre for Restorative Approaches in Youth Settings, Mortimer, Berkshire.

Howard, J.A. (2013) *Distressed or Deliberately Defiant? Managing Challenging Student Behaviour Due to Trauma and Disorganised Attachment.* Toowong, Queensland, Australia: Australian Academic Press Group.

Jansen, G. and Matla, R. (2011) 'Restorative Practices in Action.' In V. Margrain and A. Macfarlane (eds) *Responsive Pedagogy: Engaging Restoratively with Challenging Behaviour.* Wellington: NZCER Press.

Johnson, D.W. and Johnson, R.T. (1995) 'Why violence prevention programs don't work – and what does?' *Educational Leadership 52,* 5 63–68.

Kelly, V. (2012) *The Art of Intimacy and the Hidden Challenge of Shame.* Philadelphia, PA: Tomkins Press.

Kelly, V. (2014) 'Caring, Restorative Practice and the Biology of Emotion.' In V. Kelly and M. Thorsborne (eds) *The Psychology of Emotion in Restorative Practice.* London: Jessica Kingsley Publishers.

Kelly, V. and Thorsborne, M. (eds) (2014) *The Psychology of Emotion in Restorative Practice.* London: Jessica Kingsley Publishers.

Kim, W.C. and Mauborgne, R. (2003) 'Fair process: Managing in the knowledge economy.' *Harvard Business Review 81,* 127–136.

Lewis, S. (2009) *Findings From Schools Implementing Restorative Practices.* International Institute of Restorative Practice (IIRP) Graduate School. Available at http://www.iirp.edu/pdf/IIRP-Improving-School-Climate-2009.pdf, accessed on 11 June 2016.

Lickona, T. (2004) *Character Matters.* New York, NY: Touchstone.

Lillico, I. (2000) *School Reforms: 2000 ASPA Conference Report.* Available at www.boysforward.com.au/perspectives/school-reforms, accessed on 28 October 2015.

Manasco, H. (2006) *The Way to 'A': Empowering Children with Autism Spectrum and Other Neurological Disorders to Monitor and Replace Aggression and Tantrum Behaviour.* Lenexa, KS: Autism Asperger Publishing Company.

Marshall, P., Shaw, G. and Freeman, E. (2002) *Restorative Practices: Implications for Educational Institutions.* The University of Melbourne, Australia.

McCarthy, F.E. (2009) *Circle Time Solutions: Creating Caring School Communities. An Analysis of a Learning through Community Service Initiative Supporting Circle Time in Eight Primary Schools in Greater Western Sydney.* Sydney, Australia: NSW Department of Education and Training.

McNeely, C.A., Nonnemaker, J.M. and Blum, R.W. (2002) 'Promoting school connectedness: Evidence from the National Longitudinal Study of Adolescent Health.' *Journal of School Health 72,* 4, 138–146.

Morrison, B. (2007) *Restoring Safe School Communities: A Whole-School Response to Bullying, Violence and Alienation.* Sydney, Australia: The Federation Press.

Nathanson, D.L. (1994) *Shame and Pride: Affect, Sex and the Birth of the Self.* New York, NY: W.W. Norton and Company.

Nathanson, D.L. (1996) *Knowing Feeling: Affect, Script, and Psychotherapy.* New York, NY: W.W. Norton and Company.

Nathanson, D.L. (2000) *Shame Is the Name of the Game.* Report to the Academic Advisory Council of the National Campaign Against Youth Violence (New York, NY).

Nathanson, D.L. (2004) *Managing Shame, Preventing Violence: A Call to Our Clergy.* DVD. Lewisburg, PA: Silvan Tomkins Institute.

New Zealand Ministry of Education (2014) *PB4L Restorative Practice.* Available at http://pb4l.tki.org.nz/PB4L-Restorative-Practice, accessed on 24 November 2015.

Noguera, P.A. (1995) 'Preventing and producing violence: A critical analysis of responses to school violence.' *Harvard Educational Review 65,* 189–212.

O'Connell, T., Wachtel, T. and Wachtel, B. (1999) *Real Justice Conferencing Handbook.* Pipersville, PA: The Piper's Press.

Queensland Government Department of Communities, Child Safety and Disability Services and Department of Education, Training and Employment (2013) *Calmer Classrooms: A Guide to Working with Traumatised Children.* Available at http://education.qld.gov.au/schools/healthy/pdfs/calmer-classrooms-guide.pdf, accessed on 20 December 2015.

Real Justice (nd) *Teacher Circles Booklet.* Unpublished teacher resource.

Retzinger, S.M. and Scheff, T.J. (1996) 'Strategy for Community Conferences: Emotions and Social Bonds' in B. Galaway and J. Hudson (eds) *Restorative Justice: International Perspectives.* New York: Criminal Justice Press.

Roffey, S. (2014) *Circle Solutions for Student Wellbeing* (2nd ed.). London: SAGE Publications.

Rogers, W. (2006) *Behaviour Management: A Whole-School Approach* (2nd ed.). Lindfield, New South Wales: Scholastic Press.

Shochet, I.M., Smyth, T. and Homel, R. (2007) 'The impact of parental attachment on adolescent perception of the school environment and school connectedness.' *Australian and New Zealand Journal of Family Therapy 28,* 2, 109–118.

Skiba, R.J. (2000) *Zero Tolerance, Zero Evidence: An Analysis of School Disciplinary Practice Policy*. Research Report #SRS 2. Indiana Education Policy Center, Bloomington, Indiana.

Stutzman Amstutz, L. and Mullet, J.H. (2005) *The Little Book of Restorative Discipline for Schools: Teaching Responsibility, Creating Caring Climates*. Intercourse, PA: Good Books.

Stutzman Amstutz, L. and Zehr, H (1998) *Victim Offender Conferencing in Pennsylvania's Juvenile Justice System*. Available at http://www.emu.edu/cjp/publications/all/victim-offender-conferencing-manual/victim-offender-conf-manual.pdf, accessed on 11 June 2016.

Thorsborne, M. (2005) *Leading with Integrity*. CD. The Leadership Series, Australian Institute of Management.

Thorsborne, M. and Vinegrad, D. (2004) *Restorative Practices in Classrooms: Rethinking Behaviour Management*. Queenscliff, Victoria: Inyahead Press.

Thorsborne, M. and Vinegrad, D. (2009) *Restorative Justice Pocketbook*. Hants, UK: Teachers' Pocketbooks.

Tomkins, S. (1963) *Affect Imagery Consciousness* (Volume 2). New York, NY: Springer.

Vandeering, D. (2010) *A Window on Relationships: Enlarging the Social Discipline Window for a Broader Perspective*. Paper presented at the 13th World Conference of the International Institute for Restorative Practices, Hull, UK. Available at www.iirp.edu/pdf/Hull-2010/Hull-2010-Vaandering.pdf, accessed on 27 March 2016.

Wachtel, T. (1999) *Restorative Justice in Everyday Life: Beyond the Formal Ritual*. Paper presented at the Reshaping Australian Institutions Conference: Restorative Justice and Civil Society, The Australian National University, Canberra, 16–18 February. Available at www.iirp.edu/article_detail.php?article_id=NTAz, accessed on 3 April 2016.

Wachtel, T. and McCold, P. (2004) *From Restorative Justice to Restorative Practices: Expanding the Paradigm*. Paper presented at the IIRP's Fifth International Conference on Conferencing, Circles and Other Restorative Practices: 'Building a Global Alliance for Restorative Practices and Family Empowerment, Part 2', 5–7 August, Vancouver, British Columbia, Canada. Available at www.iirp.edu/article_detail.php?article_id=Mzk5, accessed on 3 April 2016.

Zehr, H. (2002) *The Little Book of Restorative Justice*. Intercourse, PA: Good Books.

Subject Index

Author Index

18559000R00173

Printed in Great Britain
by Amazon